HEDGE
HOGGING

HEDGE HOGGING

BARTON BIGGS

WILEY

John Wiley & Sons, Inc.

Published by John Wiley & Sons, Inc., Hoboken, New Jersey.
Published simultaneously in Canada.

For general information on our other products and services or for technical support, please contact our Customer Care Department within the United States at (800) 762-2974, outside the United States at (317) 572-3993, or fax (317) 572-4002.

Wiley also publishes its books in a variety of electronic formats. Some content that appears in print may not be available in electronic books. For more information about Wiley products, visit our web site at www.wiley.com.

Library of Congress Cataloging-in-Publication Data:

Biggs, Barton, 1932–
    Hedgehogging / Barton Biggs.
      p.   cm.
    Includes index.
    ISBN-13: 978-0-471-77191-3 (cloth)
    ISBN-13: 978-0-470-06773-4 (pbk.)
    1. Hedge funds.   I. Title.
  HG4530.B516   2006
  332.64′5—dc22
                    2005026139

Printed in the United States of America.

10 9 8 7 6 5 4 3 2 1

CONTENTS

CHAPTER TWENTY

CHAPTER TWENTY-ONE

INTRODUCTION

I n the three years since I wrote *Hedgehogging*, a lot has happened to the hedge fund world, but the people and the engulfing emotions of fear and greed that torture and compel manic behavior from the players that I write about in this book are still the same. The capital invested in equity-oriented hedge funds around the world is around a trillion dollars (up from $300 billion six years ago), with the gross exposure both long and short somewhere between $1.5 and $2 trillion. Overall performance after fees (not surprisingly, considering the strong markets since 2002) has been mediocre.

Both the birth and death rates continue to be astronomical. No one knows the exact numbers, but at least 2,000 hedge funds have closed since the end of 2004, and probably 2,500 new funds have opened. There have been triumphs and tragedies, and a few fortunate men (as far as I know there are no very rich women hedge funders) have become *filthy* rich, and many other unfortunates have been broken, sometimes brutally, on the rack of performance and marketing neglect.

Since I wrote the book, funds of hedge funds have become an even more important factor in the business. In the past decade, funds of funds have been the biggest winners in the entire investment management business, with their assets up 10 times from 1999, and with growth in the past three years in excess of 25% annually. It is estimated that there are now 2,500 of them, up from 500 seven years ago. Funds of funds now account for almost 40% of total hedge fund assets, which is far ahead of the 22% share of high net worth individuals. The five biggest funds of funds control about a third of the business, and they can flick $150 million in or out of a hedge fund at a moment's notice. Love sessions such as the Breakers Conference I describe have multiplied.

What have been some other trends? First, hedge funds have become more recognized as a noncorrelated asset class for pension fund,

foundation, and endowment money. An increasing number of fiduciaries and plan sponsors believe hedge funds in bull markets should deliver at least 80% of the return of the Standard & Poor's 500 stock
index, and in bear markets will not lose money and perhaps will make
a little. Thus, they have become a preferred diversifier and the substitute for fixed income in large multi-asset portfolios.

Second, the number of and publicity about fund accidents have
frightened many buyers. The volatility and huge losses of the previously
sacrosanct quant funds rattled them, and the collapse of some very big
funds—in particular, Amaranth, Bear Stearns, and Sowood—has put the
fear of God into investment committees, trustees, hedge fund consultants, and fiduciaries. As a result, the new institutional money is increasingly going to the giant, established so-called multistrategy hedge fund
groups. In other words, the big are getting even bigger.

At the same time, fiduciaries are looking for protection. They don't
want the grief and resulting lawsuits if one of the funds they selected
blows up. This makes funds of hedge funds more attractive, as they provide a layer of fiduciary protection.

The good thing about funds of funds is that they are managed by
expert professionals who spend their time studying hedge funds. They
do extensive analysis of the sources of hedge fund performance and
how much risk individual hedge funds are taking. They monitor portfolios and are not susceptible to promotional bullsh★★.

In addition, as I discuss in my book, they pay close attention to the sociological signs of hubris evolution. Subtle indications that a manager
might be taking his eye off the ball are a falling golf handicap, a divorce, the
purchase of multiple vacation homes, multiple foreign nannies, and a rising
social and charity profile. In other words, the funds of funds are professional.

The bad thing about funds of funds is that they abhor performance
volatility and so-called drawdowns. A drawdown is when a fund reports
a decline in net asset value for a marking period. An occasional monthly
drawdown will be tolerated, but a large quarterly drawdown can be the
trigger for a quick redemption. The funds of funds also tend to chase
performance. The results of these practices are that hedge fund managers become terribly conscious of not losing money, and at the first
sign of a soft market head for the sidelines and often get whipsawed. In
other words, they become trend followers. In my view, you are not going to produce an exceptional long-term record if you let business considerations dominate good investment decision making.

The Achilles' heel of funds of funds may be their fee structure. Often they charge a 1 percent fixed fee and 10% of the profits. Combine that with hedge funds that are assessing 2% and 20%, and the investor has some hefty hurdle to work through. Large amounts of money under management and high fees spell eventual performance disappointment. I will bet hedge fund fees will be considerably lower five years from now.

The third trend involves the disasters of the big quant funds in August of 2007. For a long time computer-driven, black-box investing had seemed to be in a relentless ascendancy. Strange, reclusive, bearded physics doctorates who effortlessly could do complex data mining using powerful computers were the new, new thing. Experienced investors with judgment, intuitions, and complex reactions to the economy were dinosaurs. It all seemed so simple. Back-test, massage the data, discover patterns, and then identify and buy cheap stocks based on fundamental valuation criteria and be short expensive stocks. Throw in a little momentum analysis for timing and some leverage for performance, and the portfolio was bound to be a moon shot regardless of what the overall market was doing.

Then came the summer of 2007. Volatility increased, and suddenly the quant funds had more leverage than their risk budgets permitted. As a result, they began to reduce their holdings by selling their long positions and covering (buying back) their shorts. The trouble was that their models all had generally produced similar stocks so they were long and short the same names. Compounding the problem was the bias of these giants to small- and medium-capitalization stocks. This process created a marvelous virtuous circle when the quants were getting floods of new money but a vicious circle when they had to shrink their portfolios. They had to sell the stocks they owned and buy back the shares they were short, so consequently their longs were going down while their shorts were soaring.

The result was a devastating meltdown in July and August of 2007. The big, famous quant funds suddenly had disastrous falls in value. As frightened investors withdrew capital, the vicious circle became even more vicious. Declines of 20% to 30% in a month were common, which generated frantic redemption notices from their investors.

There were all kinds of secondary consequences. A Midwestern quant whose nickname was Super Cruncher and who was famous for wearing T-shirts to the office suddenly came down with Bell's palsy. This is an affliction where you get crushing headaches, your eyes water, your tongue thickens, and one side of your face is paralyzed—hardly the impression you want to create when you meet with clients during a time of very rough performance. A rumor spread that he had experienced a stroke, and redemptions soared.

Another well-known quant, a relatively young man who liked to call himself "an evidence-based investor" and who luxuriated in an immense, sprawling house in the new hedge fund capital of the world, Greenwich, Connecticut, took the whole debacle very seriously and became depressed as his theories and performance unraveled—so seriously, in fact, that it affected his sexual potency. His wife began to suspect that he must have a girlfriend. Angered by his neglect, she fled with the children in his G-5 to her family's home in San Diego. His depression deepened. Who knows what the outcome will be?

The moral of the quant meltdown story is that quant value investing works as long as too many people don't do it. To paraphrase one of my favorite quotations: "Ignore the investment past and you will lose an eye; invest based on the past and you will lose both of them." The stock market is a sadistic, contrary, changeable beast and nothing is forever.

The other big trend is the high failure rate of new funds. It has become increasingly difficult to raise money. A friend of mine—let's call him Dan—left J.P. Morgan Investment Management in 2005 with a great record in small- and mid-cap stocks. He got $15 million from the hedge fund incubator Julian Robertson and a few million more from some friends and family. Since inception his performance has been spectacular, and his prime broker last summer offered to take him on tour to raise money. In June, July, and August he made over 100 presentations. The results to date? Zippo. As Dan puts it: "They got me a lot of dates and about half the girls kissed me good night, but not one asked me to come in and spend the night!"

This is why so many new funds go out of business after a couple of years. They just can't get to an asset size to cover their overhead and make ends meet at home. Five years ago, just starting a hedge fund got you attention. Now there are so many funds out there that unless you shoot the lights out, no one pays any attention. And, make no mistake, once an investment guy does his own hedge fund things and drops out of business, it's not so easy to land the next job.

So in the hedge fund world "it's still the same old story, a fight for love and glory, a case of do or die as time goes by." Buy sheep, sell deer.

CHAPTER
ONE

The Triangle
Investment Club Dinner
Hacking Through the Hedgehog Jungle

I went to the Triangle Investment Club dinner at the Century last night. There were about 25 guys there, about half from hedge funds and the other half very aggressive long-only managers. The age mix was about half and half, too. There were plenty of distinguished oldies with curly gray hair and husky voices who roll their words, but also a lot of sleek-looking young guys who talk very fast. Young or ancient, everyone there was a big-time investor running public, competitive money of one type or other.

Triangle is an investment club of mostly guys who have dinner once a month to exchange ideas and take one another's temperatures. I don't go that often. You must be in the mood. You have to be capable of putting (and keeping) your game face on because, although everyone is ostensibly friendly and jovial, the members are some of the most intensely competitive people in the United States. There is definitely an edge to the interaction and conversation. It's not exactly a relaxing, friendly evening with old tried-and-true comrades in arms.

It was the usual routine. We stood around with drinks for half an hour or so and gossiped mainly about how tough it was to make

1

money. I chatted with Jonathan, a big-time hedge fund mogul who must be worth a billion dollars and flies everywhere in his own Gulf Stream. I've known him since he was a young analyst at Tiger, Julian Robertson's legendary hedge fund. I like him. He is one of those guys who tells you exactly what's on his mind.

Tonight he is shaking his head. A week from now is his oldest daughter's tenth birthday, so last night he asked her what she would really like for her big double-digit birthday. She looks at him and says, "I can ask for anything?" He says, "Yes." She says, "You won't get mad? My wish involves an airplane." He's stunned. What has he wrought? Poor little rich girl! She wants her own plane. With trepidation he says, "Okay. What is it?" "Daddy," she says, "I'm almost 10 years old, and I've never been on a commercial airline flight. All the other girls at school have. What I really want is for you to take me to a real airport, check in, go through security, get searched, stand in line, and fly commercial to someplace. Daddy, never having done it is really embarrassing." Hedgehogging with children is not easy!

KIBITZING, GILDING, AND SANDBAGGING

Then we go in to dinner at a long table with candles and fresh flowers, and immediately Leon, who had the chair last night, gets things going and we begin to go around the table. In no more than four minutes, each guy is supposed to elucidate his favorite stock or concept and the reasons why. Everyone takes notes, and there is a lot of kibitzing. Because there are many mammoth egos present, the chair has to be ruthless about cutting speakers off or we would be there all night. There are some guys who say they get a lot of ideas out of the dinner. I don't find that I do, but you do come away from the evening with a sense of what the mood of the members is and what the hot areas are.

Last night I got a sense of confusion. The mix between longs and shorts was pretty balanced. Some of the stories boggle the imagination, with lots of aggressive supposition. With energy hot, one young guy told a fantastic tale about a Malaysian wildcat oil company that had a structure at offshore Borneo, which rivaled the North Sea. Sure! A mutual fund manager told of a new surgical process that cuts the risk of impotence from prostate surgery by 75%. Then there are the usual market-cap-toeyeballs stories about new and old Internet adventures, and wondrous tales about everything from health-food chains to nanotechnology.

It is assumed you're going to be recommending what you already have a position in. Most guys announce their positions before talking. As always, there was a lot of cynical, sardonic byplay, with certain notorious offenders being accused of gilding (as in gilding the lily) and an occasional joking cry of "Sandbagger." *Gilding* is just what it sounds like—when you dress up your story to take it to the party by exaggerating the fundamentals in your favor. In other words, if you are plugging Symantec and making the case that it's cheap because it's going to have big earnings next year, you might, in the spell of the evening, jack up your earnings estimate from $3.50 a share to $3.75, when even $3.30 would be a minor miracle. But who can forecast earnings of an exotic tech company anyway, and why not dream a little?

Gilding is a relatively minor offense because, to some extent, everybody does it all the time. The members have very sensitive built-in BS detectors, so egregious gilding backfires and tarnishes the credibility of the gilder. Also, members who know the story being presented have no compunction about rudely interrupting and correcting the gilder. This can be quite embarrassing, but it's all part of the charm of the evening. If a guy tells a good, original story and nobody interrupts, it means that the tale is at least fresh and maybe for real.

Sandbagging is a much more serious crime. You can even get kicked out of the club if you're caught red-handed, *en flagrante* so to speak. Sandbagging is when you tell a story and egregiously gild it, hoping to attract buyers at the same time you are actually secretly selling the stock. It's one thing to promote the story of what you own or are short, and as noted, most members make it clear that they have a position one way or the other in the merchandise they are talking about. It's quite another to sandbag. Sandbagging is dishonest, cheating, a violation of the rules of the money game.

JUST BECAUSE YOU'RE A SNAKE DOESN'T MEAN YOU'RE NOT A MONEYMAKER

One guy who used to be a member, Richard, was always suspected of being a sandbagger, but it's a capital offense and very hard to prove, and as long as nobody got hurt, it was overlooked. Richard, incidentally, is one of those guys who insists on being called Richard and not Dick.

Now there are some slick, slimy guys in the big-time hedge fund business who traffic in stories and even in forms of inside information. Richard is as slick and slimy as they come, although he has a smooth, cultured, Harvard veneer, wears fancy suits, and talks with a hint of a Boston accent. But just because you're a snake doesn't mean that you are not a moneymaker. Richard has been around for a long time, and one of the other members was even in business with him for a while. That ended in a nasty lawsuit. Richard once arrogantly described himself as a self-made man, and his former partner interjected, "and you worship your creator." Richard is very smart, very obnoxious, and has made a lot of money, mostly for himself. He tells a stock story with great certainty and precision, and so I guess that's why we all put up with him for so long.

Years ago, Richard and I played singles tennis four or five times. It was a horrendous, mind-twisting experience, even though I knew I was better than Richard. If a shot I hit was in but close to the line, he would often, but not always, call it out. If he hit a ball that was clearly out but only by a couple of inches, he would walk up toward the net and stare at the spot. To a certain extent, it was intimidating, and you found yourself hesitating on out calls if they were close. When I got a run of points going, Richard would insist on sitting down and retying his shoes for five minutes. Sometimes, he would miscall the score, always in his favor.

I talked to other guys about it, and they had the same problem. One guy told me that Richard once wanted to start a set over when his opponent was ahead three–love. The problem with confronting Richard was, were you going to make a huge scene and accuse him of cheating? No, it would be too ugly, with people on adjacent courts listening in and thinking that you are both total jerks. So you end up playing carefully and not hitting balls close to the lines. Each time I played him, I resolved it would be the last, but he would press me to play again. As I said, I definitely knew I should beat Richard, but the cheating and the byplay were so unnerving, and my mind was so bent that the fourth time we played, he won, which further enraged me, especially since he immediately told the other guys about it as if it were the usual thing.

Richard finally went a shenanigan too far with the Triangle group. One night a couple of years ago, he told an intriguing story about a company that had secretly developed a weight-loss drug with no side effects that really worked. He rattled off the names of compounds nobody had ever heard of. You took a pill twice a day, and presto, in a month you had lost 10 pounds! Obviously, such a drug would be an absolute blockbuster with obese Americans! He told us he had seen the results of the blind tests, and he cited data from the Stanford Research Group and the AMA. Food and Drug Administration (FDA) approval was imminent. A number of the guys knew of the company, which was a legitimate biotech with some real scientists but a flabby balance sheet. It had announced it was working on a weight-loss drug that was promising, but the biotech analysts, of course, were skeptical.

Guys were intrigued by the story. When they work, biotech stocks can be moon shots. Richard was asked a lot of tough questions, and he handled them well. I told you he was a smart, savvy guy. "Look," he said, "the former chairman of Pfizer is a director of Stanford, and I've known him for years. We all know nothing is a sure thing in genome land, but he tells me extensive tests show the pill works wonderfully with rats, and best of all, they haven't found any side effects to speak of. The rats pee a lot more than normal, but their dispositions don't change. Do what you want. I've got a big position, and I'm adding to it."

The next day, some of the guys put in buy orders and were a little surprised when they got filled quickly and in size. Surprise wasn't their emotion two weeks later, when the company suddenly announced one morning it was withdrawing the FDA application. Apparently, the drug did cause rats to lose weight, but it also gave them inoperable, incurable stomach cancer, resulting in death. The stock price instantly collapsed. I was at the next meeting, which Richard did not attend. At dinner, one of the guys, John, told how he had been suspicious when his order got filled in a flash, so he had checked who the big seller was. It was the broker Richard always used!

The members looked at each other the way I suppose the apocryphal Western posse looked at each other when they finally figured out who was the cattle thief. John is a large, serious man with big hands, and during cocktails at the following month's dinner, he and a couple of other guys confronted Richard. Richard squirmed and said he had sold only a little stock to lighten his position. "Get out of here, you piece of crap," said John quietly, and Richard did. He doesn't come to the dinners anymore, and I heard he had moved to Los Angeles.

IT'S A JUNGLE OUT THERE, AND THE HEDGEHOGS ARE KILLING THEIR GOLDEN GOOSE

Anyway, after dinner last night, some of us sat around and gossiped about hedge funds. The members of the Triangle, opinionated veterans of the investment wars, are not shy about expressing their opinions, and we all have known each other for years. The insults flew like shrapnel on a bad day in Baghdad. It began when someone remarked that there are now 8,000 hedge funds in the United States, and that hedge fund capital has exploded from $36 billion as recently as 1990 to probably around a trillion dollars today. A long-only manager sourly said something along the lines of the following: "The golden age for hedge funds is about over, and it will end with a bang, not a whimper. The larger capital and the bigger talent pool now being deployed by hedge funds mean that the pricing of everything from asset classes to individual securities is under intense scrutiny by manic investors, who stare at screens all day, have massive databases, and swing large amounts of money with lightning speed. This has the effect of bidding up the prices and reducing the returns of all mispriced investments. Obvious anomalies now disappear, almost instantly. In effect, the alpha available for capture by hedge funds has to be spread over more funds with bigger money, resulting in lower returns on invested capital for hedge funds as an asset class. Risks will also rise as hedge funds have to take larger, more concentrated positions. You greedy hogs are in the process of killing your own golden goose. It's not only endangered, it is about to die. "

"Don't you wish," one of the hedge-fund guys replied from the bottom of his brandy glass. "The golden goose was plumper and sturdier than you think."

"Global macro is headed for a bust," another guy said, looking at me. "Too much rookie money. You had better make it quick." I just stared at him.

"It's a jungle out there in macro now," he went on. "There are so many macro players and momentum investors, they're bumping into each other. There must be a couple of hundred new macro hedge funds formed in the last six months by guys who think they are the next Stan Druckenmiller or Lewis Bacon. Some of these guys are so green, they can confuse you with their stupidity, and they are big and clumsy, so they can hurt you if you bump into them. And then, stumbling around are the proprietary trading desks of all the big investment banks, plus various rogue central banks like Bank Negara and the Nigerians. Last week, I got crunched between an Asian central bank and some rookie hedge fund guy who panicked on his first macro trip. It's all very disorienting!" The guy, despite his alleged bruises, looked tanned and rested, so I ignored him.

"It's like the money game; our nice old game is being played at faster and faster speeds by bigger and rougher guys, so it's getting tougher and more dangerous all the time," another hedge-fund guy said glumly. "Everybody is on steroids. The violence level is soaring. It's like the NFL."

"As more and more funds are unable to earn sufficient excess returns to justify their fees," another guy said, "the love affair with hedge funds is bound to cool. But not before all that excess capital takes its toll on the performance record and exalted reputations of the big stars. The alpha pool of the whole hedge fund industry is not growing, but the number of guys trying to drink from it is. Ask not for whom the bell tolls; it tolls for thee."

"I'm not so sure the alpha pool isn't growing," I argued. "As all these new, naive, trigger-happy crazies, long on aspiration and short on experience, enter the business, a lot of them will get creamed. Then their losses will expand the alpha pool for the rest of us." I noticed one of the veterans was looking at me kind of funny, as though he was thinking, "Who are you, punk, to go talking about naive talent?"

"Leverage, leverage, leverage—that's what is going to wreck you guys eventually," said the long-only guy. "Actually, since LTCM with its huge balance sheet and various forms of tail optionality (whatever that means) blew up, hedge funds have been reducing leverage. Instead of them, it's their investors, both individuals and the fund of funds, who are putting on the leverage. The clients of the fund of funds are unhappy with the meager returns they are getting, so the fund of funds goes to the bank and borrows. And the banks, particularly the European ones, are falling all over themselves to offer credit to their wealthy individual clients to leverage up their hedge-fund holdings. Theoretically, it makes sense. A basket of diversified hedge funds has lower volatility than one fund, so why not leverage it up to magnify the returns?"

"Yeah," said somebody else. "It makes sense until a bolt from the blue, a tsunami wave, a two- or even three-standard-deviation event happens, and then the you-know-what hits the fan. The hedge fund basket has a 10% drawdown not in a year but in a month, and a big leveraged fund of funds could be down 15% in a flash. What happens to the whole hedge-fund universe then? I'll tell you what. The frightened fund of funds clients redeem, the fund of funds in return have to redeem from their hedge funds, and the whole asset class does an extreme shrink. Furthermore, there are no safe havens. The long–short market-neutral funds get killed, too, because when they have forced liquidations, their longs go down and their shorts go up."

"Meltdown," said the long-only guy, "not just for you perps but for everyone else and me too." The evening was over.

CHAPTER

TWO

The New Hedgehogs May Have Been Golden Boys, but They Still Bleed Red

A s I mentioned before, for every hedge fund rags-to-riches story, there are at least two to three rags-to-rags or rags-to-riches-to-rags tales. In 2004, an estimated 1,000 funds went out of business. Despite media sensationalism, there are very few spectacular blowups, in which a fund goes down in flames like LTCM or Bayou, but there are a lot of slow, lingering deaths. A couple of guys start a hedge fund and raise $10 million or even $50 or $100 million. Their fee is 1.5% fixed on assets and 20% of the profits, but they can't survive on the fixed fee. They have a lot of overhead in space, accounting, computers, back office, and technology. Then they have three analysts and a trader to pay salaries to, plus hard dollars to fork out for Bloomberg terminals and research services. The fixed fee doesn't even cover the overhead, so there is no money left for the partners. Unless the partners have some money to begin with, they have nothing to live on.

Their future then depends completely on the fund's performance over the first couple of years. If the fund does well, the partners earn the 20%, get more money, and wear smiles to bed. If they really blow it in the first year, everybody redeems their money, and they're gone with barely a ripple. But if they just dog along for a couple of years with mediocre performance, then no new money comes in, and it's tough at the office and austere at home: 20% of nothing is nothing. The New York research firm of Bernstein estimates that the 200 biggest hedge funds have 80% of the total industry's assets. The rest of the horde are just dreaming of a hot streak that makes them viable.

I personally know of a dozen funds that were started in the past few years by very successful analysts or savvy institutional salespeople. They were the golden children of the great bull market, and they made a lot of commission money in the late 1990s, which they spent with luxurious abandon. They are attractive guys and gals (not many gals, as a matter of fact), but to some extent, they confused charm, a low handicap, and a bull market with investment brains. Flushed with success, they embraced a voluptuous lifestyle that included everything from wine cellars to jet time-shares. They all seemed to have windblown blond wives, multiple children, starter castles with eight bedrooms and four-car garages, ski houses out West (Vermont is *déclassé*), and a brace of Scottish nannies. Add in private school tuition at $20,000 a crack for even nursery school, annual dues at four or five famous golf clubs, and lots of help, and you get some serious embedded overhead.

THREE GUYS FROM GOLDMAN SACHS

Take the case of three successful guys from private wealth management at Goldman Sachs, who a couple of years ago formed a market-neutral long–short equities fund. They had been big winners at Goldman. One had a real nose for tech stocks, another was particularly good at trading IPOs. But being successful brokers, which is what private-wealth-management people really are, and making a lot of money wasn't sufficient. Brokers are a little grubby. Wives aren't elated to tell another wife that her husband is a broker. So these guys aspired to run a market-neutral hedge fund and be stock pickers. Were they investors or asset gatherers at Goldman Sachs? Mostly the latter, I suspect. *Market neutral* means that a fund's net exposure ranges from maybe 30% net long to 10% net short, volatility adjusted. Market neutral is fashionable because the good practitioners produce consistent, low-risk annual returns in the 7% to 12% range.

Sorry, but I think market neutral is a tough racket, particularly quantitative market neutral. There are too many people doing the same thing. In the 1980s, Morgan Stanley had a series of market-neutral funds that were run off different fundamental and quantitative models. All had boy geniuses at the controls who had made big money on the trading desk or had built a model that worked great on paper when they were dummy back-tested. In live action, none ever produced with real money. One allegedly used a computer to take stock selection to the third derivative and fifth dimension in color. There was color all right. The color of the P&L was a deep shade of red.

Anyway, this attractive trio from Goldman opened on January 1, 2001, with $100 million and lost only 10% over the next two years, which wasn't bad considering the bear market. Then in 2003, they were too cautious and bearish, and the fund went up only 5%. So for the first three years, they had no profits to take 20% of, no draw to live on, and families that were still living high on the suburban-New York hog, so the personal overhead was eating them alive.

Then one of the three partners, the one with the big house in Rye and all the nannies, quit and went back to Goldman in private wealth management. The trouble was all his accounts had been reassigned and he had to start all over again. The other two hunkered down. They let go of their two analysts, pared back on overhead, and transitioned their children to the Greenwich public school system. But as their investors heard about the departures and confidence that the firm was holding together began to dwindle, they were slowly but steadily bleeding assets. The point is that this firm's portfolio hadn't done badly at all; nevertheless, it was about to become history.

SUPERSTAR IAN SLEEPS WITH HIS PORTFOLIO—AND GRINDS HIS TEETH

Another somewhat similar case was Ian. I wrote this six months ago, so bear that in mind as you read this little essay and the addendum. For two years, my two partners and I shared office space with Ian, a brave companion from our Morgan Stanley days. Ian is in his late 30s and is a lean, ascetic-looking guy with a shaved head. He is very bright and analytical. He talks fast and passionately, and all four of us have been

good friends for a long time. I think I know Ian well. He is the quintes-
sential, hard-core, investment true believer. He is the hedge-fund version of Howard Rourke in Ayn Rand's great novel *The Fountainhead*. A
man searching at all costs for *the truth* of his profession.

Ian went to Berkeley and then, like my partner Cyril, was hired by
Bankers Trust for its analysts' program. He was there five years, until my
other partner Madhav lured him away to join Morgan Stanley's emerging markets investment team. Ian put together a fabulous record in
emerging markets. By the late 1990s, he was a managing director and
running the entire investment side of Morgan Stanley's large and very
profitable emerging markets business, reporting to me. We regarded him
as a young superstar, and as 2000 drew to a close, I pressed very hard to
get him paid big money because he was crucial for the business, because
he had so much potential, and because I knew he was restless. At the
end of 2000, for the first time, Ian received a huge bonus, part in cash
and part in deferred compensation.

The day after he got paid in January 2001, he came to see me and,
sheepishly but very sweetly, told me he was going to resign to start his
own global hedge fund. I was disappointed, a little hurt, and very surprised. I felt manipulated, but on the other hand, that's the way the
compensation game is played. I tried hard to talk him out of it. I told
him he had a great job. Why in the world would he leave now? I knew
Ian had a wife and three little children, that he had bought a small
house in the Hamptons and an apartment in New York, and that he
didn't have any real capital of his own to launch a hedge fund. I also argued that he didn't have the credibility to raise money for a global
hedge fund. Why didn't it make sense to stay at Morgan Stanley for a
few more years, make and save more money, and build up his knowledge base on global markets, so that he could raise some serious capital
if a hedge fund was what his heart was set on? Of course, I hoped that
over time, he would come to his senses and stay put.

It was all to no avail. He was adamant, determined no matter what
the cost to become a true, practicing global investor. As it turned out,
the costs were very high. By leaving, he forfeited well over $1 million
of incentive compensation. In the months that followed, he found that
raising money was almost impossible unless he gave up equity, and
even then it was tough. In order to have some capital to invest, the
maniac sold his apartment and house in the Hamptons and moved his

family into a grubby rental. God only knows what austerities he imposed on them. He opened his fund in March 2002 with a pittance of $8 million.

Ian's style evolved into a combination of global macro and global stock picking. He will own or short bonds, currencies, commodities, equity indexes, or individual stocks. Since he began, his performance has been up and down. In the years since he started, he is slightly ahead after fees of the MSCI World Equity index and is doing even better versus the S&P 500. However, the monthly numbers have been erratic. He will have a month when he is up 10% and then three or four months back-to-back when he's down 3% or 4%. In November 2004, he jumped 17%. His capital now is up to $25 million, but he hasn't attracted any substantial money, I guess because of his volatility. In addition, as a purist, he is unwilling to make a deal with any of the money raisers who would require giving away part of the ownership of his fund.

I love Ian's intensity. He sleeps with his portfolio, and his wife says there are nights when he grinds his teeth in his sleep. His is the only other hedge fund to which I have given family money. I gave him money because I am so impressed with not only his head and his heart, but also his discipline and intellectual purity. Ian has come to the conclusion that at Morgan Stanley, he was letting external sources dominate his time rather than controlling it himself.

"Here I was," he says, "taking phone calls, listening to analysts chatter, going to lunches, dinners, meeting with strategists who were talking at me. They controlled the agenda. I'm basically a pretty nice Western guy, and being rude, cutting people off once they get into their babble doesn't come naturally. But I want facts, not opinions. I came to the conclusion that I was much better off not seeing anyone, and that the best use of my time was to read newspapers, trade magazines, factual stuff, and some research. To really focus, I needed isolation reading and solitary studying, with the freedom to discard immediately what is junk or irrelevant to my investment thesis."

That's what he does. He reads and probes all day long. Ian never gets on an elevator without a stack of research in his hands. In the office, he is like a hermit monk alone in his cell, searching for truth. Does this mean Ian is going to be a big winner? Not necessarily, but it is the right way *for him* to give himself the chance to be a big winner, and I'm willing to bet some of my own money that he will succeed.

Postscript: April 2005. Ian came to me today and told me that he has, after much agonizing, decided to give his investors their money back; in other words, to close down his fund. I was utterly shocked. I knew he had been struggling the past few months. In early March, he thought equity markets were breaking out, and he covered his shorts the day before the market rolled over and declined for 11 straight days. I knew he was now down 16.5% for the first four months of 2005, but he had come back from big downs before. After all, he had been up 22% gross in 2004, after being down more than 10% at one point during the year. Since inception and after all fees, his investors are still up 10%, while the S&P 500 has returned 12.65% over the same period. Not a brilliant performance, but hardly a disaster.

Ian is discouraged with the volatility of his performance. It has made it virtually impossible for him to attract assets. But, he tells me, this is not what is driving his decision to pack it in. It's because the pressure of living so intimately, so intensely with his portfolio (and dying a little on the bad days) has become intolerable. He has so much at stake that every wiggle wrenches his insides. He is a solitary investor, working alone, in isolation—but at this point, he doesn't have the emotional and financial stability to deal with the stress. Maybe, if he had had an investment partner to share the burden with, it would be different.

Winston Churchill, whose career had its up and downs and also was plagued with bouts of depression, spoke of the huge, foul-smelling black dog with breath like the sewer, which appeared uninvited and sat heavily on his chest, pinning him down. There is an investment black dog, and when you are doing badly, it comes and sits on your chest in the middle of the night, and on Saturday mornings, and on sunny spring afternoons in the office. It's almost impossible to banish the black dog when he gets on you. He plagues your life. We all have visits from the black dog from time to time, but Ian has seen a lot of him in the past three years. In his final letter to his investors, he wrote:

> *On a more personal/psychological note, it is painfully obvious that I never recovered from the fund's devastating first seven months. Getting caught on the wrong side of the worst seven-month period in equity market history in 30 years was not a great way to start a hedge fund. And while we soldiered on and caught a decent portion of the bounce, I remained somewhat scarred from the experience, and at the sight of my*

own shadow as ready to throw on shorts or sell my longs. . . . So to compound the negatives, I have also been running a business whose medium- and long-term prospects were challenging at best. And this intrinsic business fragility can often leak into the psychology of investing. It makes you feel as if you are perennially one bad quarter away from having to pack it in, which is hardly the solid foundation upon which to make medium-term investment decisions.

I'm convinced Ian is a winner. At this moment, he is totally burnt out. He has taken one day off in the past three years, but now he plans to take time out to reassess what he is going to do with the rest of his life. For the past three years, he has spent a large part of his day staring at Bloomberg screens. The trouble is that there are another 1,000 smart, obsessive people staring at the same screens. It has become a grossly overpopulated loser's game, and Ian told me that he doesn't want to spend the rest of his life this way.

Ian is going to be okay. He is going to beat the black dog. Ian is happily married with three little boys, but he told me his family relationships have suffered. Screen staring, the loneliness of his style of running money, plus a tough market environment have just plain worn him out. But honestly, do I feel somewhat betrayed for the second time? Yeah, I do.

GRINNING GILBERT LOSES HIS GRIN

Of course, as you would expect after a bubble like the one that happened in the Internet and tech space, there also have been hedge funds that went out of business with a bang, and a few that have disappeared with a whimper. Then there were some that burst with a bust in the pocketbook for the investors and with a whimper for the manager. In some cases, the whimpers are sad. There was a guy who was known as Grinning Gilbert because he was always grinning when he talked to you. He could be telling you that his best analyst had just quit or that his biggest long had missed on earnings, and he would be saying it with a huge, beaming smile. It was a friendly, sincere grin, and Gilbert was a very sociable guy. Everybody liked him.

Anyway, that's neither here nor there. In 1996, Grinning Gilbert was maybe in his early forties and was laboring as a portfolio manager at Lord Abbett when he quit to form his own hedge fund. Grinning Gilbert didn't have any money to speak of, and he only raised a pittance initially, but he hired three young analysts and opened his own shop. Grinning Gilbert was a story stock, momentum investor, and he alone made all the investment decisions. In the hot markets of the late 1990s, he increasingly concentrated on tech and Internet stocks. Performance was volatile, but 1997 was huge, and 1998 was OK, and the fund grew. By 1999, Grinning Gilbert was running around $500 million and making some serious money, which he plowed back into his capital account in the fund. That summer, he moved his offices to Greenwich and paid something like $10 million for a big old stone mansion on Round Hill Road, which is about as fancy an address as you can get. It was, to say the least, an aggressive move because $10 million was probably half of his net worth at the time.

Now, Grinning Gilbert's wife Sharon is an aggressive, ambitious personality. She performed a full cannonball into the Greenwich social pool, which is not so easy since there are numerous other families that also desire maximum splashes. Sharon signed up for all the requisite charities and expensive nursery schools, and she instinctively discerned the Greenwich lifestyle. She insisted on a real Scottish nanny and a personal trainer, and that they buy a share in Net Jets. But most of all, she began to pour money into their new property. The interior of the old house was gutted and was rebuilt, complete with every modern architectural flourish, including a two-story-high screening salon and a family room with a massive fireplace and a cathedral ceiling. Her architect designed a wine cellar for the remodeled basement that could stock 5,000 bottles, surrounding an ornate dining room with an antique table that could seat 12. An electronic dumbwaiter connected it to the kitchen. Why she ever thought she would want to have a dinner party in the basement was beyond me, but she did. In any case, it took a year for the rebuild, and the combination of the purchase and the construction put another substantial dent in Grinning Gilbert's still immature net worth.

The family finally moved in on July 1, 2000. Grinning Gilbert was a little nervous about all the new overhead he was acquiring, but as long as the fund kept cranking, he figured he would be okay. Besides, the markets were cranking and he was hot. "What are you going to do?" he said to me with a shrug and a big grin. "The lady wants an estate." Their oldest boy was up for admission to the hot day school, Brunswick, and his prospects looked bleak until a trustee whispered in Grinning Gilbert's ear that a seven-digit pledge would work wonders. Meanwhile, his firm had accumulated some additional overhead as well. There were now five analysts, a chief operating officer, a client-relations person, an office manager, and four secretaries.

The straws were mounting on the camel's back even as dark clouds were gathering. For the year 2000, Grinning Gilbert's fund was down 15%. As I said before, 20% of nothing was (and is) nothing. Grinning Gilbert suggested to Sharon that they defer the new terrace and major landscaping scheduled for that spring, but Sharon angrily argued that if they did, it would be very embarrassing because it would appear as if they had run out of money when their grand design was only half completed.

By the summer of 2001, the retreat in tech and Internet stocks had turned into a full-scale rout. Grinning Gilbert's portfolio was stuffed with moonbeams whose prices were collapsing. By September, he was down another 30%. His investors, most of whom had signed up fairly recently and, therefore, had missed the glory years, began to assail him even as they withdrew their money. Some even talked of lawsuits for gross negligence. One Tuesday, in early October, after a morning when his longs were down and his shorts were up, and after several limited partners screamed at him, Grinning Gilbert told his secretary, with his usual big smile, that he was going home for lunch and would be back by two o'clock. It was a golden, early fall day, with the leaves just beginning to turn, and Greenwich must have looked beautiful as Grinning Gilbert drove home up Round Hill Road, with the magnificent houses and fields rich and indolent in the soft sunlight.

When he got home, Sharon was at a benefit, and Grinning Gilbert had lunch served by the cook on the porch with CNBC on. Apparently, that day there was a lot going on at the old homestead. Seven men with a backhoe were planting mature fir trees, at $20,000 a shot, to create an avenue effect to his driveway. On the back lawn, ten Mexicans were working on the new terrace. A truck was unloading Belgian Block for the new driveway, and an electrician was in the basement installing indirect lighting in the wine cellar. Somewhere, he could hear children laughing. Overhead at home, overhead at the office, leverage, redemptions, and a declining portfolio. It all must have got to Grinning Gilbert.

After lunch, he went up to his bedroom, drew the curtains, and went to bed. He put in wax ear plugs, pulled the covers up over his head, and stayed there. When Sharon came into that dark room at about four, he told her he was very tired and was not getting up for dinner. His secretary called, and a little later, one of his analysts needed to talk with him. He wouldn't take either call. Grinning Gilbert just stayed in bed. In fact, he stayed in bed with the curtains drawn, living on toast and soup for the rest of that week and right through the weekend. He refused to talk with anyone from his office, didn't watch CNBC or look at a newspaper, and seemed to have no interest in the children when they came to visit him. By Friday, two of his biggest investors were demanding to know why he wasn't in the office.

Who knows what really happened that weekend in that dark room between Grinning Gilbert and Sharon. Did he talk to her about his losses, about overhead? The facts are that, on Tuesday afternoon, Sharon went to the office and told Grinning Gilbert's traders to close all his positions, locking in a 30% decline. She informed the 12 employees that the fund was being liquidated, and that they would be paid through the end of November. Sharon talked to the lawyers and the accountants, and she generally took charge. The investors were notified the following week. Grinning Gilbert never came to the office again.

I wasn't really close with Grinning Gilbert, but I heard what had happened from one of his analysts, with whom I played tennis. The analyst said he hadn't heard from Grinning Gilbert since. He was bitter. I called Grinning Gilbert at home and got Sharon (whom I barely knew) both times. I didn't know what to say to her. She said he was out but would call back. He never did. I heard other guys who were even closer to him had similar experiences. And he was a very sociable guy.

Grinning Gilbert and Sharon put their house on the market a few weeks later. That fall, the Greenwich real estate market was slow and soft, but six months later, they sold the property for $7 million—but who knows how much they had put into it? And they had a mortgage to pay off. They subsequently moved to San Diego. I don't think Grinning Gilbert is coming back.

WHAT HAPPENED TO THE HOT, YOUNG TECH GUY

Then there is the case of a young tech guy I knew at a big firm who, in the run-up to bubble, was really hot. He was (and still is, as far as I know) a homespun, attractive guy who will talk your ear off about tech. At the pinnacle of his moment in the sun, he wore blue jeans and sandals to Greenwich cocktail parties, while carrying his baby around in a back-pack. His office was stacked with research reports and prospectuses, which I'm pretty sure he never read, because all day long, he feverishly worked the phone on the whisper network, gossiping and trying to get an edge on earnings releases or who was going to recommend what the next day.

He was fast on the trigger, and in the boom years, his performance was spectacular. He used all the tricks of the late 1990s to get those numbers. He traded intensely, which created a lot of commissions for the brokers and which, in turn, got him big allocations in hot IPOs. Then he put all the IPOs derived from the business of all his accounts into one public fund (which, incidentally, he had most of his own money in), and when the IPOs went to big premiums, he flipped them and got a huge performance boost as a result. He used that fund as his representative account. If anyone asked, he claimed the IPOs weren't suitable for his institutional accounts. It wasn't illegal then, but it wasn't exactly Marquis of Queensbury, either.

He even came as a guest to the Triangle Investment Club dinner a couple of times. Because he was so hot, the grizzled vets listened respectfully and shook their heads in wonder. Maybe the world had passed them by.

In early 1998, the young tech guy quit the big firm and used his record to raise $45 million for his own hedge fund, which, in reality, was just a leveraged long tech fund. That first year he was up 40%, and in 1999, he was up a dazzling 65%. I figure he must have taken home $30 million. In 2000, the money gushed in, and he began with $600 million. That November, he came to the big tech conference in Santa Monica in a G-5 with his wife, two children, a nanny, his wife's parents, and a cousin who was his personal trainer. He had been nicked by the price declines of that summer, but he still believed he was invulnerable, touched by stardust, anointed by the gods. Just as friendly and talkative as ever.

After 2001, which was another bad year, he was bloody but un-bowed, but in 2002, he was taken out to sea and drowned. It seemed as though everything he owned sank to the bottom of the ocean. Most of them were dreamers or promotions, and a few were outright frauds. He had stocks that over a couple of years went from 150 to 3. By year's end, his fund was down something like 80% from its high-water mark, which meant he would have to go up almost 400% before he would start earning an incentive fee.

In January 2003, he closed down and walked away with, I hear, maybe $5 million, which was what was left of the compensation he had earned in those two great first years. He told people he was going to take some time off and start over again fresh, without the dead weight of a high-water mark. So far he hasn't resurfaced. Now they tell me he lives in Malibu and surfs all day long.

The point of these vignettes is that starting and managing your own hedge fund is such a personal and intense endeavor that failing can really put a dent into your life and psyche. Forever!

THREE

Short-Selling Oil
The Crude Joke Was on Us

I f hedge funds didn't sell short, all they would be is just leveraged long funds that charge high fees. As you would expect, leveraged long funds are prone to extreme swings in performance. In fact, this is what many hedge funds morphed into in the 1970s and then again in the late 1990s, as two great secular bull markets were expiring. However, bona fide hedge funds are committed, perpetual, investment short sellers. In other words, they are always short to some extent because there are always stocks that are overvalued *relative* to other stocks. In theory, at the very least, they are going to earn the spread between the difference in the performance of their longs versus their shorts.

That said, professional hedge funds do two different kinds of short selling. One is to sell major indexes short to hedge long positions or to protect the fund if they are bearish. Many of the best managers use this tactic. They are very confident they can apply fundamental analysis to select stocks that will go up, but they have learned the hard way that picking stocks that will go down is considerably more difficult. Currently, the hedge fund industry in general is disillusioned with its ability to earn alpha on the short side. Shorting indexes is passive, they concede, but shorting individual issues or sectors is hazardous.

Nevertheless, specific short selling has its appeal. There are far fewer short sellers than there are long investors, so the short space theoretically should be less populated and, therefore, more inefficient. This is intellectually attractive to those investors who relish being different. Another reason that the short space is less inhabited is that it is temperamentally stressful; being short something always leaves the seller with an uneasy, queasy feeling. The old saw, "He that sells what isn't his'n must give it back or go to prison," echoes back across the centuries. However, short selling appeals to the contrarian instincts of investors, especially those with a skeptical and sardonic view of the innate intelligence of humankind. Thus, the practice endures, but with a relatively high number of casualties.

The other type of short selling involves the few dedicated short-bias hedge funds. As this is being written, a guy I know who runs a $500 million short-bias fund tells me that he thinks total short-bias assets currently under management amount to about $3 billion, down from $6 billion a couple of years ago. Funds of funds sometimes employ short-bias managers, because such funds are uncorrelated with other types of hedge funds. The short-bias guys usually divide their positions into investment shorts and frauds.

Investment shorts are situations in which rigorous security analysis identifies companies whose business prospects are either deteriorating or are materially worse than what is priced into their stocks. The short seller might stay short stocks like this for years, although the short seller may trade around his position. Coca-Cola (KO) is an example. In 1998, a short-seller guy became convinced that Coke was playing with its earnings because a company with a 3% sales growth could not indefinitely deliver 15% earnings gains, as was being advertised by management and analysts. (See Figure 3.1.) He studied the soft drink industry, went to Coke's analyst meetings, and talked to bottlers. Everyone was convinced KO was a true, 15% trend-line growth stock. He found five different reasons it was more likely to be a 5-percenter, went short Coke at a price in the mid 80s, and has been short ever since. It's been a fine short sale, as the company couldn't fulfill expectations, and management turnover resulted. The shares currently trade around 43. Now that everybody hates the company and its management, he, contrary soul that he is, is considering covering his short. This guy likes to sell short and stay short on big, famous stocks that have gone up a lot and

FIGURE 3.1
Coca-Cola Stock Price, 1986–2005

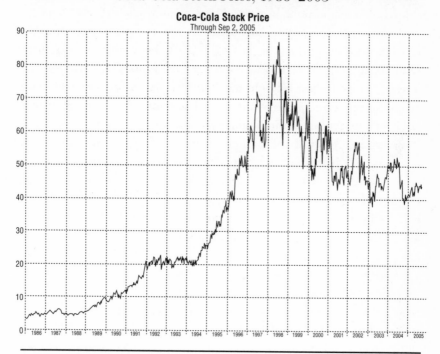

Coca-Cola Stock Price
Through Sep 2, 2005

Source: FactSet Data Systems

that the institutions love. He studies *Fortune* magazine's list of the most admired companies for new victims.

By contrast, *fraud shorts* are just what they sound like, and they can become big winners because reality and the truth do tend to eventually prevail. However, such shorts can be dangerous if they get overcrowded. When the short interest is very large, nonfundamental developments can result in painful squeezes. For example, a number of hedge funds get short a fraud. The fairy tale that has been spun by the promoters is unraveling, and short interest rises rapidly. It becomes hard to borrow the stock. In the meantime, one of the hedge funds that is short gets a big capital redemption and, therefore, has to cover its short in the fraud. This results in a run-up in the stock price that has nothing to do with the validity of the negative investment thesis.

TORTURED BY SHORTING OIL

From time to time, poor, benighted investment souls such as us become
entangled with a position that cruelly abuses and tortures. When you
first find and study an investment opportunity, be it long or short, there
is the thrill of discovery. You are excited by the possibilities, and you enter the relationship all bright-eyed and bushy-tailed, bubbling with
great expectations. It's almost like the first flush at the beginning of a
promising love affair. We commence our investment relationships full of
confidence in the intensity of our analysis and the profundity of our
reasoning. We harbor dreams of magnificent profits, but then, by some
quirk of fate, suddenly your intriguing new love transforms into a dark,
irrational beast that turns on you with savage fury. When this happens,
that wild snarling creature, that one position, can dominate the performance of your portfolio and your investment life. As the agony is pro-
longed, you become obsessed with this abusive relationship, and it can
even overwhelm everything else in your real life.

We were tortured unmercifully by a short position we took in oil in
May 2004, when the price was about $40 a barrel. We did all our usual
analytical work and model building. Our reasoning went like this:
Other than a brief war-related spike in 1990, both the nominal and real
price of oil were back to the highest levels since the early 1980s. World
production and inventories were rising, and the strategic oil reserve was
nearing peak capacity. Consumption, we postulated, was probably de-
celerating as both the world and the Chinese economy slowed. China
was crucial, because it alone accounted for 31% of the increase in global
oil consumption between 1992 and 2002 and more than 50% in 2003.
Change at the margin, we argued, was what drives prices. We constructed an elaborate oil price regression model that showed the equilibrium or fair value price of oil at $32.48 to be ridiculously precise.
Most energy experts maintained it was even lower, pricing out somewhere in the high 20s.

At the same time, bullish sentiment on oil was very elevated, and
the open interest in crude oil futures was huge. We believed that much
of the open interest represented speculative longs that were in the trade
because of trend-following models. In other words, they were momentum investors who bought oil mindlessly (in our opinion), simply because the price was going up. Of course, we realized that there was

serious risk from terrorist strikes that could disrupt Middle East production, particularly if Saudi Arabia, the swing producer, was hit. At the time, the experts generally agreed (and our models confirmed) that there was an $8 premium in the price, but they didn't agree about how vulnerable Saudi Arabia's production facilities were.

As we studied the terrorist factor, we believed that pipeline sabotage would not seriously disrupt production because the installations could be quickly repaired. A sudden revolution in Saudi Arabia would disrupt the world economy and financial system and send the price of oil to 80, but what were the odds of such an event? Very low, we postulated. We also knew that because there was less spare production capacity in the rest of the world than there had been in the past, temporary shutdowns would cause price volatility. Our monthly letter for May 2004 said, "We recognize that this oil short is a dangerous position, and we have meticulously calculated the risk-to-reward equation and sized our position accordingly." Oil has a volatility about double that of the S&P 500 stock index, and we computed that if we had a short position equal to 12% of our capital, we were well within our stated value-at-risk position limits.

DEEP ANALYSIS CAN GET YOU IN DEEP TROUBLE

All our analysis was for naught. We misjudged demand, failed to anticipate the intensity of the hurricane season and political developments, and were less respectful than we should have been of market psychology and its effect on price momentum. We first sold oil short in May at around 40, and we squirmed as it promptly rallied to over 42. Then on the last day of June, it fell to 36. That afternoon, we actually considered covering some, but we didn't. Our analysis indicated oil was still materially overpriced. Why lose our position?

We were just plain wrong. Oil prices proceeded to climb and began a virtually vertical ascent as terrorism and sabotage in Iraq, a tax dispute in Russia, a strike in Nigeria, and a presidential recall vote in Venezuela roiled the market for crude. Convinced that these were temporary disruptions, and reassured by announcements of increases in OPEC production, we increased the size of our short position. Our fundamental analysis and our model continued to say that the equilibrium price of oil was somewhere between 28 and 32 a barrel. Inventories were building, OPEC was pumping, and the world economy was slowing. We reasoned that if oil could overshoot its equilibrium price, it could also undershoot. We still loved our short.

Furthermore, we were confident that the huge rise in the price that had already occurred would eventually cause conservation and the substitution of alternative sources of energy.

From the beginning, our practice had been to write a detailed monthly letter to our investor partners to keep them fully informed of our thinking and performance. Unfortunately, despite our pleas for confidentiality, the letter got passed around via e-mail, so our performance and positions became known. In our July letter, we stressed that we were value, not momentum, investors. In our process, when the price of an investment goes against bias by more than 15% in the case of a commodity, it triggers an automatic review of the fundamentals. Following that review we either have to add to the position or close it. As value investors, if the fundamentals have not changed, our inclination is to add to the position in question, not close it, because the price change has actually made it more attractive, not less. Investing on the basis of value, not price momentum, is our religion.

Warren Buffett articulated this philosophy best with his manic-partner analogy. At a talk I attended, in one of his musings, he expressed it something like this:

> *Suppose you are an equal partner in a good business with a manic-depressive partner named Mr. Market. From time to time, Mr. Market will only see the favorable factors affecting your business and will then become so euphoric about the prospects of the business that he will come to you and offer to buy your half at a ridiculously high price. So, of course, you should sell it to him.*
>
> *At other times, seeing only trouble ahead for your firm, he becomes deeply depressed and in his despair offers to sell you his share at an outrageous discount to its intrinsic value. Then, you should buy it from him.*

Buffett went on to say that it was irrational, the height of foolishness, to sell an asset you were confident was undervalued just because its price was falling. In other words, Mr. Market can be an old fool (or maybe a young fool) who, from time to time, becomes hysterical. Sometimes, in his madness, he sees ghosts. At others, he imagines the good fairy touching him with her long golden fingers.

> *You are perfectly free to ignore Mr. Market or to take advantage of him, but it will be disastrous if you fall under his influence. Suppose the price you could sell your home at was quoted every day. For several months the quotation steadily declined. Would you then sell your home, the home you were comfortable in and satisfied with, just because its price was declining? Of course not! In this sense, an attractive investment is similar to a home you are happy to inhabit.*

Mr. Buffett's value philosophizing sounds eminently sensible, but it doesn't work when you are trafficking in commodities and you have short-term-performance sensitive clients. On August 19, the price of oil hit 48, equity markets were reeling, and we were down 7% for the year. The next day the *New York Times* ran a story, complete with a picture of me looking bedraggled, that reported Traxis was suffering substantial losses from its oil short. Furthermore, the tone of the piece was that I was a loser, which, because everybody I know reads the *Times*, did not exactly lift my spirits. That weekend when I went out to dinner at the country club, I sensed people watching me, but when I tried to meet their eyes, they looked away.

YEARS OF LOVE GO DOWN THE DRAIN

Immediately, a storm broke upon us. One of our largest investors, for whom I had done well over a number of years and who had committed to Traxis right at the beginning, called to tell me he was withdrawing. It was like a surprise punch in the stomach, which hurts most because you don't expect it. A fund of funds that was a major investor e-mailed us that we were crazy and were violating our fiduciary responsibilities. A woman, whose money I had successfully managed for 30 years and who was a close personal friend, called to tell me she couldn't take the volatility and wanted out. In other words, 30 years of confidence went down the drain in a couple of months, even though in 2003 we had performed really well. Finally, a market letter writer who had obviously seen our July letter about Buffett and Mr. Market wrote a snide, mocking piece about the folly of being a value investor and how I should have learned by now to buy strength and sell weakness. The disconcerting thing was that, for that time and that commodity, he was right.

I had experienced similar episodes of cascading negative feedback in the past. When you have been wrong for a while and the world is screaming that you are crazy, it seems as though the *tipping point* of the bad spell is signaled by a deluge of abuse and some significant account closings by long-time clients. It never fails. To be a valid signal, the blows have to be more than flesh wounds; they must actually draw blood. You must have stomachaches and wake up in the night sweating and worrying. Your smile has to feel as if it were pasted on.

I wasn't the only one who was suffering. My partner, Madhav, began having a recurring nightmare in which he was in a client meeting trying to explain our oil short, and he was unable to express himself coherently. The clients looked at him with disgust. Another partner's wife also was worrying and was following the oil price moment to moment, as intently as we were. My daughter Wende said to me, very sweetly but with just the hint of an edge, "Now, Dad, tell me again, why is it you are short oil?" I thought at the time that these were all signals that the turn in our fortunes must be near.

Sure enough, in the last 10 days of August, oil fell from its high of 50 to 42.50. We exhaled a great sigh of relief. A highly regarded technician wrote that the Fibonacci wave count he employed showed a final climax in oil at precisely 48, to be followed by a bear market. The first break would be to 42, and then there would be an exhaustion rally that would peak around September 20. The momentum buyers would be drained out of oil. Once again, in the arrogance of our intellectual conceit, we did not cover any of our position because we suspected that the bubble had begun to burst, and that the dynamic hedgers (traders who employ computer models to buy what's going up and to sell what's going down), who populate the commodities markets, would be sellers, not buyers, on the exhaustion rally. However, to protect our position from a bolt from the blue, such as a terrorist strike, we did buy an out-of-the-money call on oil.

However, our respite was short-lived. The emotional signal I thought I had received was only transitory, which goes to show that nothing—no signal, no single indicator, sociological or Fibonacci—is infallible. The gods simply were not with us because, in September, along came an unprecedented run of hurricanes. It was the hurricane season to end all hurricane seasons. Of course, we knew August and September were hurricane prone and that severe storms could cause the offshore producing rigs in the Gulf of Mexico to be shut down, but there hadn't been a really devastating hurricane for a number of years. However, that was ancient history. Now, suddenly, beginning in mid-August, a record four major hurricanes in quick succession smashed into Florida and churned up the Gulf of Mexico. The oil markets reacted to each one, and meanwhile, there were pipeline bombings in Iraq, and the Russian government continued to torture the Russian oil giant, Yukos, and its majority owner, causing exports of oil from Russia to be delayed and disrupted. These events resulted in the oil futures market surging to a new high of 50 by the end of September.

At this point, our memories and and experience kept telling us that at the top, the validation of immense price rises becomes most strident. Moreover, there is a *coping mechanism* in life that is almost a force of nature. I read again the magnificent comment of Barbara Tuchman way back in the dark ages of the 1970s when there was much talk of the Club of Rome and its theory of a permanent shortage of natural resources. She said

> *The doomsayers work by extrapolation; they take a trend and extend it, forgetting that the doom factor sooner or later generates a coping mechanism . . . you cannot extrapolate any series in which the human element intrudes; history, that is the human narrative, never follows and will always foil the scientific curve.*

Nevertheless, we wondered if all this palaver was just our desperate rationalizations, and if it were we, not the oil speculators, who had gone mad.

We were also well aware of the dangers of what the social psychologists call *confirmatory bias*, in other words the tendency to collect all the information that agrees with your position and to ignore the information that doesn't. Behavioral theory teaches that the best antidote to this bias is to listen to the opposite side of the case and then dispassionately to identify the logical flaws in the argument. It is unlikely that this exercise alone will compel you to change your mind, because data is not processed impartially. People accept data that supports their initial beliefs and reject information and interpretation that doesn't. In an attempt to keep an open mind, we studied intently every bull story on oil we could find. Meanwhile, the oil price kept working irregularly higher (see Figure 3.2.), and we bought a call on oil to partially hedge our short position.

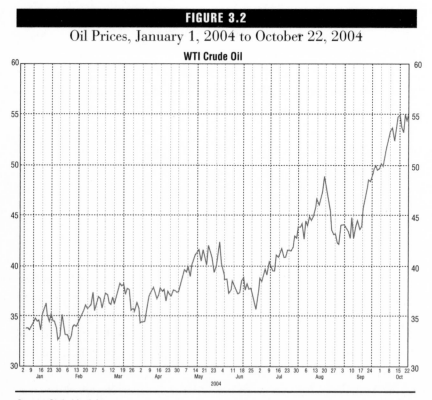

FIGURE 3.2
Oil Prices, January 1, 2004 to October 22, 2004

WTI Crude Oil

Source: Global Insight

WHAT I LEARNED FROM THE EARLY 1900s: THE MARKET HASN'T CHANGED THAT MUCH

While we were being tortured by our crude short, various people attempted to give me succor of one type or another. Guys I know who are professional commodity traders effusively offered advice, most of which was to buy strength and sell weakness, in other words to go with the flow. They unabashedly told me their short-selling trading tactic invariably was "Don't fight a losing position. If it doesn't show you a profit, cover it." Not very helpful, because we were and are value investors.

In my agony, I took out and reread passages from my trading bible, *Reminiscences of a Stock Operator* by Edwin Lefevre. The book was first published in 1923 and is long out of print, but it can be bought from time to time on the Internet. There is little doubt that the stock operator who is the narrator in the book was the legendary Jesse Livermore. The late Gerald Loeb, who wrote *The Battle for Investment Survival* ("Put all your eggs in one basket and then watch the basket"), and who often acted as Livermore's broker, told me that Livermore had used Lefevre as his scribe for *Reminiscences*. Regardless of who actually wrote it, the book is the distilled trading wisdom and market anecdotes of a professional trader operating in the frantic milieu of pools, tips, manipulation, and tape reading of the first third of the past century. Markets haven't changed that much a century later. It is, by far, the best trading book ever written.

Livermore was a fascinating character. He was a boardroom tape watcher and trader in the style of the times, but he was also very sensitive to market sentiment and value. He stressed how crucial was a deep understanding of human psychology and the interplay of greed and fear. Trading was much more about human nature than tips and hunches. In the early 1900s, he came out of nowhere to make his first big killing trading grain from a Chicago bucket shop. He sidestepped the panic of 1907 and came to Wall Street in 1908 with $3 million, which was a decent fortune in those days. Handsome, dapper, and articulate, Livermore bought a seat on the New York Stock Exchange and proceeded to challenge the Wall Street tycoon establishment. The great financiers like J.P. Morgan disdained stock-market operators, but a man like Livermore could rattle their cages.

Livermore was a bear by disposition, and in 1915 he went short stocks and suffered heavy losses. However, realizing he was wrong, he reversed his position and made big gains in the 1916 to 1919 bull market, but so did a lot of other people. However, he really distinguished himself by anticipating the sudden and brutal postwar depression and crash that wiped out so many businessmen and speculators. In 1919, he sold everything, went short, and although he was early, eventually made a fortune in the bust that followed. In 1922, Livermore had a big hit in grain, and in the early 1920s he managed the infamous Piggly-Wiggly pool that ignited speculation and ignited the bull market. However, his inherent bearish bias and his sense that greed was in total ascendancy kept him from fully participating in the madness of the late 1920s. Loeb once told me that Livermore was a great admirer of Walter Bagehot, the first editor of *The Economist*, and often cited this stupid-money paragraph from Bagehot's essay on Edward Gibbon:

> *Much has been written about panics and manias, much more than with the most outstretched intellect we are able to follow or conceive, but one thing is certain, that at particular times a great deal of stupid people have a great deal of stupid money. . . . At intervals, from causes which are not to the present purpose, the money of these people—the blind capital, as we call it, of the country—is particularly large and craving; it seeks for someone to devour it, and there is a "plethora"; it finds someone, and there is "speculation"; it is devoured, and there is a "panic."*

Livermore wanted to be there, short of stocks, when the "stupid money" was "devoured," as he was convinced it always would be— eventually. I am fascinated with his credo of being an investor/trader. In the book, the protagonist for Livermore, the Old Turkey, sounds like Buffett's spiritual father as he repeatedly preaches "sitting tight" with a position you really believe in. "Don't over-think it and don't over-trade. Men who can be both right and sit tight are uncommon," says the Old Turkey. "I found it [this principle] one of the hardest things to learn. But it is only after a stock operator has grasped this that he can make the big money."

The Old Turkey, like Livermore, is essentially a professional trader in commodities and stocks. However, again like Livermore and unlike the plungers and the peacocks of that speculative era that was coming to an end, he understood that, without the cover of a pool or inside information, trading was essentially a zero-sum game but that investing could be a winner's game.

Without faith in his own judgment no man can go very far in this game. That is about all I have learned—to study general conditions, to take a position and stick to it. I can wait without a twinge of impatience. I can see a setback without being shaken, knowing that it is only temporary. I have been short one hundred thousand shares and I have seen a big rally coming. I knew it would make a difference of one million dollars in my paper profits. And I nevertheless have stood pat and seen half my profit wiped out without once considering the advisability of covering my shorts to put them out again in the rally. I knew that if I did I might lose my position and with it the certainty of a big killing. It is the big swings that make the big money for you.

Of course none of this "sitting tight" means that if the fundamentals of your investment deteriorate, you don't sell your long or cover your short. As John Maynard Keynes famously said, "If the facts change, I change my mind, sir. What would you do, sir?"

We have an investor who has been a commodity trader all his business life. I read him the Old Turkey's quotation. "Yeah," he said, "and you know how Jesse Livermore ended up?" I said no. He told me. "After being bearish in the late 1920s, Livermore finally capitulated in mid-1929, went heavily long, and was virtually wiped out in the Crash. Some years later he committed suicide in the men's room of The Biltmore." I don't know if that is true or not.

Meanwhile oil continued to work higher.

FOUR

Short Selling Is Not for Sissies

O ne evening in mid–October 2004, at the height of our oil agony, I went to dinner with some hedge-fund friends. We got to talking about short selling and bad trips. One of the guests, I will call him The Veteran, related the story of Jock Robinson. I had heard the name, but I never knew the man.

THE PRINCE OF BLACKNESS

Jock Robinson ran a very successful hedge fund in the late 1970s and early 1980s, which was a time when markets were swinging back and forth in a broad trading range, creating a productive environment for shorting. Unlike now, in those days there were very few professional hedge-fund short sellers, so the venue was inefficient. Jock was a fastidious analyst and a good long investor, but he had the soul of a dyspeptic cynic and was a truly great short seller. He loved to dissect financial statements, deciphering obfuscating footnotes, and identifying the flaws in a company's business projections. He thrilled with righteous indignation when he discovered accounting tricks and financial pie in the sky. It was as though as a child he had been bitten by an accountant.

His specialty became taking giant short positions in story stocks that had been promoted with what were wildly optimistic projections at best and frauds at worst. As time went on and his exploits on the short side became known, someone christened him the Prince of Blackness and the moniker stuck. "Yeah," said the Veteran, "when the Prince really got going on a short position, he didn't just have some skin in the game. He had his whole ass in the game."

According to the Veteran's story, Jock worked as an analyst and then as a portfolio manager at the Morgan Bank, and then started his own hedge fund in the late 1970s. Jock ran it as a sole proprietorship with a small group of smart young analysts who did his legwork for him. His performance was good, because his longs mostly went up and his shorts went down. His fund grew, and the Prince became rich, at least by the standards of that era.

THE CARIBBEAN CASINO SAGA

At the time of this story, Jock had a huge short position in the shares of a company I will call Casino Resorts. The company had a number of rundown hotel properties around the Caribbean, but it had been a consistent money loser for years. The stock had bumbled along on the American Stock Exchange between 3.50 and 1.50. In 1980 a group of Miami real estate operators bought control of Casino Resorts for a pittance and issued themselves millions of options. They had in mind a major stock promotion.

Shortly thereafter, they purchased Blue Island, a barren island just off San Juan, Puerto Rico. They built a bridge to the mainland, and at the time of this drama were in the final stages of the construction of a mammoth resort. The main hotel was being built, as they described it, "in an arching, sweeping curve designed to draw you in with its promise of great expectations," and its entrance was surrounded by soaring fountains that danced to classical music. A long, winding aquarium with exotic fish was built into the lobby and entrance halls that led you gently but inexorably to the restaurants and casino. Behind the hotel were three spiral swimming pools set in lavish gardens supposedly inspired by Versailles and a twelfth-century Augustinian Cloister. These attractions were designed to distract guests from the unpleasant realization that there was no beach because the coastline of the island was so rocky. Two user-friendly golf courses had been completed.

The prime attraction at Blue Island was going to be the Stardust Casino, the Caribbean's biggest and most lavish, which was scheduled to open February 1 in time for the peak season. The casino itself was different because it had a domed roof that allowed natural light, which, during the day, created a late afternoon soft sunlight effect and, at night, with the stars, was supposed make the players feel that anything was possible. An elaborate aroma system was planned for the casino to disseminate a robust but gentle ambiance into the players' souls.

The source of the money for all this investment was more than a little mysterious, and there were rumors in San Juan that there was laundered drug money behind the huge bank loans. The completed parts of the complex had been in operation for six months and were losing money hand over fist, because the location was poor and tourists didn't want to be stuck on an island. The promoters' story was that when the casino was in operation, occupancy at the hotels would soar, the restaurants would be packed, and the island would become *the* destination for the rich and famous. Furthermore, the radiation effect would raise occupancy rates at the company's other hotels. The shares began to show some life.

As the Casino Resorts promotion gained momentum, a major public relations firm was hired, and an elderly former politician of New York joined the board. The public relations firm recommended changing the name of the company to Treasure Island Properties, and this was accomplished. It was whispered into a hairy ear that, if they got behind the story, Johnson & Company, a somewhat sleazy Wall Street investment bank with a high stress sales force, would become the company's investment banker and that a large equity offering was planned. Shortly thereafter, Johnson & Company issued a glossy research report projecting earnings per share of $2.00 in 1982, and with a full year of operations, $5.00 in 1983, and potential profits of $10.00 a share when the entire multiresort complex was functioning.

With the report circulating, Johnson & Company sponsored a series of lunch and dinner meetings in New York and Boston in which management confirmed the projections in the research report. The numbers were ridiculously optimistic and assumed enormous volume and profits from the casinos, much higher room and occupancy rates, and the introduction of gambling at the company's other hotels. Of course, the reality was that hotels associated with casinos usually offered low rates to attract gamblers, and gambling was not legal on the sites of the company's other properties. The stock rose to 10, and, in November 1981, on the back of all the hoopla, a $200 million secondary offering of shares was sold to the public. The stock levitated to 16. Nobody seemed to care that the company now had 40 million shares outstanding, a market capitalization of $640 million, and tons of debt.

This was exactly the kind of promotion that Jock relished and had made big money shorting. He went to the lunches and innocently asked penetrating questions. However, he made a point of not pressing too hard. He didn't want to scare off the public, who was lapping up the story, and alert other short sellers. He sent his best analyst to Puerto Rico to check out the facility and another to visit the other properties. The other properties were dumps, as he suspected, and as he dissected the numbers, he became convinced the earnings estimates were ridiculous. Meanwhile, he immersed himself in studying the economics of the gambling industry.

The motley crew masterminding the Treasure Island promotion continued to beat the drum loudly. They persuaded the American Stock Exchange to change the company's ticker symbol to RICH. Then they signed up Lord Howard of Dunnymead as chairman. His lordship was a corpulent, 50-year-old, failed investment banker, who had been asked to leave a prestigious British bank for undisclosed reasons, rumored to be either lying or lechery or both. He had a most aristocratic accent, dressed like a peacock, and carried himself like the Guards officer he never had been.

However, Lord Howard was no fool, and he negotiated a very substantial compensation package for himself, including the grant of a large block of stock options. He also fully understood the mechanics of a promotion.

At the investor lunches, sponsored by Johnson & Company in New York, at which Lord Howard presided, Jock's presence was noted and his reputation discovered. As Jock's short position increased, his questioning became more aggressive. On one occasion, when Jock politely but persistently probed the company's revenue and profit projections, Lord Howard lost his composure and finally cut Jock off with "Sir, this venture is for investors who have foresight and imagination, not for cynical Shylocks searching for a pound of flesh. I know who you are, sir. You are the Prince of Blackness. There is no place for your kind here. You abuse our hospitality." Jock flushed and left, but he was deeply offended by the Shylock crack, and, to some extent, the affair became a personal vendetta. The animosity deepened when some of Jock's disciples began to sell the stock short.

In mid-December 1982 Treasure Island Properties officially opened the Stardust Casino with a rush of celebrities, entertainment, and extensive TV and newspaper advertising in New York, Miami, and Atlanta. Lord Howard presided at the ceremonies, jowls swollen with self-importance, a voluptuous bored airline stewardess, who sipped Stolichnaya laced with bitters, on his arm. Large crowds thronged the Casino over the holiday weekends, and the hotels were sold out. The company had let it be known that the payouts at the tables and the slot machines initially would be very favorable, and newspapers in Miami, New York, and San Juan ran interviews with some of the winners who extolled Treasure Island. Of course these stories had been carefully orchestrated, sometimes with money changing hands.

Buoyed by all the excitement, RICH rose from 20 to 25, but Jock was not concerned. The opening had been a big hit, but, as Jock pointed out, why wouldn't it be? Management had handed out hundreds of freebies. He viewed the high attendance as inflated by the opening hoopla and sent an analyst to monitor activity. The analyst learned that many complimentary rooms had been allocated to athletes, beautiful people, travel agents, and even call girls to get the action going. The work Jock and his analysts had done proved conclusively that the company could not possibly fulfill its public projections, and, in fact, was presently still operating at a loss. He sold short another 200,000 shares.

The Prince had never married and in fact had never shown much interest in women. Now in his early fifties, he fell heels over head in love with a much younger woman. He told friends he had finally found his true love, his soul mate, and he planned an elaborate trip to the Far East. In early February 1983, Jock and his lover left for their Asian tour. They had eagerly anticipated this time together, and Jock's fiancé was adamant that they must discover if, away from the business stimulation of New York, they could live happily together. His office in New York was told to call only in the case of the most dire emergencies. The couple's first stop was Jakarta. At the Mandarin Hotel, his analyst called to inform him that now, four weeks after the opening of the Stardust Casino, big crowds were still evident. Furthermore, there was gossip in the New York and Miami press that this was a casino to die for because the odds were so favorable for the gambler. Even the slots paid off big. Travel agents, some of whom owned the stock, were promoting Treasure Island very aggressively. The company announced that profits in the first two months had been well in excess of expectations. RICH reached 28. Jock put in an order to sell more.

As the chatter spread about the money to be made at the Stardust Casino and the women to be experienced on the island, the crowds soared. Every room at the Treasure Island hotel was booked, and tourists were staying in San Juan and going to Treasure Island for the scene. The restaurants were jammed. The company announced that even though gambling payouts were richer than in Las Vegas, they were beating profit projections because of the high level of activity. Volume in the stock was swelling, and more analysts were initiating coverage of the company. RICH had become the hottest trading stock on the American Stock Exchange.

By now Jock was at a remote Amman resort on Bali and was out of touch. Earlier he had told his traders to sell another 200,000 shares if the stock ever got to 35. It did, and his order was executed. He was now short a million and a half shares. From Bali, the lovers flew to Singapore. It was now the end of March, and Casino Resorts announced that by next winter it would be opening another casino of similar scale at its property on Nassau in the Bahamas. Earnings projections for 1984 would have to be increased substantially. The shares hit 38, and at the Mutiara Beach Hotel on Penang, one night at 3 A.M. the phone rang. Jock angrily answered it, to learn that his prime broker had been unable to borrow the last 200,000 shares he had sold short except by paying a premium. The bulls were trying to squeeze him. Jock slammed down the phone.

FRANTIC CLIENTS AND HOSTILE BROKERS

By the time Jock and his woman got to Amanpuri in Phuket, Thailand, Jock was having trouble sleeping because he was being awakened three or four times each night by calls from New York. With the price of RICH rising, his position was getting bigger and bigger, and his prime broker wanted more margin. Furthermore, his short position had become common knowledge, and the Treasure Island consortium was boasting about cornering the Prince. The redoubtable Alan Abelson, a close friend of Jock's, had interviewed Lord Howard, who had said Jock was "a blind fool" and that the stock was going to 100.

Then came a fortuitous bolt from the blue. The monthly SEC release of insider activity revealed substantial selling of RICH shares by senior management, including Lord Howard himself. Abelson wrote a sardonic, sarcastic piece in *Barron's* questioning the accounting and the projections. The price of International Resorts promptly dropped like a stone from 38 to 30, and Jock felt much better. However, the company announced that the insider selling was merely to enable certain members of the management group who had borrowed money to fund the company to pay off their bank debt. Nevertheless, the shares didn't rally, and Jock felt the bubble had been burst.

In late March, Jock flew to Hong Kong where he had booked a suite at that grand old landmark, The Peninsula. Abruptly RICH shares took off again. The *New York Times* ran a long story in the Travel section on the charms, winnings, and values at Treasure Island. The reporter, his girlfriend, and her parents, at the invitation of the company, had spent a long weekend at the resort, and when it came time to pay, the hotel charged them only for phone calls. The gambling public now believed the Stardust Casino was a gold mine, and the whole thing began to assume some of the characteristics of a nineteenth-century gold rush.

Some tourists came just for the scene, and what a scene it was! Old ladies fought and scratched for a slot machine and cursed each other, and men went to gross extremes to keep their places at the tables. Some wore receptacles so they didn't have to go to the men's room to pee, but others who were less well prepared urinated into their pants while standing at the tables or into nearby spittoons. Although these happenings made for colorful stories, they didn't enhance the ambience, and management took action. Security personnel forcibly removed the most egregious offenders. Brokers talking up the stock spoke of earnings of $7.00 a share, which, of course, was ridiculous, but nevertheless the stock kept relentlessly climbing, reaching 60 in mid-April.

Jock was now both seriously worried and, he confessed later, scared. He had a persistent upset stomach. In spite of his deep personal happiness, the burden of his losses was weighing on his psyche. The shares he had borrowed were being called back from him. In some cases he couldn't make delivery, and he was being bought in by hostile brokers, pushing the price even higher. On May 15, RICH hit 80. Jock had lost more than $100 million. His hedge fund had always performed well, but this was the early 1980s, and huge money had not gone into hedge funds. Jock was running a little more than $400 million, and with the devastation of the RICH trade, the fund was suddenly down 22% for the first four months of 1983.

He began to get frantic calls from clients and redemptions, and, as he did, he had to buy back RICH shares to cover his short or allow the position to become an even larger percentage of his fund. Jock was a very gutsy guy and a plunger, but he was shaken. Sensing a death spiral, rumors were started by traders that there was a run on his hedge fund, and that he would be forced to liquidate it. If so, they reasoned, he would have to buy back all the RICH shares he had sold short, propelling the price even higher. His prime broker was demanding even more margin as the position grew, and Jock was forced to sell other stocks in his portfolio, so the RICH position was now almost 40 percent of his total portfolio. As rumors spread of his predicament, buyers came into RICH thirsting for the kill, and the stock touched 90. He was caught in the ultimate killer vicious circle.

Unfortunately, there is no happy ending to this story. By May 18, Jock had had enough. He told his trader to begin buying back RICH shares to cover the short position. His trader was very good and worked the order carefully, but, inevitably, the story circulated that Jock was covering. The stock spurted another 10 points. On May 25, reluctantly, Jock flew back to New York, skipping the visit to Kyoto he had been anticipating. By May 30, he had covered his entire short position but with a staggering loss. On June 1, he sent a letter to his investors, informing them of the damage and that he had bought back most of his short position. He offered his investors a July 1 withdrawal.

As this news spread, the price of RICH plunged. By the middle of May, it was down to 60, and on July 1, it was trading at 45, despite a new round of higher earnings estimates by analysts. However, it was too late for Jock. His fund was down to $80 million, of which $20 million was his. Reluctantly he discharged all but one of his research analysts. He, effectively, was out of business. Over the next decade, he ran his own money and that of a few true believers. He did very well. At our dinner, the Veteran said that Jock was currently worth well over $100 million. But he was finished in the hedge fund business. He was forevermore the guy who got cornered in RICH.

The real irony was that in the long run, Jock was totally right about both the earning power of the company and the stock price. After the initial flurry, the odds at the Casino were stacked back in favor of the house, and, in the years that followed, the property was a meager success. So much stock had been issued that earnings per share never even reached $2.00. Eventually another property was opened, but it never prospered. Too much competition. As for the stock, the price of RICH drifted down, and by 1985 was in the mid-teens, and by 1990 it was trading between 10 and 5. However, the bad guys won. Lord Howard and his associates exercised most of their options in the 50s and made big money.

THE AGONY GOES ON AND ON

Hearing the story, of course, made me feel very uneasy. There were so many moments in Jock's story that I could identify with. As October unfolded, the oil price worked higher, surpassing its old peak of $48 and bouncing around the low 50s. From time to time it would have two- or three-day corrections that we would rejoice in as signs of the beginning of the end, but it would always rebound. On October 21 we sold part of our call, booking a nice profit, but leaving us more exposed. Sure enough, two days later, crude set a new closing high above 55. We gritted our teeth in public and ground them in private. At a dinner party in Greenwich, I found myself stammering as I tried to explain our rationale for being short oil.

Then, suddenly, on October 27, oil broke when the inventory numbers that come out every Wednesday showed a bigger increase than expected. However, it wasn't a huge surprise and, in fact, right after the release, oil rallied for a few minutes. Then the price collapsed, at one point being down 6% on the day. A few days later the Bank of China surprised markets by raising interest rates, and oil fell again. There were yips of joy in our office, but I couldn't help wondering if these were brief moments of respite such as Jock had experienced that spring 20-some years ago.

Oil continued to work lower through the first two weeks of November, but as November ebbed and oil churned, the question that continued to haunt us in the wee small hours of the morning was this: Were we being brave, resolute, fundamental investors or stubborn madmen? As we talked to our clients, it was apparent that, if we were wrong, and oil went to new highs, we were going to be regarded as inflexible maniacs, who should be discarded into the trash heap of flash-in-the-pan, flamed out hedge-fund managers.

On December 1, oil finally cracked. The weekly inventory figures, which are released every Wednesday at 10:30 A.M. showed an 8-million-barrel increase, which was a much bigger rise than the 3.5-million-barrel gain that had been anticipated. Because inventories had also exceeded forecasts the previous week, we viewed this as quite a bearish development and were somewhat disappointed when the price fell only $0.75 on the announcement.

Then it began to drift lower, as traders digested the impact of two substantial increases in a row. The erosion continued throughout the afternoon until, at the 2:30 P.M. close, oil reached a low of 45.50, down 3.64 for the day. We were elated but immediately began to wonder if we should now cover at least a portion of our position. The next morning, oil busted again, and by midday was down another 5%.

That afternoon, a rumor made the rounds. George Soros was passionately opposed to the reelection of George W. Bush. He had campaigned against Bush and spent God-only-knows how much money. The new twist was that he had invested $5 billion buying oil futures in the month leading up to the election with the objective of souring the stock market, the economy, and general voter sentiment prior to the election. If he also believed oil was going higher, it was not inconceivable that he would take a gigantic position. Soros has never been reluctant to use his wealth to throw his weight around. The chatter was that with this sharp break he was getting margin calls and was liquidating his position.

I didn't believe the rumor. Soros is far too smart and dispassionate to mix business with politics. While recognizing that it takes courage to be a pig, we decided that, after all the travail we had suffered, it was the better part of valor to cover about a third of our short. We bought it in at a little over 42. The trade had been unsuccessful, but at least we had a measure of redemption. I felt like a great rock had been lifted off my chest.

The very next day, there was another story, but this one was true. The Singapore-based subsidiary of a Chinese company, China Aviation

Holdings, announced it had a $550 million loss from derivatives trading in oil and was being forced into insolvency. The Soros rumor and the China Aviation bankruptcy reminded me that, invariably, when the price of a major global commodity has a violent move, rumors and bodies floating belly-up come to the surface.

On December 8, the inventory figures showed another build, bigger than expected. However, over the next few days, oil ministers from the OPEC countries issued press releases saying that the price of oil had fallen sufficiently and that production should be cut. In fact, on December 10, OPEC announced it was reducing its production by a million barrels a day. We shuddered because we still had most of our short. After the announcement, oil briefly rallied but then plummeted to a new low of $40.71 a barrel, down more than 4% for the day. We covered another third at $41.00.

As Figure 4.1 shows, in mid-December oil had another sharp rally.

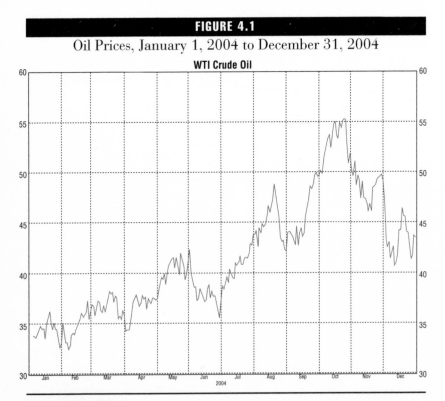

FIGURE 4.1

Oil Prices, January 1, 2004 to December 31, 2004

WTI Crude Oil

Source: Global Insight

Cold weather, an inventory drawdown, trouble in Saudi Arabia, and a new bin Laden tape all contributed. Then, two successive weeks of big inventory increases and the weight of the poor market action pushed the price down again, and on the last days of the year, oil hit $42 again. On December 30 and 31, we closed our position. All in all, the oil short and the long insurance call had cost us a little over two percentage points, but its real costs had been intense personal anguish and suffering and considerable damage to our relationship with a number of our clients.

On the morning of January 3, 2005, the first day of the rest of our investment lives, oil opened down 4.5%. Although we didn't know it, from the beginning, the crude joke was on us. Short selling commodities is not for sissies.

CHAPTER

FIVE

The Odyssey of
Starting a Hedge Fund

A Desperate, Frantic Adventure

t the end of 2002, after much reflection and discussion, Madhav Dhar, Cyril Moulle-Berteaux, and I decided to create a
hedge fund. We called it Traxis Partners (Traxis is a word we
manufactured that means nothing). We were friends who had
worked together for years at Morgan Stanley Asset Management, and
Morgan Stanley graciously offered to assist us, both with the back office
operations and in the marketing of the fund.

At the start of the long climb up the hedge-fund mountain, I
strongly suspected there would be an abundance of stress, strain, anxiety,
and maybe ecstasy. At the beginning I had high hopes but many worries
and scant conviction that the new hedge fund we were proposing to
launch would succeed. I knew this would be an extended moment I
was going to experience only once, and I decided to keep a log of the
journey. Looking back, it is simply the chronicle of the anxiety and indignities of the process.

Starting a new hedge fund is a desperate, frantic adventure. There is
a lot of anxiety involved even though you wear your sales face day and
night. The founders have to spend their own money to acquire office

space and create the administrative, trading, accounting, and legal infrastructure of a business. Sanitized offering documents to entice investors
without arousing the SEC have to be prepared. Founders also have to
find and hire analysts, traders, and a chief administrative officer. However, their primary objective must be to meet prospective investors and
raise capital. In our case, we decided that the heavy marketing program
would begin in February 2003, with a launch date for the fund of June
1. Although we had talked with a few friendly souls and even received
some early commitments from some, our money-raising offensive really
began in early March. Here is what I wrote in my diary that spring
about the process.

BIG-TIME MONEY RAISING AT THE BREAKERS

March 2, 2003 and the odyssey of raising money begins. Madhav, my
partner in illusion, and I flew to Palm Beach for Morgan Stanley's fabled hedge-fund conference at The Breakers. This conference is widely
considered the prime event at which to raise money because it attracts
the biggest, richest collection of hedge-fund buyers in the world. I had
never attended before. It is an amazing event. There must have been at
least 500 people in attendance, overflowing the richly appointed meeting rooms and lawns of the great hotel by the ocean.

After an elaborate opening dinner and a couple of investor panels
with various hedge-fund managers trying to talk smart and appear brilliant, there were two long days of nonstop group presentations and one-
on-one pitches with another fancy dinner the second night. The
intensity and the hustle level were incredibly high. Everybody was on
the make. The conference is organized and paid for by Morgan Stanley's
Prime Brokerage division, and its sole purpose is to bring together
prospective investors in hedge funds with the funds that either clear
through or (like us) are going to clear through Morgan Stanley. Morgan
Stanley's prime brokerage guys made a big deal of my being on an investment panel and of our being given a major slot to present at the
conference.

Morgan Stanley is the biggest factor in the very lucrative prime
brokerage business. The firm's prime brokerage business is an extremely
well managed, big fat gold mine. Why is it *so* attractive? Because it is a

direct beneficiary of the growth of the hedge-fund industry, which has been, by far, the most dynamic segment of the asset management space. The money managed by hedge funds has grown from $36 billion in 1990 to more than $1 trillion by the end of 2004, and no business that the world's investment banks are involved with has anywhere near those growth and profitability characteristics. However, there are so many new entrants trying to buy their way into the business by poaching people that the bloom is beginning to come off the rose. Some large hedge funds, in an effort to spread the wealth around, have more than one prime broker.

What do prime brokers do? They provide securities to cover short sales, make margin loans, clear trades, provide reporting services and custody assets, provide research, and help with money raising. A fund's prime broker executes roughly 25% to 30% of its hedge-fund clients' transactions, and most provide a daily net asset value (NAV) and a rudimentary risk management system. The prime broker will find a new hedge-fund office space, an operations officer, and traders, and it will also provide basic accounting systems. How do prime brokers make money? First, they earn from commissions and order flow, and hedge funds now account for about one-third of total trading volume. Second and most important, hedge funds are a captive source of demand for the lucrative securities and margin lending activities from which a prime broker locks in a fat spread. Morgan Stanley has the biggest prime brokerage book, and its volume and profits have been growing at around 20% per annum. It's now a major and cherished profit contributor to the firm, with revenues currently well over $1 billion.

The competition for clients among the prime brokers is about service and back-office infrastructure, but it is also about so-called capital introductions. Prime brokers legally can only introduce hedge funds to prospective investors; they can't actually make pitches or solicit clients. Only the hedge funds themselves can do that. Morgan Stanley has been helpful in critiquing our presentation and advising us on office infrastructure. In the months to come, the prime brokerage will organize lunches or dinners for us with prospective investors across the United States and in London, Geneva, and Hong Kong. At these functions, we will tell our story. After that, about all Morgan Stanley can do is call the prospective investor and ask if they would like to hear more. In addition to the Breakers conference, Morgan Stanley and the other prime brokers have various conferences for new managers throughout the year in the United States, Europe, and Asia, but the meeting at The Breakers is the big one!

I viewed the conference with trepidation. While at Morgan Stanley, I had certainly peddled to plenty of blasé, semiskeptical audiences, but I had also accumulated my allocation of hubris, and I was a little disconcerted to be in Palm Beach grubbing for money with all the other twerps. I envied the superstar hedge-fund guys who have a surfeit of capital and don't deign to appear at conferences. It is only we struggling mortals who want money who come hat in hand. The superstars have marketing managers who organize their own annual meetings with their investors, complete with elaborate presentations by the messiah himself and his entourage. In the glory days of Tiger, Julian Robertson took this venue to new heights, with glittering formal dinner dances following annual business sessions in wonderful settings like the Temple of Dendur at the Metropolitan Museum of Art, the Duke of Wellington's house in London, and a chateau outside Paris. However, hedge-fund investors are not fools, and parties are not substitutes for performance. Julian's investors liked the parties, but they loved his performance even more.

The group presentations are grindingly repetitious. The day is divided into 45-minute segments with 10-minute intervals, and the crowd circulates from one room to another. Madhav and I made the same basic presentation over and over to groups of 10 to 30 people. The skeptical faces gaze up at you, and by the fourth or fifth rendition you are varying the routine to keep yourself from going batty, but by then you can't remember what you have or haven't said.

On the second evening at The Breakers, there is a cocktail reception on the terrace. The night was clear with stars and a moon, but cold for Florida. Moët et Chandon champagne and the best California chardonnay flowed under a cold, pale moon with a vast crowd of beautifully dressed people milling about, gossiping in many tongues about the rise and fall of hedge funds and their managers. In this milieu, a Swiss accent is worth an automatic 50 IQ points, and an Oxbridge tongue is worth 25. Plain old American is definitely *déclassé*.

There is plenty to chatter about. Hedge funds and their managers have the career expectancy of rock stars. A fund whose performance elevates it into the top 20 of all funds based on assets under management has less than a 50% chance of remaining in the top 20 for three years. The average life of a fund, like that of a National Football League running back, is only four years. Each year about 1,000 hedge funds close because of indifferent performance and the inability to get to critical mass. In fact, in 2004, a thousand new hedge funds were formed and about a thousand closed down, not with a bang but a whimper.

There are many tribes at the conference. First, there are *the professionals*, who come from the big funds of funds, foundations, endowments, and pension funds. They have bored, cynical stares and limp handshakes. This conference is purely business to them, and they are here to appraise the horseflesh. The American men wear suits and have sweaty armpits. The women are tall and lean and plain. By contrast, some of the Royal and Ancients from the big London FOFs have striped blue shirts with white collars and double-barreled names and chins. The Swiss, with their pinched lips and dark blue business suits, seem aloof and cynical as they chatter away at each other in French and *Schweizerdeutsch.* This group of professionals are the serious seekers with the big money. They could give us $25 million or even $50 million at a crack, but they are notorious for redeeming their money at the first sign of any faltering. We have chosen to have a clause in our partnership agreement that prohibits withdrawals for the first year. After that, investors can get their money on a quarterly basis. There is also a provision for emergency withdrawals. However, the Swiss make no bones about not liking our first-year lockup.

Then there is the rest of the crowd, *the amateurs*, mostly wealthy individuals and small, wannabe funds of funds. Germans with bulging eurobellies from family offices mingle with bloated Arabs in pale suits and white shirts, their handshakes as cool and clammy as snakeskin. Former investment bankers exchange distinguished lies with portly ex-diplomats, permanently deformed by self-importance. Wrecked old Texans with faces like road maps, sour breath, and fitted Hawaiian shirts chatter with fast talking private wealth bankers from Miami with pompadours and slicked back hairdos. Retired, vastly rich investors with private jets, homes in three climates, and Botox-smoothed foreheads name-drop and talk about their golf games as their bored wives and sleek and skinny girlfriends, social X-rays suffering from *anorexia richiosa*, babble about dude ranches and plantations. Wealthy divorcées and widows with artificial brightness in their unpouched eyes and hard, chiseled faces and tucked stomachs and bottoms, work the crowd. Are they looking for a man or a hedge fund? They have smiles for you like cold leftovers. However, these amateurs are well worth cultivating because their commitments to a hedge fund are stickier. If you charm them, they may even ride out a rough patch, which a big fund of funds is unlikely to do.

I felt estranged and disoriented. I began to perspire in spite of the cold moon. In my previous life at Morgan Stanley, I could go to an investment dinner almost anywhere in the world, at which the guests were investment professionals, and know some of the people, but here it is a completely different crowd. I recognized virtually none of them except for the hedge-fund guys themselves, and they were too busy hustling prospects to chat. I drank chardonnay and had desultory snatches of conversation with restless people who seemed to have the attention span of hummingbirds as their eyes darted around the crowd. Not knowing anyone and not being an extrovert, to say the least, I found it hard to hustle. Madhav, who is an ebullient people person, was flourishing and had already vanished into the crowd.

JIM THE TRIGGER: INVEST FIRST AND ASK QUESTIONS LATER

Suddenly a familiar face loomed up out of the cocktail party mist. It was Jim, a guy I knew from the past, a guy a lot of people refer to as Jim the Trigger. When he is working, Jim is an investment manager like me. People in the business call him the Trigger, as in *hair trigger*, because, as a portfolio manager, he reacts so quickly to a story. This sobriquet is not necessarily flattering; invest first and ask questions later is what is implied. "Ready! Fire! Aim!" is the Trigger's modus vivendi. In a bull market, when the mongrels are running, it works great. In tougher times like now, it's not so effective.

The Trigger is a handsome guy in a sleek, sculptured, California sort of way. The top three buttons of his fitted shirt are unbuttoned, and his sports jacket clings to his shoulders. Our eyes meet. Jim's are haunted and a little mad, but who is not a little deranged on the terrace of The Breakers in the spell of a perfect starlit evening with wine and money flowing like music?

The Trigger's career has experienced a few undulations. He is always into what is hot, but sometimes gets there a little late or just before it gets cold. The Trigger is and always has been a *momentum* investor, *a player* in the parlance, and his strength (and his weakness) is that he has no memory for pain. He unfailingly gravitates to where the fast money is, and he is capable of putting up enormous numbers in a hot, trending market. However, in the past he has often followed the lemmings over the proverbial cliff. I like him, though, because, in the heat of each moment, he truly believes his own bullshit and doesn't pretend to be anything other than what he is—a stock jockey.

I first knew the Trigger in the early 1980s when his aggressive growth-stock fund was loaded with whisper stocks like the small oil exploration companies and drillers with names like Three Guys and a Rig. He was up 40% in 1979 and 65% in 1980, and the money came pouring in. But then in 1981, when oil overnight went from being black gold to just another commodity, the Trigger's fund was down 55%. He almost lost his job, as I remember it, but in 1982 and 1983, he came back and shot the lights out with the small tech and emerging growth stocks, his "beloved athletes" as he called them. In those days he would go to a company presentation, meet the adolescent storyteller, listen to the pitch, come out saying, "The kid's a gifted natural athlete, a winner," and then buy a couple of hundred thousand shares without ever seeing a number.

Subsequently, when his beloved athletes died horrible deaths and the moon balls crashed in the mid-1980s, the Trigger actually did get fired, but he has a great sense of the game and he always gravitates relentlessly toward relative strength. Value was in and growth was out, and he knew he had to change and find new faces to fall in love with. He caught on with a value investing firm called U3—for Undervalued, Underowned, and Unloved—which also did risk arbitrage. However, value was too slow for his blood; the Trigger needed emotion and momentum in his life. It was hard for him to truly fall in love with a dirty industrial dog just because it was cheap.

I remember at the time his telling me, "Value sucks and Ben Graham was a loser. Buying cheap stocks on book value analysis is for small-minded accountants. I miss the adrenaline rush from an up stock or running in the shorts with a tail." This was sacrilege, because (just in case you don't know) Benjamin Graham is the god of value investing and wrote the bible, a book called *Security Analysis*. So the Trigger left U3 for an emerging markets boutique, and for a while he actually lived and operated out of Hong Kong and Eastern Europe. Then came the Thai baht and Russian debt busts, and the emerging markets became the submerging markets.

Almost as if it were foreordained, he migrated back to tech in the late 1990s. Tech was the perfect milieu for the Trigger. Before tonight, I had last seen him in late 1999 when he ran a tech fund for a big, very aggressive mutual fund company in Denver. Those were the days when the new-issue market was on fire, and the Trigger was giving spellbinding speeches around the country about tech, Internet productivity, and a new era. The public was pouring money into his fund, and the Trigger was riding high on the hog. That day he had come for lunch with a young, statuesque woman on his arm who drank Stolichnaya straight-up. I wondered why he had brought her because she was obviously bored with the stock talk, although occasionally she shot him languid, but amorous glances.

The Denver mutual fund company stocked smart, quick, fast-talking, momentum guys and gals who had heard every story long before I did. I remember going to visit them once during those days, sitting in a conference room with half a dozen kid portfolio managers who looked so young and fresh and innocent that you expected them to still have braces on their teeth, and realizing that I had nothing to say that interested them. They thought I was a useless, old fuddy-duddy, and that afternoon I felt like one. They didn't care a P/E ratio about valuation, fundamental change at the margin, or the economy. They wanted stories about up stocks. They wanted action, stocks on steroids. As the meeting went on, I realized they weren't at all innocent. They were baby-faced killers and it was I who was the innocent. The Trigger's fund, stuffed with new issues, was up 85% that year.

But then the bubble burst, and in a flash, the Denver mutual-fund company lost half its assets. The Trigger's fund fell 75% in 18 months, and then there were lawsuits because the vast majority of the money came in after the big year, not before, and when the Trigger was on the road talking up tech, many of his statements were embellished and extravagantly optimistic, to say the least. The chief investment officer of the mutual fund company resigned, the SEC unexpectedly did an audit, and the Colorado attorney general who wanted to be a western Spitzer came calling. That year there were no bonuses. The Trigger told me he knew he was in trouble when they cut his salary, and then the new chief investment officer gave him a leave of absence. More likely, he was fired, I thought.

"The fun is out of tech," he told me. "It's no use being fast and having good reflexes anymore. Every punk kid running tech money is fast, too, and the inside information game from management is dead. There are so many of us in the tech space, we collide with each other. The short side is just as bad. Everything is discounted ahead of time. It's impossible to make money." He sighed. "Three years ago I could bench-press the world; now I'm too depressed to even work out." I wondered what he was doing at The Breaker's conference.

"I'm going into the hedge funds of funds business," he said, brightening. "One and a half percent plus 10% of the profits. What a deal! Now I've got to mingle and charm." He gestured toward an elderly blue-haired woman tottering on the arm of a younger man. "She's a fox," he said, "a very old fox, but nevertheless a fox. I'm shooting for 10 big ones from her. We're going to have a nice little dinner and hold hands."

I like Jim because he is a totally transparent, genuine exploiter of bubbles and doesn't pretend to be anything else. "I've always had a great nose for craziness," he says, "and craziness is where it's at." But when Jim tells me about a stock and says "You can't lose" in that invincible tone of voice, a little bell starts ringing, faintly but insistently, like an unanswered telephone in the back of my head. He can be very dangerous.

THE FUND OF FUNDS IS A TOUGH CUSTOMER

The conference itself was hard, grinding work. No afternoon golf or tennis. I bugged out on parts of our investor meetings because Madhav is much better at selling Traxis and himself than I am. The representatives of the funds of funds are the most rigorous examiners. It's estimated that there are now almost 1,000 funds of funds, and as a group they are the biggest buyers of hedge funds but also the most fickle. After they have intensely probed and poked you, some will stick with you even if you falter; others will dump you at the first sign of a drawdown (a decline in your net asset value). As I said before, the Europeans supposedly are the worst but the truth is everyone in this business is performance happy. Considering the fees they are paying, why shouldn't they be?

A fund of funds typically selects and manages a diversified portfolio of hedge funds that it sells to individuals or institutions that don't feel capable of making the choices and then monitoring the funds themselves. They run all kinds of analytics on the individual hedge funds and on their overall portfolio to monitor risk and exposures. A couple of years ago, LTCM, a big hedge fund run by a bunch of pointy-headed Nobel Prize economists, blew up when a series of three standard-deviation events occurred simultaneously. The media loved it and published the names of all the supposedly smart, sophisticated individuals and institutions who had lost their money. Everybody was deeply embarrassed, and ever since the big institutions have been obsessed with risk analytics and throw around terms like *stress-testing portfolios, value at risk (VAR)*, and *Sharpe ratios*.

The funds of funds employ sophisticated quantitative analytics to add value by strategically allocating among the different hedge-fund classes. The hedge-fund universe is usually broken down into seven broad investment style classifications. These are event driven, fixed-income arbitrage, global convertible bond arbitrage, equity market-neutral, long/short equity, global macro, and commodity trading funds. Each has its own, unique performance cycle. One year a fund of funds will be heavy in macro and long/short equity funds and be out of or have very little in equity market neutral and convertible arbitrage. The next year the allocation will be completely different. Getting these style shifts right can make a substantial difference in the performance of an individual fund of funds.

The funds of funds also claim they have developed programs that combine sociological and statistical data to give early warning signals so they can time switches from one manager to another. There is no question that hedge-fund managers can run out of emotional gas. They are prone to performance bursts when they are hot, often followed by cold spells, but these swings are not easy to time. However, as one veteran fund of funds manager said to me, "Actually, that quantitative stuff is all window dressing BS. What we do is similar to being the manager of a major league baseball team. The trick is to have the intuition to take your pitcher out of the game just *before*, not *after*, he's been hit hard."

Most funds of funds focus not just on the raw performance numbers but also on the sociological factors. They monitor whether the successful hedge-fund managers in their stables are getting lazy and complacent as they get richer. They watch for divorces, third homes, and falling golf handicaps. Owning a share in Net Jets is okay, but buying your own G-5 is not. They don't even like their guys to get too interested in charities. One fund-of-funds guy heard that Madhav's wife was pregnant with triplets and brazenly suggested in front of 20 people that Madhav's ability to focus would be materially diminished by this event. Madhav, I thought, had a great answer and it wasn't, "*Inshallah,*" "Fate, buddy," or "That's show biz." He looked the guy right in the eye and said that the additional financial burden was a great motivator.

The funds of funds charge a management fee of between 100 and 150 basis points, and most add a percentage of the profits levy of between 5% and 10%. It's a heavy burden on their investors. You can work out the numbers for yourself. In the most extreme case, suppose the hedge funds in the fund's portfolio have a decent year and make 20% before any fees. After the standard hedge-fund fee of 20% of the profits plus 1.5% of assets, your gain is down to 14.5%. Then the fund of funds socks you for an additional 1.5% of assets and 10% of profits, so your 20% gain has shrunk to a return of a little more than 11.7%. In most cases, though, funds of funds' fees work out to be less than what I just described, and I think that, except for a handful of big money, sophisticated investors who have the resources to do it themselves, the professionally managed funds of funds are worth the double fee. For amateur dabblers, they are essential!

The numbers show that the funds of funds do a good job of picking the better horses and avoiding the losers. And there are chronic underperformers and losers. For example, over the five years that ended in March 2003, the median of all hedge funds compounded at 7.8% a year while the S&P 500 was declining 3.8% per annum. The median FOF returned 6.3% over that same period. In a tough environment, they certainly earned their fees. However, if as a buyer of hedge funds you could achieve the performance of the seventy-fifth percentile hedge fund, you would have earned 12.7% a year whereas the seventy-fifth percentile FOF did *only* 9.2%. By contrast, the twenty-fifth percentile hedge funds returned 3.2%, while the twenty-fifth percentile fund of funds earned 3.9%. In summary, the funds of funds are effective diversifiers. Trying to cherry-pick one or a few individual hedge funds is a challenging task that requires luck as well as knowledge. For big institutions, the funds are an important layer of fiduciary insulation.

To a certain extent, the funds of funds have to make life difficult for the hedge funds they invest in to justify their fees. In this sense they are like their ancestors, the consultants, who plague the institutional money management business. The magazine *Institutional Investor*, in an article in its June 2004 issue, extravagantly entitled "Funds of Funds Make Life Less Lush for Hedge Funds," argued that the future belongs to the funds of funds: "As they grow the funds will exert even more influence on the hedge fund industry as a whole, moving near-term performance front and center, especially for new managers. This is probably good news for investors. For hedge fund managers, the happy ending is harder to find."

Professional investing is about performance, just as professional sports is about winning. However, the obsession with short-term performance is never good, either for investors' returns or for investment managers' performance. There is an element of luck in the investing game. Even the best investors have slumps. In fact, the time to invest in a good fund is after it has had a bad patch—*as long as nothing has changed.* A friend of mine named Russ has run a big hedge fund for years with spectacular success. However, even though he knew that tech stocks were ridiculously priced in the spring of 2000, he thought they had a little more juice; he didn't sell and got killed when they collapsed that summer. His big investors pulled out, and he took six months off. I knew he was angry with himself and determined to restore his reputation. When he started again in the fall of 2001, I was sure he would have some great years. He did!

My guess is that, in the years to come, there will be fee pressure on the funds of funds. The double fee is a heavy burden for the client to work through. On the other hand, even the larger pension funds are reluctant to venture into a broad exposure to hedge funds without a layer of insulation, so big, new money will keep pouring into the analytical professionals who know the hedge-fund world. Some very savvy investors believe funds of funds are the way to go for wealthy individuals and small institutions. They argue that the funds offer considerably less risk and better, more stable returns than equities, and that, from current levels of interest rates, high-grade bonds offer total returns in the mid single digits at best. They ask, "Why would you want to own bonds, anyway?" As for the great mass of small, fringe funds of funds, there are too many dilettantes, too many laid-off investment bankers, too many former institutional salespeople, too many loser brothers-in-law setting up shop. It smells like venture capital or private equity in 1998 and 1999, just before the bubble burst.

In the spring of 2001, I wrote an essay for Morgan Stanley's Investment Perspectives called "The Quest for Alpha and Endangering the Golden Goose." Alpha is just a fancy word for excess returns above that of the market. My point was that the hedge-fund universe with its various strategies is prone to minibubbles. There are times when a particular subsector, like convertible arbitrage a couple of years ago, is underpopulated and the securities are inefficiently priced. Then suddenly, for some reason, that sector will begin to generate high returns. In this extremely entrepreneurial business, large amounts of investment capital and many new entrants very quickly flock to the *in* sector.

For example, when convertible arbitrage got really hot, guys from trading desks and even convertible arbitrage salespeople left their jobs to start new convertible arbitrage hedge funds. With so many more professionals entering the field, almost simultaneously, the securities in the sector became much more efficiently priced, so the excess profits diminished. Even if they didn't, there are many more funds trying to feed on the same amount of profits. Or you could say that with more and bigger horses drinking from the same alpha pool, all the horses get less water. Eventually, the convertible arbitrage minibubble popped. For hedge-fund investors, chasing after the latest hot sector is a loser's game. As noted, because most funds of funds make tactical changes from one sector to another, if they are adroit, they perform an additional valuable function.

SEARCHING FOR THE NEW MESSIAH

Whatever their affiliation, the buyers at The Breakers are all obsessively searching for the new messiah: a boy George Soros, suave, handsome, and an investment genius with the same *seeing eye*. The trouble is that, even if they find their prodigal wunderkind, the odds are he eventually will be spoiled by wealth and adulation (even though George hasn't been). Success inevitably breeds hubris in one form or another, and in the hedge-fund business, arrogance eventually levels the exalted. Hubris leads to private jets, multiple golf clubs, homes in the south of France and Nantucket, and young wives. However, when certain guys get rich, they retire to follow some childhood dream to save the world. Some just want out of the hedge-fund pressure cooker and are content to run their own money and study eighteenth-century French literature. Others want to make a splash as political activists or philanthropists. Soros, for example, doesn't want to be remembered as a great speculator who beat the Bank of England but as a philanthropist and the philosopher who discovered the theory of reflexivity.

As an asset class, hedge funds did their job of preserving capital during the three bear market years. In 2000, with the S&P 500 down 9%, the weighted average of all hedge funds returned 9%. In 2001, the comparable numbers were −12% and +7%, and in 2002, they were −22% and +6%. Although there were some hedge funds (and not just short-biased funds) that posted 20%+ gains in those tough bear market years, there were also a lot of big funds that were down 5% to 20%. Although this performance in general was far better than that of long-only managers who, in 2002, were off at least 20% to 25% (minus 40% or more for tech guys), it was disappointing for those investors who believed their funds could actually make big money in both bull and bear markets. The mood of the crowd at that first Breakers conference I went to was sullen but not mutinous—yet. As it turned out, that year, 2003, was a big up year in equity markets, and hedge funds in general did less well than the long-only managers who stayed fully invested. However, their allure was not diminished, and the money continued to pour in throughout 2004.

As for the 40 or so hedge-fund managers in attendance at The Breakers, there were many different investment religions represented. All of us oozed glib confidence because we had to, even though the prospective buyers had that disdainful, faintly jaded look of people who already had heard every conceivable investment pitch known to man or woman. They regarded us with a condescending curiosity. The very hot hedge funds with the best performance that the buyers really wanted to get into didn't deign to grace a mass meeting like this, because they didn't need to. The funds of funds and the endowments were begging them on hands and knees for admission. In fact, access to the hot funds is part of the competitive edge of the best and the biggest funds of funds.

It was a long three days. At the meals and cocktail parties, there was endless hustling and preening. The chatter was mind-numbing and to some extent mindless. The funds of funds hustled the foundations and wealthy individuals, and the hedgehogs hustled everybody. When it was over, I had no idea whether we had raised any money. (As it turned out, we didn't get much on our initial opening but later on it paid off.) There was so much competition and so many slick presentations, I didn't feel that we had differentiated ourselves or made a compelling case about why investors should give us money. Although we told our story of macro investing with as much passion as we could muster after 15 straight presentations, and we shamelessly brandished our record and credentials, I didn't sense fascination or much commitment in the faces of our audiences. No one came up to me at the breaks and said breathlessly that they were in. A few said they would like to see us again. At the end of Thursday, we crept back to New York on JetBlue exhausted, with our tails between our legs.

HEADACHES, INSOMNIA, AND GLOOM

By *March 17, 2003*, we were back in New York wrestling with the creation of the infrastructure of accounting, legal, office management, and hiring of our fund. It was an incredible amount of work, even though Morgan Stanley was assisting with the setup of operations. For the average new hedge fund, the burden on the partners must be immense, and, of course, this is why it takes most start-up funds six months to a year to get going.

Over the next few days, we revised and polished our marketing presentation once again. We gave the new presentation one morning to Morgan Stanley's Private Wealth Management group. I had been warned that numerous people wondered about my motives, so I began with a straightforward summary of why I was leaving the firm to do a hedge fund. I said something to the effect that by June 1, I would have been 30 years with Morgan Stanley. Furthermore, leaving when everyone still wants you seemed like the thing to do rather than waiting to get pushed out. I told them I was not interested in golf or cruises to the Greek Isles, but above all I was doing it because professional investing was the best game in the world, and I relished the competition. In addition, I said, it was the only game where age may actually be an advantage.

"What do you know about short selling?" somebody asked. I told them how, when I ran a hedge fund, Fairfield Partners, in the late 1960s, we sold short the retailers and the chemicals, both of which at the time sold at 30 times earnings when the market was at 17 times. In other words, they were priced as growth stocks even though they were cyclical companies. In addition they were expanding capacity excessively. Over several years, both groups' P/E ratios collapsed as their earnings went nowhere. Then I told them how I learned from the computer-leasing stocks and the conglomerates that, when bubbles burst, the hypes and the junk stocks that the crazies thought were growth stocks usually go to $3. Why $3? No reason. It just seemed to be a magic number. I also told them how we experienced the pain of selling short the Nifty Fifty too early and then covering them too soon. Short selling gave you headaches and insomnia, but at least I was no virgin.

Meanwhile, as March 2003 unfolded, the market environment for equities was horrible, what with the impending Iraq war, the desultory economy, and the seemingly endless stream of corporate greed scandals. It was as though the bears had all the passion and all the arguments, and the bulls were in desperate retreat. Experience teaches that, by definition, the bottom of a bear market has to be the point of maximum bearishness. If so, we had to be close. The U.S. equity market had sunk to just below the lows of the previous summer, and most other markets in the world had broken through their two 2002 bottoms. For the technicians, this was a very bad sign, suggesting a break to lower lows. Strategists on CNBC were raging about the S&P 500 going to 500 (it was then 760), and a serious student of valuation, Andrew Smithers in London, called to say his work on replacement-cost book value showed incontrovertibly that U.S. equities were still 30% too expensive.

If we were right, however, and markets were either close to or at a major bottom, then it would be a great time for us to start. The issue was whether at a time like this we could raise any significant money other than our own. With a fourth down year for equity markets looming, the mood of the Morgan Stanley brokers was gloomy.

One evening, walking to Grand Central Station to get my train to Greenwich, as I passed the cocktail lounges and bars where the babbling, smiling young salespeople, traders, and analysts flirt and lie to each other, I was struck with how oblivious and unconcerned they all seemed. Didn't they know that a war was beginning in the Middle East? Were they unaware of how fragile the world economy was? Didn't they realize that their jobs could be at risk—not just for six months but maybe forever? Weren't they worried? The chatter level seemed as high as ever. The faces were as bright and questing as ever. I thought of the lines from W.H. Auden's wonderful poem *September 1, 1939*, which was published at another time of deep gloom when Hitler's Panzers seemed invincible and the world was on the brink of war. Auden, sitting in a dive on 52nd street, wrote of how "Faces along the bar/Cling to their average day:/The lights must never go out/The music must always play". He spoke of how after a "low and dishonest decade" his generation's "clever hopes expire"; now, two generations later, the Morgan Stanley brokers were uncertain and afraid as their clever hopes expire. But it is always so. We can't afford to get frightened or gloomy. The die is cast.

CHAPTER

SIX

The Roadshow Grind
Blood, Sweat, Toil, and Tears

This chapter is a diary of my road show. It chronicles the grind, some of the indignities, and the travail of the process of raising money for a new hedge fund. After the diary, I then discuss the anxiety of actually launching and my memories of an earlier investment adventure.

PETER THE GREAT:
AN INVESTMENT NYMPHOMANIAC

April 5, 2003: One of the investment bankers called today. The legendary arbitrage LBO private-equity guy, Peter the Great, might be interested in putting some money into the fund. Obviously, I'd heard of Peter the Great, because the epic story of his rise on guts, gall, and brains from a Cleveland blue-collar background is well-known. The mere rumor that he was buying could set executive paunches and putters quivering from Shinnecock to the Los Angeles Country Club. I was excited.

The vast reception room at Peter the Great's office suite has a huge

Oriental rug and fine antique furniture. "Peter is obsessed with getting into Blind Brook, and he has this idea that merchant banking is classy," confided the investment banker. "He's got a couple of phony Englishmen at roll-top desks in the other room, but they're just a front." On the paneled walls were framed English fox hunting prints. One of the husky young men in the reception room took our coats. "Former Special Forces," the investment banker whispered. "Ever since Peter read that Bill Gates had ex-Special Forces as bodyguards, he had to have some, too. Very big on the cloak-and-dagger stuff. Code names, disguises, secure telephones. It's like you're in the CIA."

As we waited, the banker told me more about Peter. "Very tough, competitive guy. He's an edge player. Was a wrestler in college and before a match he would chew garlic so he would smell horrible on the theory it might just slow the other guy down for a second. The guy is limelight obsessed. He wants to be the bride at every wedding and the corpse at every funeral. He's the only 50-year-old billionaire I know who still cheats at golf. Moves his ball in the rough. Compulsive about multitasking and redundancy. Always tries to do at least two things at once. I hear he has a stationary bicycle built into his limo so he can work out, read the paper, watch CNBC, and get driven to work all at the same time. Claims he sleeps only about four hours a night. Runs a real sweatshop here. Half of his analysts burn out and end up in communes in Oregon."

One of the Special Forces took us into Peter's office, a huge room with a panoramic skyline view and a massive structure in the middle, which was half desk, half control center. There was no chair, but there was a Stairmaster by the desk and a set of gold-colored weights in one corner. Peter himself was a lean, deeply tanned man, coatless but beautifully dressed, with a Countess Mara tie and red suspenders. Someone had been chewing at his fingernails, though, because they were right down to the nub.

"Welcome to Battlestar Galactica," he said, gesturing at the console, built into the control center, in which numerous screens were flashing prices in different colors. The lower screens were divided into 20 sections, and, on each, a researcher or trader could be seen. Peter showed us how he could talk directly to any one of them or put anyone's face directly up on the big screen. He spoke quickly and in bursts of words. "They can't get away from me, and they can't see me unless I want them to. I fired one guy who picked his nose repeatedly on my time. Discipline and control are the keys to this business."

A phone rang. We could hear snatches of the conversation, which seemed to involve whether somebody's wife was having an affair. Peter abruptly hung up. "When these corporate preppies try to block me, they better be ready to go to war!" he shouted. "My guys can dig up anything, and I'll use it. The chairman's wife is fooling around with a tennis pro," he said disgustedly, "and they think they are going to get away with trying to crown-jewel me. What is this? The Yale–Harvard game? That crud won't be able to show his face at Augusta when I get through with him."

The investment banker seemed to love it, even though I knew he had gone to Yale. "Go get 'em, Peter. That's why you're so great. How can they say LBO funds are parasitic vultures that produce nothing when you're doing creative stuff like this? Big companies shouldn't be run by clowns whose wives fall for guys in short pants. You're the market economy at work, at the cutting edge of reforming the nature of capitalism, America at its best."

Peter nodded and looked at me. "Now, tell me, what do you do? What do you want?"

I went into an abbreviated version of my usual Traxis pitch, but abruptly he cut me off.

"How many bets do you usually have in your portfolio?"

"Somewhere between 20 and 25. We do use leverage so we want to have some diversification."

"I don't believe in diversification. I don't like people or wines equally, so why build a portfolio equally? Own monster positions of what you really like and leverage them up, or else you're only practicing. It's all greed versus fear, and risk control is a misallocation of energy."

I was tongue-tied. He went on: "My master is my purse! You'd better believe it! Everything is for sale except my kids and maybe my wife. I'm an investment nymphomaniac. He who has the most money when he dies, wins. But I want to do good in the world, too. With the amount of money I give away I should be a trustee of the Museum of Natural History and the Ford Foundation instead of those stingy stuffed shirts they have on their boards."

He looked at me intently. "Did you know I give a lot to charity—religious studies, funding scholarships for black kids, work on reincarnation.

The press never mentions it. They just yack about how many people I fire when I buy a company. It's a conspiracy. " Suddenly his mood changed. "But I have to jump. Thanks for coming by. Good luck!" The phone was ringing again.

"The reincarnation studies," the investment banker said disgustedly as we waited for the elevator. "Probably he's interested so he can find out who he is coming back as and then he can leave his money to himself. Good luck."

Seems ominous that everybody is wishing us good luck.

NONSTOP PRESENTATIONS: FROM STIMULATING TO LISTLESS TO SKEPTICAL TO HOSTILE

April 6, 2003: The road show with all its grit and grind began today. Road shows are part of the landscape in the money-raising business. They're just what it says. You take the show, the pitch, on the road. Nobody ever said it was fun. We started with three days in San Francisco jammed full from breakfast to dinner with meetings with institutions, groups, and wealthy individuals. Some of the sessions such as the one we had with the Stanford Endowment were stimulating because of the investment interaction; others were listless for one reason or another, and at some of the group sessions we faced hostile, skeptical questions. I guess it's all part of the money raising game.

April 7, 2003: Today was nonstop presentations. One of the Morgan Stanley Private Wealth Management (PWM is an elite group of brokers that concentrates on investors that have substantial assets) guys took us to Silicon Valley. Among others, we saw the three founders of one of the hottest (and now coldest) venture capital firms, Placemark Capital. The reception room walls were covered with the framed tombstone announcements of transactions they had completed in their glory days. It seemed a little sad because so many of the companies they had created failed to survive.

The three still very rich partners looked subdued, like guys who have recently had a death in their immediate family (remember, this is April 2003 and the Nasdaq is hovering around 1,200). They listened to our story politely. We asked them how their portfolio companies were doing. No sign of a rebound yet, they murmured. Corporate buyers are very cautious. I asked if there wasn't a huge amount of deferred demand because businesspeople had cut back so severely on information technology spending since 1999, and there had been a lot of technological progress since then. No, they said, very little true innovation had occurred in the past few years, just upgrades. There was no reason for a revival of spending on hardware or software. I think they are too gloomy.

April 8, 2003: We had four separate meetings with very wealthy individuals. All had been big investors in small technology stocks and were licking their wounds. They weren't hostile to us, but my sense is that they are risk averse and paralyzed into inactivity by their losses. Investing money in a new hedge fund is not an appealing thought. My only consolation is that this disdain, although a bad omen in terms of money coming in, is probably a good sign for our initial performance.

This evening, at the dinner for us organized by Prime Brokerage, we made our usual presentation and then took questions. As always, we said we hoped to have long-term returns in excess of the S&P 500, but that our back-testing indicated volatility approximately comparable to that of the S&P 500. In other words, if our long-term rate of return is going to be about 15% per annum, our annual returns should fall in a range of +30% to zero—in other words, 15%, plus or minus 15%. A woman from a big fund of funds stood up and said she thought our volatility estimate of 15% was about right, but it made us unsuitable for many investors. With that kind of volatility, she said, at some point a 10% down month was likely, and 10% drawdowns invariably triggered big withdrawals from investors and a *vicious circle* effect on fund performance: in other words, a redemption crisis. Another happy thought!

April 9, 2003: We flew to Houston this morning and had a group lunch with 20 private wealth management clients that went well. A lot of rich, savvy guys who asked tough questions, but they seemed interested in what we had to say.

The private wealth management people at Morgan Stanley are an elite group of salespeople and investment managers who service wealthy individuals and smaller institutions. They are sophisticated, tough, and greedy. In other words they respond to financial incentives. However, in general, their real loyalty is to their clients rather than to the firm because their clients are their long-term meal tickets. They usually are effective and discriminating in using us, but occasionally we get abused. This afternoon was one of those times.

After lunch, Madhav and I were taken to visit a very successful, elderly oil operator whose Morgan Stanley contact alleged that he was a billionaire and a very likely prospect. The billionaire met us in his reception area, oozing charm. He clapped me on the back and told me I looked "younger than springtime." He looked awful, so I was tongue-tied. We went into an office the size of Madison Square Garden and proceeded to give a summary of our pitch.

"Wonderful story," said the billionaire when we had finished, "but, boys, I got some problems. I have a couple of dry holes off Venezuela, and the Nigerians just nationalized my company in that hellhole. The other thing is that since my girlfriend left me, I'm a lonely old man, so for company I go to all these charity balls here in Houston. Everyone thinks I'm rich as Croesus so they hit me up for contributions. I have some huge gift commitments I've got to fund. So, in other words, boys, right now I've got a severe liquidity crisis. I'd love to be with you fellers, but this year I can't swing it." He gazed at us mournfully and we gazed back.

He finally broke the silence: "Plus I got prostate cancer. I'm getting radiated through those damned seeds. Do you know what it's like walking around with seeds in your crotch?" He then proceeded to tell us in excruciating detail about the diagnosis, treatment, and history of his prostate cancer. His lurid description of the rectal exam had me squirming and Madhav looked ill.

Afterward, the embarrassed salesman fled, and Madhav and I got lost walking around the ghost town that is downtown Houston on a hot spring afternoon. We didn't talk about the meeting. There really was nothing to say. We both had experienced bad days at Morgan Stanley, but then you knew that at least you were still going to get paid. We were acutely conscious of the hard fact that unless we collected some assets, we were going to be out in the cold. When we got back to the hotel, we went to the gym.

I am addicted to working out. I think it's the best medicine for keeping your sanity, particularly when times are tough. Ideally playing a competitive sport or climbing a mountain is even better, but neither is easy to organize at the last moment in Houston, Texas. I am also addicted to reading, but the writing has to be good, or at least lean. I am a gourmet of words. While lifting weights or running I listen to books on my iPod. My taste is eclectic, ranging from novels to history. When I am truly absorbed in a wonderful book, it actually motivates me to go to the gym. Most of my nonbusiness reading gets done while sweating. I also get a lot of research reading done on the StairMaster. The nice thing is that no one interrupts you.

FINALLY, WE GET A BREAK: DINNER WITH A TRULY GREAT INVESTOR

April 10 we were invited to Fayez Sarofim's house for dinner. Fayez is my age, and we have been friends for years. His investment management firm, Fayez Sarofim & Company, has had a superb record, and Fayez is a truly great investor. He runs his firm with an iron but benevolent hand and is quite conservative. The firm has grown to be a large business. On the other hand, he loves to speculate in his personal portfolio. He makes giant macro bets and uses big leverage. I have always thought he would be great running a hedge fund. I was very skeptical that he would have any interest in Traxis, and I suspected the salesman was just using us to get face time.

"Absolutely not," said the guy. "Fayez told me he was definitely interested." I am amazed. He doesn't need us, but I knew dinner with Fayez would be a treat, both gastronomically and intellectually.

Fayez's spacious house is loaded with fine impressionist paintings, young children from his most recent marriage, and piles of research reports. In his elegant, paneled library there are stacks of reports on the floor, on the sofa, and on the coffee table. Despite a bevy of servants, charming disorder envelops the house and grounds. Bicycles, basketballs, and roller skates are piled on the porch, and here was this rotund, slightly rumpled, elderly Egyptian pharaoh in a dark suit and wearing a vest presiding serenely over the carnage. The clan and the entourage seemed completely happy and utterly at ease.

We had a wonderful, elaborate dinner with Fayez and his oldest son, who is in the firm. Fayez is a baroque character. He has always had impeccable taste in restaurants, wine, food, cigars, art, and stocks. He has both an ample waistline and a lot of money to show for it. He has invested his clients' money in high-quality consumer growth stocks that have world-class franchises and that don't have to reinvent themselves every five years the way tech stocks do. His criteria require that they also generate free cash flow so they can buy back their stock and raise the dividend. He argues that in a slow-growth, low-inflation, low-interest-rate world, stocks with these characteristics will have great scarcity value and will sell at very high P/Es, just as they did in the late 1950s and early 1960s.

This has always been his investment style. Buy and hold great growth stocks. "My favorite holding period is forever," he says with a wry smile. The only difficulty is that companies with these characteristics are hard to find and usually are very expensive. We talked about Pepsico. Fayez thinks its earnings can grow 12% per annum even though its revenue growth is more like 6% to 7% and it is in very competitive businesses. He is convinced that management is exceptional.

Fayez is also very enthusiastic about the shares of the large U.S. drug companies. Relative to the rest of the market, these stocks are currently as cheap as they have ever been. He argues that while they face more regulation, are suffering through a new-product slump, and probably won't grow as fast as they have in the past, the drug companies remain great growth franchises. With their legal problems, he views them as being in a similar sold-out position as Phillip Morris was a decade ago. Growth, says Fayez, is about earnings and dividends growing faster than inflation, so the shareholder increases the purchasing power of his or her income stream from the investment. He mentions Merck shares he bought 30 years ago for an elderly cousin. The current dividend is now twice her cost. I calculate that over that period, Merck's dividends have risen three times as fast as inflation. What a marvelous way for a taxpaying individual to compound purchasing power!

That said, identifying which of the current crop of growth stocks are going to be the long-run winners is a far more difficult, nay, almost impossible, task. Bernstein, the New York research firm, did a study of the likelihood of a company maintaining growth status years into the future. The frightening results are in Table 6.1. Over the past half century, your odds of identifying a growth stock you can hold for 20 years are 4% and only 15% for 10 years. Even for 3 years, they are just a little more than 50%. Healthcare (in other words, big pharma) and consumer staples have somewhat higher success ratios. And what the study doesn't say is that when a growth stock falls from grace, the landing is not just hard, it's usually a crash. However, Fayez has his own magic. His portfolios for wealthy individuals have very low turnover, and his

TABLE 6.1
Likelihood of a Company Maintaining Growth Stock Status

	All Sectors	Major Growth Sectors				
		Technology	Healthcare	Consumer Staples	Consumer Cyclicals	Financials
1955–2003						
3 Years	58%	55%	57%	69%	61%	46%
5 Years	37	36	38	48	44	24
10 Years	15	14	23	24	18	8
15 Years	7	7	13	16	7	4
20 Years	4	3	9	9	3	2
1980–2003						
3 Years	51%	55%	57%	57%	55%	41%
5 Years	31	35	37	45	39	23
10 Years	12	10	19	27	16	8
15 Years	5	4	7	18	4	2
20 Years	2	2	4	5	1	1

Source: Sanford C. Bernstein, Inc., Strategic and Quantitative Research Group

5-year growth stock persistency record must be around 60%, which is spectacular.

It was a marvelous, stimulating evening swapping ideas. My partners were charmed by Fayez. The food and wine were magnificent. However, once again I question whether we had raised any money, as I know how Fayez loves to speculate with his own portfolio. He didn't ask us anything about our macro process, besides.

Addendum: At any rate, I was wrong: Fayez invested with us. We were honored.

SIZE IS THE ENEMY OF PERFORMANCE

April 10–12, 2003: From Houston we went to Atlanta and Palm Beach. Were there any scintillating moments? Not really. My impression is that wealthy individuals don't know what to do with their money. They are discouraged with their current investment advisers, but changing means uncertainty. They say there is no place to hide. They think bonds will be losers because long-term interest rates will be rising soon. On the other hand money market rates are lower than inflation, which means you are losing money in real terms. It is hard rationally to argue with them, but I suspect that when everyone thinks there is nothing to do, it means that there is a lot to do—probably in equities.

In Palm Beach I did have one interesting meeting with a guy named Sean from Lighthouse. Lighthouse is a young fund of funds with an excellent record. One of the first presentations we made months ago was to Sean in New York, and he was very encouraging. Sean is probably in his mid 30s, a tall, lean guy with an open face and an affable manner. I instinctively like him. He is very professional, and he makes it clear that he is ruthlessly managing a portfolio of hedge funds. His only loyalty is to his portfolio and to his investors. Personal relationships with hedge-fund managers have nothing to do with it. He will dispassionately reduce or eliminate managers based on his judgment just as impersonally as we would sell an investment we had lost faith in. As the second Adam Smith (Gerry Goodman) put it, "The stock doesn't know you own it." The hedge funds you own do know you own them, but your personal relationships with them shouldn't have any effect on your judgment to stick or redeem if you're in the money allocating business.

Sean talked about how he had found that even successful hedge funds had relatively short performance lives. Not only is size the enemy of performance, but success and wealth cause the principals to suffer from either hubris or retirement. Obviously, both are fatal from his point of view. It is very hard for even the most talented hedge-fund practitioners, who are by nature obsessive, to survive success, he said. Hedge fund investing is so demanding, and strong investment performance is so exhilarating that many of the best investors fall victim to fatal attacks of hubris, burn out, or get distracted.

April 16, 2003: Madhav and I flew the red-eye to London. Hyde Park was green and glistening in the spring sun. We had two and a half jam-packed days of presentations arranged by Morgan Stanley's prime brokerage people with wealthy individuals, institutions, and funds of funds. We also interviewed a young Russian guy for an analyst. Sergei seems bright and ambitious, and he has that lean and hungry look. Our third partner, Cyril, knows him well, shared an office with him at Morgan Stanley, and is a big booster. Madhav and I are not so sure. I wonder about analysts in general. If you have them, you then have to figure out things for them to research, listen to what they discover, and occasionally even do what they suggest. Are they a distraction or an asset? I am not sure. One of the very best hedge-fund managers once told me he makes all his analysts communicate with him by e-mail because it's difficult to end face-to-face conversations without appearing to be brusque and rude. It also creates a record of their work, which comes in handy at the end of the year.

Managing money is about one thing: performance. You are not trying to win a popularity contest, and you certainly don't want the hired help wasting your time. The same applies to not squandering time on pleasantries with salespeople. Their job is to chat you up. Your job is to ingest information and make good decisions. The hedge-fund guy I just mentioned is the toughest, fastest conversation terminator I've ever known. When he thinks he has extracted the meat from a conversation, he just says, "Thanks," and that's it.

TRAVELS WITH CHARLIE

The first night in London, Madhav and I had dinner at the Barclay with Robert, an old friend, who has successfully managed a global hedge fund for a long time, even though he is only in his late 40s. Robert has run his fund as a sole proprietor, and the stress has taken its toll. He now has a chronic back problem, and he travels so much he is always in one stage or another of jet lag and insomnia. His marriage gradually dissolved. Tonight he had dark blue circles under his eyes and seemed despondent. (Afterward, I said to Madhav that Robert needed either a partner or a wife. Madhav said, "No! All he needs is some warm, cuddly performance to sleep with.")

He is right! Even though Robert's long-term record is excellent, his key investors are restless despite all the money he has made for them. After a good run in the late 1990s, he has had three small down years in a row. His assets have fallen from more than $1 billion to $400 million. At this moment, Robert is reluctant to take a strong position, either bullish or bearish, because he worries that if he is wrong, his remaining clients will think he has truly lost his touch and will withdraw. I told him this was a dangerous strategy because, if the markets rallied and he missed the move, the clients would be equally upset. As you would expect with the high fee structures they endure, hedge-fund investors are a demanding and mercurial breed. They have no loyalty, nor should they; you are only as good as your most recent performance. But this is fallacious thinking. If the manager is good and is still committed, poor recent performance is an opportunity to add money, not take it away.

Addendum: Robert subsequently got his investment and personal acts back together. He entered into a romance with a beautiful young model, and either because of her or in spite of her, his fund ended up 25% in 2003. Then in 2004, everything went right, and his fund gained 38% in what was a very tough year for most other investors. So far, in 2005, he continues to prosper.

April 18, 2003: We took the early morning flight from London to Geneva. The day was warm, and Lake Geneva sparkled in the sun as the great fountain hurled a plume of water high into the sky. We made a presentation at Pictet et Cie, the biggest private bank in Geneva. I have known the Pictet partners for 30 years, and they are classy people. The former senior partner, Pierre Pictet, is an old friend. The family still controls the partnership. Pictet has a big fund of funds, but it was hard to tell whether the staff was being polite, curious, or was truly interested. The current senior partner, Charles Pictet, attended the meeting, which was flattering. However, his cell phone kept ringing, which was a distraction; even worse, he didn't turn it off and kept answering it—not a sign of consuming interest.

We then walked across the bridge in the fresh spring sunshine to the Four Seasons Hotel, where we had a lunch presentation with 35 polite but skeptical Swiss. Again the question: "Is it true, Mr. Dhar, you are going to be the father of triplets, and won't that be a distraction for you and a negative for the fund?" Madhav had a new answer this time. "The best advice I have had is from another father of triplets. He told me, 'Leave for work early and get home late.'" The Swiss apparently didn't think it was funny, because nobody laughed but me. I had the definite sense at the lunch that the crowd was curious to hear our pitch and was interested in our view of markets, but was unlikely to invest on the first go.

We had additional meetings that afternoon, at dinner, and then the next day. There are relatively few hedge funds in Geneva, but there are a large number of funds of funds, which are run by the private banks. I am impressed with the professionalism of the Swiss banks. They are perceptive analysts, and they are client oriented.

Afterward, I went to France for the weekend to visit my daughter and her family on their farm. I had forgotten how bucolic the deep French countryside is with its orderly hedgerows, stately plane trees, and old-fashioned stone houses. In the midst of the rabble of children and horses, there was serenity.

MEETING MARGARET THATCHER

April 22, 2003: I have been in London the past few days slogging back and forth pitching potential investors. Today is my last day in London, and Julian Robertson, an old friend and companion in the battle, has arranged for me to call on Margaret Thatcher at her offices in Prince's Gate. I have always revered her. It is not an exaggeration to say that at a time of extreme distress and crisis, she saved and reformed Britain and then re-created its place in the world. In addition, she was the intellect behind and articulator of Ronald Reagan's strategy of economic and military competition with the Soviet Union. In the end, this strategy bankrupted the Soviet Union, caused the collapse of the Soviet system, and brought an end to the Cold War. She articulated a vision of the world that Reagan only sensed. Remember the famous picture of Thatcher speaking at dinner in Number 10 as Ronald Reagan, seated next to her, stares raptly up at her. Reagan sent her the picture with the following inscription in his own hand. "Dear Margaret, As you can see, I agree with every word you are saying. I always do! Warmest friendship. Sincerely, Ron." He meant it! In 1990 she bucked up the first George Bush when Iraq invaded Kuwait ("This is not the time to go wobbly, George").

I first met Lady Thatcher in the mid-1990s when she was a member of Julian Robertson's Tiger Management board, which I also was on. She was so dynamic, so intensely interested in how a hedge fund worked, and such a contrast to the prominent politicians I have seen on other boards, who are charming but who don't impress you as first class minds, and who in terms of contribution are indistinguishable from the proverbial bumps on a log. Not Lady Thatcher. I remember her walking through the offices and the trading room of Tiger, radiating energy and intelligence, interrogating everyone with genuine curiosity. And when Tiger imploded and Julian chose to close his fund, without being asked, she flew across the ocean to be at the closing dinner that Morgan Stanley gave for him.

Once, in June 1998, at a Tiger board lunch in London, when I was seated next to her, she asked me what I thought of the investment outlook for Russia. I said I was selling. She took my hand and proceeded to rattle off five reasons why Russia was still a great investment. The effect of the radiance of the intellect and the held hand was my total and unconditional surrender. I cancelled the sell orders as soon as lunch was over. Unfortunately, at the time she was wrong (or at least early), because a few months later came the Russian debt and equity collapse. Several years later, at the closing dinner for Julian, I was seated at her table. The after-dinner entertainment was a self-proclaimed clairvoyant. After several ostensible triumphs, this rather obnoxious showman approached Lady Thatcher and loudly announced to the room that he was now going to read the baroness' mind. She regarded him with disdain and pity and gave him a thin smile. "Not likely, young man, not likely," was all she said. The room roared.

Today she was as elegantly dressed as ever, and as usual, she appeared as if she had just been to the hairdresser. She sat in a big armchair with the light behind her and offered me coffee. Looking at her I couldn't help but recall François Mitterrand's remark that "she has the eyes of Caligula but the mouth of Marilyn Monroe." At seventy-seven, the lady's health is a little frail, and she has suffered several small strokes, but the wisdom and passion are still there.

First, I somewhat lamely asked Lady T (as her staff calls her) a silly question to the effect of who were the most impressive figures she had encountered over the years. I did not get a puffball answer. Well, Ronald Reagan was a great one, she said, and it was easy for lesser men to underrate him. His style of work and decision making were detached, but he laid down general policy directions and expected his subordinates to execute them. "Ronnie understood the really big things like taxes, Russia, and the Cold War." He was self-confident and good-natured, she said, and never pushed himself forward in international meetings. In addition, he was a superb speaker with "this most wonderful voice." She was very fond of him, she said. Did I know how he was? Did Nancy still feed him dinner every night? She liked Nancy a lot, too. Of course, I had no idea whether Nancy still fed the President every evening.

Mikhail Gorbachev also was impressive. He was not like the elderly, wooden Russian *apparatchiks* Thatcher had known. He smiled, laughed, spoke well, and was a sharp debater. They became friends, almost confidantes. Then came the surprise. She had very high regard for Raisa Gorbachev as well, who was smart and well-informed. When the Gorbachevs came to Chequers for a weekend, Lady T found her in the library reading Hobbes's *Leviathan*. Raisa also spoke good English and translated for her husband. She was more liberal and open-minded than Mikhail: Once Lady T instigated a lively argument between the Gorbachevs about the definition of the working class. In retrospect, she is convinced Raisa had great influence on her husband and played a major role in the Soviet transformation.

I asked Lady T how dangerous she found the world today. There is always danger, she said, but it's not as hazardous an environment as it was during the Cold War years. There was a moment toward the end when the Soviet Union was breaking down financially and morally under the pressure. Both the military and the regime knew their days were numbered, and there was great danger that they might lash out in one final death-spasm. Terrorism is a menace, she said, but progress is being made. We cannot equivocate. We cannot appease. We have to be tough. And then she said with that wonderful voice and accent, "The tyranny of terror cannot stand the breath of liberty."

Afterward I called on Arnab Banaerji at 10 Downing Street. Arnab was chairman of one of the big British investment management firms and is now the private secretary to Tony Blair. He is a very intelligent, charming man. He showed me around Number 10. What a wonderful old house with such stately rooms and so much history! The offices and meeting rooms have old pictures of great events, and the walls of the main staircase are decorated with the simply framed portraits of previous prime ministers in ascending order, with Lord North close to the bottom. The whole building fairly reeks of understated history and empire. Number 10 is such a refreshing change from our eternally egocentric White House, which always has publicity pictures of its current inhabitant plastered all over the West Wing walls.

GLOOM AND DEPRESSION BACK HOME

May 6, 2003: I am back in raw, rainy, bleak New York, its blacktop shimmering under a low ceiling of gunmetal gray clouds. We continue to see a lot of potential investors, but the mood of our prospects seems depressed. We also are down. We are like manic-depressives and go through violent mood swings from ebullience to despondency about our opening size. Very little capital seems to be actually signed, sealed, and delivered, perhaps $100 million, apart from my family's money. Everyone keeps telling us initial size doesn't matter. All that counts, they say, is performance with the money once we get it. However, I find it disconcerting that early forecasts from the Prime Brokerage people were that we would romp into business with $800 million plus. Mouth bets! We will be lucky to end up with $250 million the way things are going.

Tonight I took the 8:11 train from Grand Central, and just after the 125th Street station, we stopped for some undisclosed reason. I gazed blankly out the window into an asphalt playground. It was a sweltering hot, sticky New York evening. Kids were lounging around smoking, talking, and bouncing balls. Over in one corner, a teenage guy was practicing medium-range jump shots at a bent hoop with no net. Two young girls with long pigtails, who I guessed were his sisters, were rebounding for him, and he had them firing the balls back to him. Their throws were erratic, but he would run them down, then catch and shoot. The air was thick, and the sweat was pouring off him. As I watched, he hit four long jumpers in a row. I stared, entranced. The train lurched forward, and I began to lose him. Suddenly it became significant that he hit one more before I lost sight of him. Off balance, he drained it! Everything was going to be all right.

May 15, 2003: More gloomy news today. Two large endowments we were counting on for big money informed us they would not be able to invest on June 2, each for a different reason. On the other hand, the positive response from former Morgan Stanley managing directors has lifted my spirits. In particular some long-time friends have made substantial commitments, which really makes me feel good. Today we hired Sergei, the young Russian Madhav and I had interviewed in London, so our research team is complete for the time being.

May 22–23, 2003: At the Field Club this weekend six different people, some of whom I knew well, offered to invest with the amount ranging from $500,000 to $2 million for Traxis. Later, on reflection, the euphoria faded as I suddenly realized that if we performed badly, it was going to be awkward and humiliating. Last year, my friend John's firm had some poor stocks. John is a great value investor, but he had turned over a number of accounts to another manager who got suckered into value traps. Anyway, John felt so bad about the losses, and at his country club there were so many friends whose money he ran, that it was embarrassing for him to go there. He said it was like he had leprosy. In fact, to avoid painful moments, he joined the very expensive Golf Club of Purchase where he didn't know many people, so he could play golf in peace and tranquility. John is a very serious and conscientious man.

May 23, 2003: This has been another long week of presentations. Private wealth management is doing a great job of getting us in front of people, but my sense is that we are getting a number of $500,000 and $1 million investors and nothing big. The legal people at our bell-cow, lead-investor pension fund are giving us an excruciatingly hard time on terms and details. It is particularly frustrating because their early support last August was the spark that got us going.

I know the head guy of this pension fund well, and I had managed money for him for years. He is a smart man and a sophisticated investor, and that August day in 2002, I sat in his air-conditioned office perspiring as I told him what we were about. I didn't know whether he would be angry or supportive. "We will give you $50 to $75 million locked up for three years," he said without hesitation. Madhav was there with me, and we left glowing. He gave us the confidence to proceed. This present disappointment shows how raising money is full of surprises—some good, some bad, some just a result of bad timing. You never know who is going to come through in the end.

Meanwhile, the equity markets are acting well, which is disconcerting because we are on the sidelines. The last thing we want on opening day is to have to contend with an elevated stock market. I'm sleeping badly, and Cyril has a persistent cold.

CHAPTER

SEVEN

The Run-Up
and Haunted by
Remembrances and Doubt

I n the run-up to actually having and investing the money, I am
haunted by memories of things past. I suppose you could say I
was born with a silver investment spoon in my mouth. My father
was a very successful professional investor who was the chief investment officer of the Bank of New York and who was on a number
of corporate boards. My parents gave each of us three boys a portfolio
of about 15 stocks worth roughly $150,000 when we became 18, and
we were encouraged to learn about what we owned and ask questions. As we got older, there was always lots of talk around the dinner
table about markets and the economy. I wasn't much interested. One
year my father organized a family stock-picking contest. We each had
to pick five stocks. I finished last, and my mother, who knew or cared
nothing about the stock market, was the winner. Her approach was
to select companies whose products she liked or that had sentimental
attraction. For instance, two of her big winners were Procter & Gam-
ble and Iowa Power (she had been born and raised in Iowa). I was
disgusted.

A.W. JONES WAS THE PIONEER

By the time I got to Yale, even though it was peacetime, military service was compulsory, and I chose the Marine officer training program. I survived two summers of the physical and mental torture of the dreaded Platoon Leaders Course, and graduated from Yale in June 1955 as a second lieutenant USMC. Basic School at Quantico was 10 months and even tougher, and afterward I was sent to Okinawa as a platoon leader in a rifle company. It was peacetime, and I never heard a shot fired in anger. I liked the Recon and Escape & Evasion schools, and I enjoyed the physical life of the Marines. When I was discharged in 1958, like a lot of other young guys who didn't know what to do, I briefly taught English at Landon, a Washington area prep school, played semipro soccer, and tried to write the Great American Short Story. I didn't follow the stock market, although I viewed my portfolio's progress with interest. In fact I was so oblivious to economics that when the then chairman of the Fed, William McChesney Martin, came to dinner and he and my father talked about the economy, I didn't even bother to listen.

Meanwhile, my next youngest brother, Jeremy, who was three years behind me at Yale, had just returned from two years at the London School of Economics. He quickly got a job on Wall Street at the U.S. Steel & Carnegie Pension Fund, and suddenly I was out of the dinner table conversation and way behind. I was bored with playing soccer and getting rejection slips for my stories, so I went to my father and told him I wanted to be an investor. He told me to read Benjamin Graham's great classic *Security Analysis* from cover to cover, and then we would talk. I slogged through the 600 pages, underlining and taking notes. When I had finished, I went to see my dad. He took my dog-eared copy from me, handed me a new one, and said, "Do it again." He wanted me to have a deep grounding in value investing and to understand that investing was hard, grinding work.

I finished at the top of my business school class, and in 1961 I went to Wall Street as an analyst at E.F. Hutton. The silver-spoon thing comes in because the chairman of Hutton, Sylvan Coleman, was a very close friend of my father. My godfather ran Baker Weeks, the finest research firm of that time, and he also offered me a job as an analyst. I took the Hutton job for the lousy reason that it paid more: $7,200 versus $6,500.

By 1964 there was only one hedge fund, A. W. Jones & Company. It managed about $80 million in two funds. The firm had been created in 1949 with capital of $100,000 by Alfred Winslow Jones, basically to run his wife's money. Jones himself had bounced around from the U.S. foreign service to journalism without notable success. He thought of himself as an entrepreneur and intellectual. As a graduate student in sociology at Columbia, he had published a paper with the elaborate title *Life, Liberty and Property: A Story of Conflict and Measurement of Conflicting Rights*.

In the 1940s Jones had been a staff writer for *Time* and *Fortune*. By the mid-1960s Alfred Jones (no one dared to call him Al, just as no one would dream of referring to Alan Greenspan as just plain Al Greenspan) was a wealthy, snobbish, pretentious man, but he was no dummy. He conceived the idea of the modern hedge fund: a private fund that uses leverage to go both long and short on stocks, actively manages its net long exposure, and charges a performance fee. There were plenty of leveraged long pooled funds in New York before the Crash, but my father told me that none of them systematically controlled risk by hedging with shorts.

In London, John Maynard Keynes had been managing a macro fund, a long-short fund, as far back as the early 1920s, but more about that later.

Then, in the 1930s, Benjamin Graham had run a fund called Graham Newman that employed his value-based, intense security analysis approach to identify the most expensive and the cheapest stocks in the major industries. The fund then sold short and bought equal dollar amounts. It didn't work very well. There wasn't enough differentiation, and Ben Graham, although a superb analyst, was perhaps a little too theoretical in his obsession with value. The fund was often short the best companies in an industry and long the worst. Graham, like many of his generation, also may have been too traumatized by the carnage of the Crash and its aftermath to use much leverage and take risk.

Incidentally, Alfred Jones did not pretend to be an investor. He saw himself as an innovator, and a manager and collector of talent. That is precisely what he was. The investment world was still a little sleepy in the 1960s, with most of the money run out of trust departments inhabited by investment Rip van Winkles. There also were no rules about conflict of interest for analysts. Jones believed that if he could get an information edge and some smart, aggressive portfolio managers who would react quickly to news, his fund could put up big numbers versus the rather pathetic competition from somnolent, lethargic bank trust departments. He also was convinced that he could then charge investors in his hyperfund a higher fixed fee plus 20% of the profits.

His firm, A.W. Jones & Company, had several in-house portfolio managers, but he also made ingenious use of brokerage-firm analyst talent. For example, if a brokerage firm analyst made some good recommendations and developed a following, Alfred Jones would ask him or her to lunch and suggest that he or she run a model or paper portfolio for A.W. Jones to give Jones direct insight into his thinking and performance. The arrangement was that the analyst had to call one of A.W. Jones's three portfolio managers and explain his or her thinking whenever a change was made in that portfolio.

In return, the analyst's firm would be handsomely compensated through soft dollar (give-up) commissions, a percentage of which would flow directly to the analyst, because at that time the best analysts worked for retail brokerage firms and were registered. If the model portfolio prospered, the model would become a real portfolio located at A.W. Jones, and the analyst would be paid even more commissions. This was a big deal financially for the analysts and perfectly legal under the rules of that era. The better the portfolio did, the more commissions the analyst got. Jones never implicitly suggested the analyst front run his recommendation or his firm's clients, but he made it clear that analysts got paid strictly for investment ideas that worked and that A.W. Jones & Company couldn't care less about long, scholarly research reports. Moreover, Jones was ruthless. If your model portfolio didn't perform, you were gone. Alfred Jones understood the performance game and the value of getting an edge from research before anyone else did.

In 1966 he told Carol Loomis of *Fortune* magazine that he had developed a model with pairs trading within a risk management framework. I think that was a bunch of baloney. Basically Jones used commissions to develop an informational advantage and hired smart, young guys to exploit it. Fortunately Elliot Spitzer was still in diapers.

By the beginning of 1964, I had been an analyst at E.F. Hutton for a little more than three years, and I had had a couple of lucky hits. It really was luck because I was fresh out of business school. Jones was a class behind my father at Harvard and somehow heard about me, and he asked me to lunch at his club with his operating officer. His firm was not yet well known, but it was riding high and growing exponentially because it had delivered a compound investment return of 28% since its inception in May 1955. His first question when we sat down to lunch was, "When you go to pee in a restaurant urinal, do you wash your hands before or after you pee?"

I was stunned. "Afterwards, sir."

He looked at me sourly. "That's the wrong answer. You're a conventional thinker and not rational. I always wash before rather than after."

He sat there, a pudgy, nearsighted, aristocratic man in his mid 60s, and reviewed my resume as if I were one of his horses. He was intrigued that I had been a Marine officer and had played rugby for Yale. He knew very little about the market, so he really was as interested in who I was and how I answered his odd questions as in my investment candlepower. Later, I figured out that he really cared only about whether the people who worked for him could make him money, and his interest in my pedigree was only because he thought it would make his firm seem more credible to his rich, socialite investors. Over dessert he offered me a model portfolio.

During the course of 1964 I ran my model portfolio and put up some good numbers. I also became friends with Dick Radcliffe, who was a junior partner and portfolio manager at A. W. Jones. Dick was nine years older than I, and he, too, lived in Greenwich. Five years earlier Mr. Jones had persuaded him to leave White Weld and work full time for his company. In early January 1965 I began to get heavy pressure from Alfred Jones to leave Hutton and join his firm. It was an excruciating dilemma. My Jones portfolio had done very well. I was making excellent money at Hutton and at the end of 1964 had been made a partner, partly because my commission credits from A. W. Jones were so huge. I knew that if I said no to Jones, he would cut me off, which would be very painful because the Jones commissions were well over half my compensation. I liked the concept of hedge funds, but I didn't particularly like Mr. Jones.

After a while, I talked to Radcliffe about my problem. He grinned and told me he was tired of Alfred Jones, whom he found autocratic and capricious. One day that spring, we went out to lunch, and I proposed that we form our own fund. Radcliffe was very enthusiastic and suggested we locate it in Greenwich. My father was supportive but warned me in stark terms that the great postwar bull market was long in the tooth. "Stocks have done too well for too long. A 5- or 10-year bear market is a definite possibility," he warned. "Prepare your mind for that eventuality." I couldn't conceive of an extended bear market, and thought he was still dwelling in the 1930s or becoming senile.

Alfred Jones was furious when he found out about our plans. The year before, another of his portfolio managers, Carl Jones, had left to form his own hedge fund, City Associates. Because everyone who worked for Jones (including me) was getting richly compensated, Alfred Jones believed we should be both content and grateful. He promptly threatened to sue Radcliffe for breach of contract and stealing clients.

In the years that followed in the hedge-fund world, the minuet of acolytes leaving the beloved master would repeat itself over and over again. The great hedge-fund managers, the sun gods who have masterfully run huge money, like George Soros, Louis Bacon, and Julian Robertson, have all been generous in giving their talented people substantial pieces of the action. Nevertheless, the big funds are continually losing their best, most obsessed young people. In part, it's the money, but it's mostly the eternal desire to run your own show and make your own investment decisions. The Great Ones are held in awe by their acolytes, but the Great Ones, as strong, confident personalities, have a tendency to keep control of the portfolio and dominate its composition. Julian Robertson of Tiger is both respected and adored by his Tiger cubs, but that didn't stop them from leaving him to form their own funds. Yet they have endowed scholarships in his honor and truly revere him. George Soros's Quantum Fund has been a revolving door for investors. Although George is highly respected as an investor, he is known to be an imperious and highly critical second-guesser. But what would you expect?

NOTHING LIKE A PUNCH IN THE MOUTH THE FIRST DAY

Dick Radcliffe and I launched Fairfield Partners on June 1, 1965, with $9.7 million, $200,000 of which was mine. The Dow Jones Industrial Average closed on May 30, 1965, at 912. Sixteen years later it was at the same level, so my father's warning was prescient. By 1981 adjusted for inflation, the Dow had lost more than half of its 1965 purchasing power value, even when you added back in the dividends that had been paid. Anyway, on June 1, 1965, Radcliffe and I had selected a list of stocks to go long and short, and we put our new capital to work over the course of the morning. Our theory was that the right thing to do was to get where you wanted to be immediately. I still think it is the right way to handle new money, but that afternoon, speaking at a lunch in Washington, William McChesney Martin, the revered and scholarly chairman of the Federal Reserve, warned in a somber speech of the disturbing similarities between the summer of 1929 and 1965.

Then, as they would now, these comments sparked a ferocious sell-off in equities. The Dow plunged 45 points, and we lost 5% that afternoon alone. For the month of June, our first month, we lost 6.3%, compared with a drop in the Dow Jones Industrial Average of 4.7%. For the month, our longs went down 6.7% and our shorts fell only 0.45%. Various limited partners called with edgy questions, and some wondered if there was a provision for early redemption. At our low point on June 20 we were down 10%, and I was sure I was done for. How was I ever going to get another job in the investment business after a belly flop like this?

As it turned out, we had a great first year and finished up 55% with the Dow up 3.6%. The U.S. market was very selective that year, and we were short basic industry groups like the chemicals, aluminums, and retailers that sold at 25 to 30 times earnings, and long technology and medium-sized growth stocks. The investment gods smiled on us, and our shorts went down and our longs went up. Over the next three years, we continued to do well, and by June 1, 1969, the portfolio had gained slightly more than 200% compared with an increase in the Dow Jones Average over that period of just 4.7%. A limited partner who had invested $200,000 on June 1, 1965, had $543,000 after paying our fees. Our capital had grown to what at the time was the magnificent sum of $50 million. We thought we were geniuses. Radcliffe bought a bigger sailboat, we brought in a third partner, John Morton, and I tore down my old house and started building a much larger one.

Then came the deluge. By early 1970 the U.S. equity market had become highly speculative, with tech, computer-leasing, and new-era growth stocks selling at astronomical valuations. Hedge funds had proliferated. Salespeople, traders, guys you had never heard of were out raising money, and private placements were very much in vogue. In the late winter of 1970 a vicious bear market struck, with the heavy damage concentrated in the speculative growth stocks that had soared in 1968 and 1969. We were long the best of the new era stocks and short the worst, plus we were short some of the blue chip growth stocks known as the Nifty Fifty that we thought were outrageously overpriced. By May 1970, the new growth stocks we were long were getting killed, and the junk we were short inexplicably was holding up pretty well, as were the Nifty Fifty.

It was a devastating time. I was halfway through rebuilding our home, and we were living in the small cottage. I remember waking up every night like clockwork at 3 A.M., literally in a cold sweat, hearing the children peacefully breathing, and agonizing over the portfolio. Should we cover our Memorex short? Should we sell Digital Equipment? Was Recognition Equipment a real company? Would Polaroid ever go down? It was the worst agony I have ever experienced. It went on night after day after night. Stocks were getting destroyed. Our portfolio was dying before my eyes, yet I was also terrified of getting whipsawed. April and May were horrors. My father had always disapproved of our somewhat raunchy stock selection, questioning whether our new-era stocks were real companies and warning about the increased level of speculation. In late May, I had lunch with him at the Bank of New York. He was sympathetic, but when I complained that the market was irrational, he paraphrased John Maynard Keynes to me. "Unfortunately the markets can remain irrational longer than you can remain solvent. I advise damage control," he said.

We survived, but May 1970 was a lesson I will never forget. When you are managing risk in a portfolio, you always have to remember that there is a possibility of a catastrophic outcome. Markets are prone to extremes, both up and down. In good times, we all operate under the assumption that liquidity is a constant, and that if a position goes wrong, you can expeditiously exit it with only minimal damage. That spring, in the midst of tumultuous political and economic events, I learned the hard way that in a market meltdown, not only does liquidity evaporate, but prices can fall so steeply that all decisions have the potential for serious adverse consequences. I discovered that in crisis decision making, the key is to find the least bad option, but, as my father said to me afterward, "In your investment trial-by-fire, it is good that you learned the lessons of the danger of leverage and the need to cut losses. However, don't learn too much from them. Don't become like Mark Twain's frog that never would sit on a stove again after being burned and as a result froze to death."

THE GREAT BEAR MARKET—AND THE BOTTOMLESS PIT IN MY STOMACH

As things turned out, the end of our fiscal year, June 1, 1970, was the bottom of the first leg of what turned out to be the great secular bear market of 1969 to 1974. Almost half our partners gave us the proverbial black spot, as the crew did to pirate-ship captains of old when the sailors had lost confidence. Over the course of our next fiscal year, the markets rallied, and with the Dow Jones Industrial Average up 29%, we were up 67%, so we had made back everything we had lost the year before. However, the size of our fund had shrunk; understandably, many of our investors could not tolerate the volatility.

In addition, hedge funds had lost their luster. From 1970 to 1973 many hedge funds crashed and burned because they were really just leveraged long funds and as a result suffered huge declines. Other funds had bought private-equity venture-capital deals that turned out to be totally illiquid when things got tough. Another game at that time was for a fund to purchase private placements of publicly owned companies at substantial discounts with a so-called investment letter attached. The companies were usually questionable or else in desperate need of financing. The hedge fund after a few months would then mark up the private placement to the current market price even though it couldn't sell the shares. Later, when the funds got redemptions, there were large chunks of their portfolios that were mispriced and that they couldn't sell. The entry of hedge funds into the private equity space today worries me.

In the spring of 1972, Morgan Stanley had raised $10 million for us in Europe and the Middle East. I had several close friends there from Yale and from a football group in Greenwich. At that time, Morgan Stanley was a small, very high quality investment bank with an incredible blue chip list of banking relationships. The senior partners were somewhat aristocratic, but they fervently believed in hiring the best and the brightest. In those days, Morgan Stanley published no research, disdained mergers and acquisitions, and had no distribution capability of its own. Instead for each issue it underwrote, it formed syndicates of regional firms across the country. The big wire-houses were beginning to loom as a threat because they had the distribution capability and were attempting to develop expertise in investment banking.

In the securities markets, 1973 was a dismal year, and Morgan Stanley was suffering because there was no underwriting activity. The young partners who were my friends wanted to grow and to expand into new areas. The first step, they argued, was to develop research and an institutional sales force to get some placing power. I was their candidate to create a research department and investment management. In May 1973, they offered me a partnership with a 3% interest for $300,000 and a $50,000 salary. I was flattered and accepted. The firm on the day I became a partner had 27 partners, 255 employees, and $10 million of capital. In both 1973 and 1974, Morgan Stanley operated at small losses and in the summer of 1974, the then senior partner, Bob Baldwin, decreed all travel, including international, would be tourist.

Fairfield Partners survived the bear market of the 1970s and prospered until 1985 when Radcliffe and Morton retired.

Three memories of that time are what haunt me. The first is the boulder-sized pit in my stomach that June afternoon in 1965 when we lost 5% the first day we were in business. The second is the fatigue and despair of that horrendous month of May 1970. The third is the horrendous month of September 1974, when stock prices fell day after day. It was the mirror image of the early spring of 2000, when tech stock prices soared day after day.

Now, fast forward to 2003; we're bullish but tense, as shown in the following entries.

May 26, 2003: The tension is building as June 2 approaches and markets keep climbing. I woke up this morning at 3 A.M. with the moonlight pouring in, worrying how we are going to invest the money when we get it. The French say, between the hour of the dog and the wolf lies the end of all things. It sounds romantic, but it's actually just insomnia. What plagues me is that everyone tells us that it's crucial not to lose money in the first few months. This argues for a conservative stance. To get invested and then have equities fall and lose 10% would be a disaster. On the other hand, if we don't participate in a rip-roaring rally, people will be very upset with us, regardless of what they say now. Experience teaches us that the right thing to do is to get to where we want to be and feel comfortable, rather than play tactical games. We are all still bullish, so we are going to go substantially net long. The three of us agreed today that we would each separately construct a portfolio to begin with on June 2, with all the specifics about position sizes, and that we would meet Sunday afternoon to talk about it.

May 28, 2003: It looks as though we will start with $270 million of capital, not counting Morgan Stanley's contribution and my family's money which will get us up to $390 million. Of the five big money sources we were banking on way back when, only one will be with us, and he is half of what he originally said. The others either didn't make the closing because of legal issues, or there was some kind of timing problem. On the other hand, there were some very pleasant surprises. Our biggest investor, at $40 million, is a London fund of funds, and oddly we can't even remember the initial presentation. The whole money-raising experience goes to show that immediate postpresentation euphoria is ephemeral and that you can't count on anything. I am flattered but frightened that so many friends came in.

May 29, 2003: I woke up early today hearing the chirping of the tree frogs and feeling tense about the portfolio. After this three-month rally in stocks, what do we do? I keep tinkering with my version of an opening portfolio. I feel quite confident that over a couple of years we can create good absolute returns with our style and system. After all, we have done it for a long time. What is so scary is that we live or die on what happens in the next year, or should I say the next seven months, to December 31. Anything can happen in the short run. We could be cold and unlucky and look like bums. If we do poorly in this first stub year, the fund will shrink by 50%, and it will take a couple of years of good numbers to restore our credibility and attract new money. Who knows if the three of us will hang together for that process, and I can just imagine all the snide comments. The latest piece of bad news is that our big pension fund is not going to make the June 1 closing because of legal nit-picking. Cyril still has a cold and lost a filling today during an investment presentation in our office. Is it psychosomatic? Stocks surged going into the weekend, which really bums us out.

June 2, 2003: I played tennis on Saturday in Greenwich with Sam, a young guy, who runs a small tech hedge fund, and on Sunday with Phil, who has had his own hedge fund for years. Sam is smart, savvy, and hardworking. He talks with 5 to 10 tech company managements a week. He says they still don't see any real pickup in orders. He is doing some selling. He was formerly an emerging markets manager but migrated to tech after the Russia panic. Out of the frying pan into the fire, I tell him. He has some good insights about emerging-markets investing. One is that the locals in the end always get the best of the foreigners. After a panic, triggered by some political event, the locals will happily buy your shares at depressed prices. However, don't kid yourself that next time you are going to be able to sell your appreciated shares to them. The only way to take profits home from emerging markets is for foreign fools to sell at higher prices to greater foreign fools.

Phil, the veteran hedge-fund manager, is bullish. Some people become debilitated by experience and the accumulated scars of investing. Not Phil! After tennis (he won), we sat in the shade. He told me that he was the biggest investor in his fund and that, after much agony, he had come to the conclusion that he had to run the fund as though it were his own money. In other words, don't make decisions on the basis of business considerations, just be an investor. This is a very pertinent insight, because our handlers are telling us to be cautious and above all to be sure not to lose money in the first few months. I'm bullish and more inclined to go for it. Phil caught the rally and is already up 25% for the year.

Phil is a gutsy guy. In January of this year, after two bad years, he raised his fixed fee, telling his investors that he was so far below his high-water mark he needed a higher fixed fee to keep his best analysts. Otherwise, they would migrate to a fund that wasn't under its high-water mark so they could get paid if 2003 was a good year. Some of his clients walked, saying, "You've made millions of dollars in good years in the past, so you should dig into your deep pockets and pay your analysts, not ask us to." Then Phil put his whole business at risk by taking a huge net long position. Now it has paid off big. He really does run the fund as though it were his own money.

As for high-water marks, in addition to their fixed fee, hedge funds take an incentive fee of 20% of the gains for the year. However, obviously, if there are no gains, there is no incentive fee. If the fund actually loses money in a given year, the manager doesn't get paid the following year until those losses have been recouped and the portfolio is in the black. This is the so-called high-water mark. Thus, when Phil was down two years in a row, he had a big carry-forward loss to recover before his people got paid anything. This provision encourages funds with losses either to close down and restart with a new identity or go out of business. I think it is almost immoral to shut down and then restart because you are abrogating the spirit of your contract with investors.

However, some sophisticated investors feel differently, and if a manager has had a good record for a number of years and then has a bad spell, falls way below the high water, closes down, and restarts, they will give the manager money on the restart. Their theory is that reversion to the mean applies to hedge-fund managers just as it does to almost everything else. Secondly, they are betting that the restart managers will be desperately hungry. To be consistent, they should probably take money away from a hedge fund that has had a couple of spectacular years. In fact, this happened to Jeff, a friend of mine. He had a fine record for years, and then he really shot the lights out with two back-to-back 40% up-years. So what happened? Some of his investors withdrew money *because he had done so well.* Jeff didn't really care because he had plenty of capital anyway, but still it was irritating. If you're not a secure immortal like Jeff, it can be a frustrating business. You suffer redemptions if you do badly and also if you do too well.

Anyway, I went into New York this afternoon. Our office is in temporary space on the fourth floor of One Rockefeller Plaza, rented from my friend John Levin. The space is dark, dingy, shabby, and ancient. The rug in the conference room reeks of mold. I choke up every time I go in there. However Madhav, Cyril, Doug, and I have small offices with big windows overlooking the life and action of the plaza and directly into the tops of trees. The windows actually open, and the music from the bands and singers in the plaza wafts up. After years of high-altitude, sealed, sterile office environments, fresh air and street noise are very pleasant. Maybe we will dance in a bright cloud of music after all.

(As it turned out, we had to move three times in the first year of our existence, and each time our surroundings improved until finally we had our own space fitted out not luxuriously but comfortably with a magnificent view of Fifth Avenue. Perversely, our relative performance has varied inversely with the shabbiness of our locale. We did great, put up our best numbers, on the cruddy, mold-ridden fourth floor. It never fails.)

Everyone was at the office when I got there, including Phil, our trader, the analysts, and Suzanne our office manager. The mood reminded me of a locker room before a big game. You're scared of a bad break that will put you down a goal in the first five minutes. You know you can't tighten up and that you have just to play your game, but it's easier said than done. Late in the afternoon Cyril, Madhav, and I met in the conference room for a couple of hours and compared the model portfolios we had each prepared. They were surprisingly similar. Is that good or bad?

Afterward, the three of us went out to dinner at a cheap Italian restaurant in Rockefeller Center. We bought a decent bottle of Chianti, and I intoned, "So this is either the end of the beginning or the beginning of the end." Cyril said it was a pretty corny statement. As the Chianti did its work, I began to feel that we are a band of brothers about to go to war together. And war is what it is. Us against the markets and everybody else.

Bob Farrell, an old friend in the battle for investment survival and the best technician I know because he has a real sense of the history and mystery of markets, e-mailed me this wonderful passage from an obscure book written long ago (*Ten Years of Wall Street* by Barnie Winkleman.) I printed out three copies and passed it around at dinner.

> *No discussion of the interrelation of stock prices and business conditions would be complete without emphasizing that in the clash of speculative forces on the exchange, the emotions play a part which is not paralleled in the normal processes of commerce and industry. The golden mean is non-existent in Wall Street, because the speculative mechanism does all things to excess; even the reactions from the heights of phantasy (sic) and from the depths of despair are accompanied by convulsions which are distinct from the calmer tenor of business. Those who seek to relate stock movements to the current statistics of business, or who ignore the strongly imaginative taint of stock operations, or who overlook the technical basis of advances and declines, must meet with disaster, because their judgment is based upon the humdrum dimensions of fact and figure in a game which is actually played in a third dimension of the emotions and a fourth dimension of dreams.*

The writer, whoever he was, understood. The money game *is* played in the third and fourth dimension.

It was too late to go back to Greenwich. I went with Madhav to his apartment, took an Ambien, and slept poorly on the couch in his library. It seems as though tomorrow will be a particularly lousy moment to be having to put to work a big slug of new money on whose performance so much depends, but then that's investment life, its own cantankerous self.

Now is always the hardest time to invest. Always the hardest time to decipher the third and fourth dimensions.

CHAPTER
EIGHT

Hedgehogs Come
in All Sizes and Shapes

Throughout the course of a normal week, we have a steady traffic of salespeople bringing strategists, economists, and analysts to our offices to make presentations. They can be interesting and even stimulating, but essentially they are not at risk the way we are. They often mouth-bet because they can always rewrite history if they are wrong. We don't have that luxury. You can't obfuscate performance numbers. Thus, our best, most insightful intercourse is with other professional investors who have public performance records, and with whom we have become true confidantes over the years. They may still not tell us the whole truth about what they are doing, but at least they are at risk in the same game we are.

Being an investor, actually running other people's money, attracts men and women who tend to be intellectually self-confident and opinionated. A questing mind, the gambling instinct, and the ability to make tough decisions on inconclusive evidence are all essential characteristics. There are no Hamlets in the ranks of successful investors. Because performance is measured impersonally by clearly defined quantitative standards, losers don't last long. For some reason, hedge-fund investing in particular attracts baroque characters with very definite views of how the world works. In the course of time, here are some of the other players I communicate with.

IT TAKES COURAGE TO BE A PIG AND *TOTIS PORCIS*

Tim

Today Tim came to have lunch. We were flattered because he is truly a legend in the hedge-fund business. Tim is a slim, dark-haired, handsome man of perhaps 55. He speaks softly with a faintly British accent, seems imperturbable, and has beautiful manners. He grew up in Kenya on a coffee plantation, which he still owns. He is a very cultured, erudite man. For most of the 1990s, he had the best record of any major hedge fund in the world. His performance is no longer public, but he is still doing brilliantly. Tim's portfolio is so concentrated and he uses so much leverage, that his results have immense volatility. But so what? If you are a long-term investor, you should happily take a highly volatile, five-year 25% compound return over a stable 10%, but you have to be able to live with the volatility and not panic when the inevitable bad year comes.

Tim works out of a quiet, spacious office filled with antique furniture, exquisite oriental rugs, and porcelain in a leafy suburb of London with only a secretary. My guess is he runs more than $1 billion, probably half of which is his. On his beautiful Chippendale desk sits a small plaque, which says *totis porcis*—the whole hog. There is also a small porcelain pig, which reads, "It takes Courage to be a Pig." I think Stan Druckenmiller, who coined the phrase, gave him the pig. To get really big long-term returns, you have to be a pig and ride your winners.

Tim is a *macro* or top-down global investor. He studies the world, searching for investment opportunities. He concentrates on asset classes, countries, and major groups of stocks. On one day in June 2003, when he came by our offices, he was long Japanese banks, Russian equities, Treasury bonds, the euro, and Korean equities. At the time, he was short the dollar in a big way, which could mean a position three times his equity. He was also short the consumer staple stocks like food and beverages in Europe and the United States. When he lacks conviction, he reduces his leverage and takes off his bets. He describes this as "staying close to shore."

Tim's modus operandi is the exact opposite of the conventional, fiduciary wisdom. He uses immense leverage, practices enormous concentration, and has no investment organization. It requires nerves of spun steel and great inner confidence to use the kind of leverage he employs. Leverage means volatility, and it means that you have a lot less margin of error. For example, a guy like Tim could easily have his fund leveraged up four times. That means if he loses 10% on his portfolio, his equity is down 50%. Once you are down more than 20%, it's hard to recover, because you are compounding off a much lower base. Suppose Tim was down 10% overall but down 50% on his equity. If he was up 10% the next year, he would still be down 25% from inception, whereas on the same performance the unleveraged fund would be down only 1%. Besides, anytime your portfolio is down more than 20%, your head is being seriously messed with.

Tim is convinced that hedge funds, because of client pressure, have become obsessed with avoiding monthly declines in net asset value (drawdowns). As a result they employ stop-loss limits and all kinds of risk-control mechanisms that mechanically make investment decisions for them. Most of these decisions are bad. They never fight the tape and brag about how market neutral they are. As a result, they become short-term, momentum-oriented traders. He argues that this creates an opportunity for an investor who uses leverage, is willing to accept volatility, and who is long term in his thinking. "Accept volatility and concentration," he says. "Diversification is an enemy of performance."

Tim makes another interesting point. "Running a portfolio," he says, "is a solitary activity. For me it doesn't work to have partners. In the end, one mind in the dead of night has to make the buy and sell decisions." Teams, much less groups, are about compromises and they are bound to make less good decisions than an individual who is focused on one portfolio in which his own money is at stake. He says he can and often does make wrong decisions, but at least the decision-making process is uncontaminated.

You would have to truly believe in Tim to invest in his fund, and you would have to either ignore or not be disturbed by the huge performance swings. In 2002 he was down about 20%, then up more than 100% in 2003. At one point in 2004, he was up 18% and then ended up close to 40%. I suspect Tim has a few large investors who have been with him for a long time, and I'm sure he wouldn't even answer a phone call from a fund of funds. Twice a year he writes a one-page letter describing what he is thinking. It is literally one page! He publishes his net asset value once a week on a secure web site, so his investors, if they want to look, can find out how he is doing.

Tim keeps himself totally inaccessible to all but a few select strategists and analysts. He speaks with other money managers and to businesspeople who are working in the real economy. I don't think he reads much Wall Street research, but he does look at and pay attention to charts. When I asked him how he got his investment ideas, at first he was at a loss. Then, after thinking about it, he said that the trick was to accumulate over time a knowledge base. Then, out of the blue, some event or new piece of information triggers a thought process, and suddenly you have discovered an investment opportunity. You can't force it. You have to be patient and wait for the light to go on. If it doesn't go on, "Stay close to shore."

Tim usually carries about 10 positions, and argues that the proper way to invest for superior performance is to have a few big bets in which you can develop an edge and that you have real conviction in. Then you must follow them intensely. Recently he told me he had three positions. He was short the dollar by a factor of three times his equity, and he had more than 100% of his equity in Japan, half in the banks, and half in the Japan Topic Index. In addition, he had 200% of his equity in two-year U.S. Treasury notes as an insurance position. Sometimes he also owns a few exotic positions; like right now, he owns a significant interest in a North Korean bank and commercial real estate in St. Petersburg. The bank sells at a third of book value and the real estate yields 15%.

He travels continually. He is a very curious, inquisitive man. He operates almost like a secret agent. For example, Tim has big positions in Russian and Japanese banks. He isn't just content with the usual fare of company meetings and government officials in Moscow and St. Petersburg. Instead, because Russia is so much about oil, last year he went on a grueling trip for a week in Siberia, visiting the Russian oil companies. With the Japanese banks he employs a number of unconventional sources, and I know he has long-time contacts with the senior management of two of them. He goes to Tokyo probably four or five times a year.

As I said before, Tim thinks investment management is essentially a one-person, lonely, anguished occupation, and that intense personal relationships with the people who work for you are essentially disruptive and a distraction. Your focus has to be totally on your portfolio and what is happening in the world and in markets. Your objective is performance and not to build an enduring firm or develop brilliant young macro analysts. Almost all of the other really successful hedge-fund managers I know want to create a legacy, build a business that survives beyond them. Often this obsession becomes their downfall.

Tim must be a very wealthy man, but he doesn't live ostentatiously. He has a house in London and a coffee plantation in Kenya. This is an intriguing question: Why does Tim run money in this extremely stressful, highly concentrated, massively leveraged way? Why does he travel endlessly to places like Japan, Russia, and India, which are not exactly luxury locations? He has no partner with whom to share the anxiety, and his performance swings are so immense it must be nervewracking even for an impervious persona. From time to time, one hears wild stories that Tim is facing huge margin calls and is about to be carried out. Of course it is never true.

The only answer I can come up with is that he loves high-octane investing, and I know that he thinks it's the right way to manage money. He must like to travel. This quiet, austere, gentle man must thrill to the adrenaline rush of spectacular successes and be able to live with the big downs. As an investor in hedge funds, what would you rather have over five years? A very choppy 20% to 25% compound or a steady 10% to 12%?

THE BEARDED PROPHET OF THE APOCALYPSE

Vince
There is this guy I have known for years named Vince. This little essay came out of a dinner I had with him last summer.

I first met Vince in the late 1970s when he was the head trader for the biggest hedge fund of that time. Now he is retired and runs his own hedge fund. Although he has a honed market sense, Vince has always been far more than just a trader. In fact, he is much better on the giant slow ideas than the short-term twitches. No one is perfect, but he has had some great long-term calls. I could give you some big investment names who regularly check in with Vince. In 1973 he nailed the Nifty Fifty, and in 1980 he was talking about the oil price bubble bursting, interest rates peaking, and arguing that Ronald Reagan meant disinflation. He has had some big wrongs, too, particularly on Japan, and he was early on tech. He doesn't change his mind easily. Vince now runs his own small hedge fund, which is mostly his own money and a few friends who believe he may be a prophet.

Certain other people think Vince is a kook, and maybe he is a little crazy.

Some guys call him "the bearded prophet of the apocalypse," but I listen to him because he thinks immoderately, extravagantly, and in life, both financial and social, sometimes events swing to extremes that seem inconceivable to conventional minds. He has also read a lot of history; he is a big believer in Paul Johnson and his theory of the importance of "unintended consequences." When Treasury bonds yielded 15%, Vince said they would go to at least 5% before it was over. When the Dow sold at 9 times earnings, he said it would levitate to 25 times. At the time, I agreed with the direction but thought he was too extravagant.

Vince talks very fast, with great passion, and he has a manic giggle. He is part technician, part historian, and a lot mystic. Vince is Greek, an immigrant refugee, and New York tough. He never went to college and sometimes likes to appear uncouth. Once he walked into a cocktail lounge in a fancy hotel and said to the pianist in a loud voice, "Play some Picasso." The pianist stared at him. "Okay," said Vince, "play Rembrandt, instead." He has a thick beard and insists on cheek kissing, which is a prickly experience I don't much care for. He can be strident and embarrassing. He now lives outside New York, but he called me and said he had something to tell me. So he drove down and we had dinner in one of those dark, expensive French restaurants where the waiters have sensitive, aristocratic faces.

Vince thinks of himself as a prophet of social and financial change. Prices and society gravitate around a central value and in the long run revert to the mean, he believes, but human nature is wildly emotional and thus prone to disorderly excesses that cause booms and busts. In a world where communication through television and the Internet is omnipresent and virtually instantaneous, enormous intemperance occurs faster and more frequently than ever before. To him, the excesses of the 1990s have only begun to be purged, and the secondary consequences will be a social and financial revolution that will destroy another huge chunk of paper wealth and transform society. Vince has a strong religious streak, so he started by quoting Ecclesiastes to me.

> *To everything there is a season, and a time to every purpose under heaven:*
> *A time to be born, and a time to die; a time to plant, and a time to pluck*
>   *up that which is planted; . . .*
> *A time to weep, and a time to laugh, a time to mourn and a time to*
>   *dance; . . .*
> *A time to get and a time to lose; a time to keep, and a time to cast away;*
> *A time to rend and a time to sew; a time to keep silence and a time to*
>   *speak.*

"This is an evil time for America," Vince told me, his eyes gleaming points of light in all that hair, "and a time to weep; a time to lose is coming. Gross corruption and greed on Wall Street and corporate America have poisoned the golden well of capitalism. The people of the world have learned from television and the Internet that capitalism and globalization are evil systems that make the rich richer and the poor poorer. They hear that in the past 20 years CEO compensation has increased from 43 times that of the average worker to 531 times. Who knows if it is true? But people believe it."

Vince blew smoke at me (yes, he still smokes red box Marlboros). "And investors now know that the accountants were corrupt and that reported earnings of even the icons of American capitalism were manipulated by hero CEOs so they could exercise their options. Even some of the best firms underwrote trash and had analysts who were liars. Brokers were pawns and are being thrown to the wolves. Investors always knew Wall Street was a casino, but they thought that at least it was an honest casino. Instead, it was a giant sophisticated Ponzi scheme, and they were the suckers. People are not going to forgive and forget these grievous wounds in a year or two. This is secular, not cyclical."

"Yeah," I said, "but everything you say has been on TV and the front pages and is already mostly discounted. These are all the reasons why equity markets were down three years in a row. It's yesterday's news."

Vince emitted his harsh giggle. "Right," he said, "but the secondary consequences haven't appeared yet. Investors in equity mutual funds in the greatest bull market in history earned 6% a year when the S&P was compounding at 17% because, at the top, they were *sold* what was hot and what already had gone up. Now, many equity funds are down 50% from their highs; tech funds are down 70%. Gretchen Morgenson in the *New York Times* is leading a crusade against investment management companies, portfolio managers, and fund directors. It's just beginning. The class action lawyers will dig and dig and find all kinds of trash. They will reap big money. Then the redemption phase begins. It hasn't even started yet. It will take a generation to rebuild trust. Don't forget that in the 1970s, from the high-water mark, American mutual funds lost 50% of their assets, and that the Japanese mutual-fund industry lost 90% of its assets between 1990 and 2000. The aftermath of this whopper secular bear market has barely begun.

"And then there's the pension fund disaster. The people who have signed up for all those defined contribution plans have individual accounts that are hopelessly underfunded: They are time bombs. This is the aftermath of the bubble. There will be lawsuits against the bankers and brokers that will go on forever, and they will have to disgorge great hunks of capital. Their shares will sell at discounts, not premiums, to book value before it's over."

I shuddered, thinking of the Morgan Stanley stock I still owned. "I understand your concerns," I said, keeping my voice down, "but the apocalypse you talk about is not going to occur unless stock markets fall a lot further. It's easy to scream the bear case when prices have collapsed and bad things are happening, but as Warren Buffett says, betting against America has never been right."

"Buffett has become an establishment shill," Vince replied. "Stocks will fall a lot further. They are still too expensive. The U.S. economy will be slow for years: too much debt, too little savings, inadequate retirement provisions. Residential real estate is the next big disaster. People are borrowing short to invest long, refinancing mostly with floating-rate mortgages. When short rates go up, debt service payments will soar and house prices will decline. Then the consumer collapses from the double whammy of the wealth effect and shrinking disposable income. It's called civilization exhaustion, and the beginning of the decline and fall of the American empire.

"Furthermore, another bubble is about to burst. Existing home prices have been rising 7% to 8% a year, financed by Fannie and Freddie. Luxury real estate values from Park Avenue to Beverly Hills and from Southampton to Aspen will collapse. In the aftermath of every burst financial bubble in history, paper wealth of all types evaporates. It was created out of thin air, and it will be blown away like mist in the wind. The price of the average luxury condo in Tokyo fell from US$1.2 million in 1990 to US$250,000 last year. In the 1930s, the price of art fell 80%. Oriental rug prices collapsed. Delayed backlash effects are always the same. Why should it be different this time? Secondary consequences take time—years—to happen, particularly when central banks cut interest rates drastically and flood the system with liquidity. But they can only be postponed, not averted. In three years, the American economy will be in a depression, the S&P 500 will be at 500, and there will be a revolution in America. It could be a fascist revolution like Germany in the 1930s."

"Vince, you're going to crazy extremes again," I scoffed. "You've predicted nine of the past three bear markets. There doesn't have to be an apocalypse. The U.S. socioeconomic system is the most flexible and adaptable in history. The authorities have a lot of fiscal and monetary weapons and won't just sit idly by and let the U.S. economy collapse. Depressions like those in the United States in the 1930s and in Japan in the 1990s aren't just bubbles bursting; their root cause is in major policy errors. The Fed may be erring on the side of being too easy, but assuming the worst, the result should be stagflation, not depression and deflation."

"Too late! I haven't even talked about the economic impact of more terrorism. Smallpox, nuclear explosions, suicide bombers in malls . . ."

"Don't. I can imagine. What are you doing about it?"

"I have $50,000 in gold coins in a safe deposit box in a big New York bank. But I've been thinking about it. A serious terrorist strike would knock out the power sources, so I couldn't get into my vault to get my gold. Besides, these big banks are whores. And even if I could get into my vault, with all the chaos and looting going on, there would be thugs on the street who would rob me of my gold. So the best hedge is an assault rifle and canned goods or maybe a home in New Zealand."

I saw Vince recently, and his views have not changed materially. He concedes he was early on the timing, but that an apocalypse is inevitable. Why do I listen to Vince? First, because we have to be conscious of the doomsday scenario. We need at least to keep it in mind, so we can pick up clues and react if it starts to happen. Once Vince said to me: "You native Americans have lived in a unique golden age. Nothing bad has ever happened to you. Us children of European refugees are realists. We know that unimaginable catastrophes happen." Second, the guy has hit some big ones, and unfortunately there is a germ of truth in what he says. The 1930s were a wipeout. A recurrence is not impossible. I think sometimes about owning gold. It has seldom appealed to me. Gold is an investment with a negative yield and no discernible intrinsic investment value, whose price is determined mostly by fear—fear of inflation, war, and paper money.

For me, Vince is background music. As long as I have been an investor, articulate lunatics have proposed a plausible but highly improbable doomsday scenario of war, plague, or financial meltdown. There also is always a remote possibility that something horrendous will happen, like September 11, 2001, or an Avian bird flu epidemic, but you can't manage performance money on that basis.

Julian's Guy

It's the summer of 2003, and I flew with the family to Sun Valley for a family outing on Julian Robertson's plane.

Julian is a great, wonderful friend, and for years ran one of the most successful hedge funds of all time, Tiger. He now manages his own money, and incubates new hedge funds. In other words, he funds smart young investors he knows with, say, $10 million to $20 million, and houses them in his offices. He gets a share of the management fee, maybe 20%, for the funding and for providing infrastructure and space. He also tries to create a supportive environment where these young

Tigers share ideas. Julian, as a personality, is perfect for inducing this type of environment because he is so open and friendly.

Along on Julian's plane was one of his new protégés. This guy is in his early 30s, attractive, confident, and very gregarious. He went to Harvard and then to the Harvard Business School. Since then, his whole business life has been in the hedge-fund business (and his wife is a part-time trader for another hedge fund). He worked initially at another fund, started by one of the former Tigers, and then opened his own fund with help from Julian. He was up in the bear market years of 2000 to 2002, and now Julian says people are just throwing money at him.

This guy runs a long-short, market-neutral $500-million fund. *Market neutral* means that they adjust their longs and shorts for volatility and keep their exposure to the market at a very low level. In other words, they might be long 80% volatility adjusted of their equity and short 60%, so they have a net exposure on only 20% of their capital. He has seven analysts who concentrate on mid- and small-cap companies that they get to know inside-out. They short the ones they have identified as failing, the promotions, and the frauds, and go long companies that are reasonably priced and have solid business plans. He told me they presently were short about 70 stocks and long 30. I had heard only of a few of the names he rattled off. So far this year they are doing poorly and are down a few percentage points.

He was very open and told me that, in the second quarter of 2003 when the S&P 500 was up 10%, he was 35% net long. During the quarter, his longs were up 11.5%, his shorts 24%, and he made 2%. Why were his shorts up so much if they were so lousy? Not because his analysts were wrong, he said, but because there are so many long-short stock pickers, they get in each other's way, particularly when it comes to covering a short position. A company may be in trouble, but if you have too many shorts when the market is going up, you may still want to cover. Analysts don't help you at all at a market turn. He also said he was disenchanted with having so many analysts. He had become a manager of analysts, he said, rather than being a stock picker and an investor, which is what he wanted to be and what he thought he was good at. It was a very interesting conversation.

FINDING MEANING IN ALL THE NOISE AND BABBLE

Taleb

Today, I climbed 3,200 vertical feet up the winding Bald Mountain trail and thought about our portfolio in the wonderful Idaho peace and quiet. There is nothing like mountain aerobics for isolation and meditation. It's hard to have one without the other.

Probably the biggest intellectual problem an investor must wrestle with is the constant barrage of noise and babble. Noise is extraneous, short-term information that is random and basically irrelevant to investment decision making. Babble is the chatter and opinions of the well-meaning, attractive talking heads who abound. The serious investor's monumental task is to distill this overwhelming mass of information and opinion into knowledge and then to extract investment meaning from it. Meaning presumably leads to wisdom, which should translate into performance—the only thing that matters. It's nice and even good public relations to talk fast and sound smart, but basically our investors don't care a whit how articulate and well-informed we are. They care about the numbers. Managing the information deluge and separating out the noise has become more difficult because in the Internet era, there is so much more opinion and information readily available. Yet babble has always been there.

Noise and babble can be very hazardous to your investment health, and there is a massive amount of it disseminated, often with the best of intentions. As an investor, I have to deal with it every day. A guy named Nassim Nicholas Taleb who runs a hedge fund has written a book, *Fooled by Randomness*, which says a lot of perceptive things about noise and babble. One of Taleb's major themes is that the wise man listens for meaning, but the fool gets only the noise. The ancient poet Philostratus said, "For the gods perceive things in the future, ordinary people things in the present, but the wise perceive things about to happen." A more modern Greek poet, C.P. Cavafy, wrote:

> *In their intense meditation, the hidden sound of things approaching reaches them and they listen reverently while in the street outside the people hear nothing at all.*

I have met Taleb only once, and that was on Madison Avenue. The dust jacket of the book says he is the founder of Empirica Capital, "a crisis hunting hedge fund firm," whatever that is. *Fooled by Randomness* is a serious, intellectually sophisticated book, well worth reading carefully. At times, the book is condescending, as though the author had discovered the holy grail of investing. There ain't no holy grail, and the cosmopolitan tone can be somewhat off-putting. Nevertheless, there are some great insights.

At one point he explains the difference between noise and meaning with this example.

Suppose there is an excellent investor who can earn a return of 15% in excess of Treasury bills with 10% per annum volatility. Standard deviation analysis means that out of 100 samples, about 68 will fall between plus 25% and plus 5%, and that 95 paths will be between plus 35% and negative 5%. In effect, this investor has a 93% probability of generating an excess return in any one year. However, as the time scale shortens, the probability of out-performance declines drastically, as shown here:

Probability of Making Money

Scale	Probability
One year	93.00%
One quarter	77.00
One month	67.00
One day	54.00
One hour	51.30
One minute	50.17

This is standard Monte Carlo simulator stuff. Taleb's important insight, however, is that almost all investors experience more pain and anguish from losses than they do pleasure from gains. The agony is greater than the ecstasy. I don't know why this is true, but it is. Maybe it's because the investment business breeds insecurity.

But to the extent that the investor is focused on the daily or even minute-by-minute performance of his or her portfolio, as the table shows, the time of pain is inadvertently increased and the time of pleasure reduced. This is a particularly bad trade-off when moments of pain are more poignant than the times of pleasure. The problem is (and Taleb doesn't say this) that the investment pain leads to anxiety, which, in turn, can cause investors to make bad decisions. In other words, continual performance monitoring is not good for your mental health or for your portfolio's well-being, even though contemporary portfolio management systems and their suppliers strenuously promote it. Some hedge funds have instantaneous, continual profit and loss reporting on their screens. Guess what they look at all day long. Taleb argues that they would probably do better (and be happier) if they dealt only with monthly or even annual performance reporting. (Frankly, I think he is too ethereal in this assertion. Getting your performance on a daily basis doesn't mean that you are going to be dominated by it.)

Most investors think they are rational, but in fact they are prone to drown in randomness and to incur emotional torture from short-term performance swings. Taleb says: "When I see an investor monitoring his portfolio with live prices on his cellular telephone or his PalmPilot, I smile and smile." In other words, turn off the Bloomberg. When an investor focuses on short-time increments, he or she is observing the variability of the portfolio, not the returns—in short, being "fooled by randomness." Our emotions are not designed to understand this key point, but as investors, we need to come to grips with our emotional liabilities. It's not easy, Taleb concedes.

Taleb says he does it by denying himself access to information except in rare circumstances. "I prefer to read poetry," he says. "I am aware of my need to ruminate on park benches and cafes away from information, but I can only do it if I am somewhat deprived of it." He maintains it is better to read *The Economist* from cover to cover once a week than the *Wall Street Journal* every morning, given both the frequency and the massive gap in intellectual content. "My sole advantage in life," he writes, "is that I know some of my weaknesses, mostly that I am incapable of seeing performance with a clear head." However, if you are going to sit on park benches and meditate, you'd better have done some reading and listening first.

WHAT MAKES A SUPERSTAR INVESTOR?

Jake
A couple of days ago I had a long phone conversation with one of the true hedge-fund immortals. His record over the past 20 years is spectac-

ular, although, of course, like everyone else, sometimes he gets it wrong. His fund is now around $5 billion, and he does the macro overlay. He has maybe seven or eight asset class (like biotech, Asia, junk bonds, Europe, emerging markets, etc.) portfolio managers who each run anywhere from $400 million to $100 million, depending on what Jake's view of their sector is. Jake creates performance by allocating between the asset classes, and, in theory, the other guys add additional alpha by doing even better than their sector index. Sometimes Jake buys or sells an index to hedge them out. If one of his managers fails to perform, he or she gets cut. Jake is famous for being tough but fair and generous.

When you come right down to it, there are half a dozen superstar investors in the world, a number of good investors, and a multitude of what you might call journeymen. The superstars, like my immortal, consistently put up the big numbers and generally run their own hedge funds. The good investors usually outperform and have long-term records a couple of hundred basis points above the indexes after fees, which is no mean feat. As for the journeymen, they will have an occasional year when they light up the night sky, but in the long run, man, woman, or boy, after fees, they just can't consistently or predictably beat the indexes. The real bums who almost always underperform quickly are dispensed with.

This doesn't mean the journeymen are incompetent or bad people. In fact, they are usually bright, articulate, often charming, well dressed, and have a plausible line of investment patter. And you don't need to feel sorry for them. One of the ironies of the business is that professional investors whose returns are only in line or slightly better than their benchmark indexes are very richly paid compared to those in any other profession in the world. The reasons for this anomaly are that investment management is a growth business and the journeymen are achieving index returns *after* fees have been deducted, so they do have some value to their firms. Hedge-fund managers can earn even more outrageous compensation, but at least their compensation depends almost totally on performance. It is a lot like being a professional athlete.

As for the superstars, there are conflicting views on the authenticity of their brilliance. The *good* investors and even most of the journeymen are just as well educated, focused, and intense, so what is it that makes the difference? Is it genius, magic, or is there an element of luck? I think it was Warren Buffett who made a provocative comparison between superstar investors and the finalists in a hypothetical, national coin-flipping contest. It went something like this.

> *Suppose there was an All-America Coin-Flipping Tournament, and all contestants put up $10 to enter, with the prize money to be divided among the 8 quarterfinalists. Think of it! 200 million entrants and the prize money $2 billion. There would be one flip-off each week to allow the drama to build. After 6 months, there would be 32 contestants left in the tournament, each of whom would have made something like 25 consecutive correct calls. Imagine the excitement that would be created by the media!*
>
> *At this point, things would start to become a little crazy. Magazines would run features on the rags-to-riches stories of some of the contestants, and others would make appearances on talk shows at $50,000 a crack describing their unique flipping skills, ability to divine a coin in midair, and their mystic reflexive vision when it was about to land. Several would be rushing out books with titles like* How to Make Millions Flipping *and* Why Jesus Chose Me to Win. *Meanwhile angry college professors would be publishing articles in the* Wall Street Journal *about efficient markets, coin flipping, zero-sum games, and how the contest really was a random walk. Of course the contestants would be replying that if it can't be done, how come there are 32 of us who have done it? In the weeks before the round of 16, the winners would be much in demand by attractive members of the opposite sex, and some of them would be pricing ski houses in Aspen and condominiums in Florida.*

As I remember, the point of this somewhat farfetched analogy was that investment superstars are similar in a way to the finalists in the national coin-flipping contest. In other words, in a coin-flipping single-elimination tournament, by definition, there have to be some winners. They are not brilliant or gifted; they are just consistently lucky in what is basically a random series of calls. The same phenomenon applies to the investing world. How else can you explain the differences in performance when all the players are so similar? The superstars don't have bigger staffs, higher SAT scores, or any other discernible unique characteristics. The journeymen go to the same meetings, talk to the same analysts, read the same research reports, and probably most of them work just as hard.

I have a different theory. The superstars are like the horse whisperers of yore. Through the ages, as long as people have tried to tame horses so they could ride them, there has been a premium on strong, fast horses. The best horses, the strong, fast ones tend to be wild, but there have always been a few men and women who could soothe and saddle even the wildest. No one knew how they did it, and they would never explain it—maybe they couldn't. Did they carry in their back pockets the bleached bones of frogs plucked from some moonlit stream, or was it a gift from God, the way certain men can hit a baseball? Some people who saw them work said it was magic; others said they were shamans and charlatans at best and witches at worst. Some got rich, and probably a few were burned at the stake in the Middle Ages.

I don't believe for a second that the superstar hedge-fund investors are in any way similar to the random winners of a national coin-flipping contest, and I'm just kidding about them being like horse whisperers, although the stock market is as wild and unpredictable as an unbroken stallion. There have always been people who have special ways with animals. My real theory is that the investment superstars have some special magic with markets that enables them almost intuitively to do the right things most of the time. Somehow, the superstars fertilize their minds with meaning and wisdom so they, too, can "perceive things about to happen," as Philostratus wrote. This is the "seeing eye" that Churchill describes in his wonderful passage in his 1937 collection *Great Contemporaries* about David Lloyd George, the maverick prime minister, possessed of a "perceptive mind."

> *The offspring of the Welsh village whose whole youth had been rebellion against the aristocracy, who had skipped indignant out of the path of a local Tory magnate driving his four-in-hand, and revenged himself at night upon that magnate's rabbits, had a priceless gift. It was the very gift which the products of Eton and Balliol had always lacked— the one blessing denied them by their fairy godmothers, the one without which all other gifts are so frightfully cheapened. He had the "seeing eye."*

He had that deep original instinct which peers through the surface of words and things—the vision which sees dimly but surely the other side of the brick wall or which follows the hunt two fields before the throng. Against this, industry, learning, scholarship, eloquence, social influence, wealth, reputation, an ordered mind, plenty of pluck counted for less than nothing.

But to get back to Jake, that day he lectured me on time management and babble. You can't read everything and talk to everybody, he said. There simply are not enough hours in the day. As far as babble is concerned, you must be disciplined and control how you spend your time. You can't let others control it for you, which often happens in the office environment of big investment management companies. Keep your office door closed to discourage casual chatterers. Don't answer your own phone; let your secretary do it and take the message. Don't be compulsive about reading every piece of trash that appears on your desk or screen. Don't let salespeople chat you up. Their job is to talk to you. You must be rational by managing your time and not allowing others to waste it. You may have to be rude sometimes. You may have to cut people off. Your investors are not concerned if the salesperson from Goldman Sachs likes you or not. All your investors care about is performance.

Incidentally, Jake is famous, or infamous, for short conversations with babblers. If somehow you get through to him, he just listens for a few minutes, says nothing back, and then says, "Thanks" and hangs up. The caller feels like an idiot.

Unfortunately there may be a price to pay for not being Mr. Friendly. A couple of years ago Jake bought a big house in Watch Hill virtually in sight of the fabled Beach Club. Now I don't know Watch Hill, but apparently the Beach Club is where the right people go to hobnob, gaze at each other, have lunch, and swim. I suppose the beach there is sandier, the ocean bluer, and the brats better behaved because they all go to private schools. The only time I was there, the waiters certainly were surlier. In any case, Jake's wife desperately wanted to be a member, both for herself and for her children's sake, so they could build sand castles with the right children.

So Jake asks a fancy guy who is one of his investors to propose them. At the Beach Club the membership thing is done very discreetly.

The Admissions Committee discusses you *in camera* so to speak, and the candidate's name is circulated. As long as you have decent table manners, your children go to private schools, and you are willing to pay a big initiation fee, it's not too hard to get in. However if there are a few influential members who don't like you for whatever reason, your name goes on the waiting list, the years go by, and eventually you get the picture and withdraw. Unfortunately in Jake's case, the chairman of the admissions committee was the sales manager of White Shoe & Company, whom Jake has stiffed for years. Of course White Shoe & Company hasn't had an original idea for years either, and all the sales manager can talk about is golf and baseball. However, he has an exalted opinion of himself because he is a partner and his wife has inherited money, and Jake bugs him.

The problem is it isn't just him. Another guy who is the syndicate manager at Morgan Stanley thinks Jake is uncommunicative, and a man who ran an investment counseling firm that had lost clients to Jake says he is arrogant. Jealousy must have been a big factor. So to make a long story short, the proposer comes back and tells Jake there are no vacancies. After a couple of years, Jake leans on him. The guy goes through the whole routine again. This time the answer is unequivocal. No way. Not now, not ever.

Jake basically doesn't care one way or the other. He is very rich and every golf club on the East Coast is rushing him, but his wife is crushed and angry. She still hasn't gotten over it. She has to drive by the Beach Club every day and watch the fancies driving in and out. She claims Jake's brusque telephone manners have seriously retarded their children's social development. Periodically, she makes Jake's life miserable.

Art

I played golf with a couple of hedge-fund guys in Florida last winter. One was Art, a guy for whom I have great respect. Art is probably 55, rich, and also a very likeable, unpretentious person. He runs $4 billion in long/short global equities with a macro overlay. He is softspoken, very precise, and a totally controlled, disciplined guy. As an investor he is extremely analytical, and thinks through every angle, all the secondary consequences of his investments. He has a reputation as a good, fair leader to work for and for not being a screamer. In fact he is so softspoken and analytical it is almost impossible to imagine him losing his temper or raising his voice.

I regard Art with awe because he survived a horrendous first year. When he opened his own fund maybe 12 years ago, he had very little capital of his own and was taking a huge career and family risk. He raised $50 million, which wasn't bad for that time. Right out of the box he was down 25% that first year. He got the market direction wrong, and a lot of little stuff went against him. Half of his investors quit, and everybody thought he was history. But he hung in there and the next year was up an astounding 82%. Over the following 10 years he compounded at 20% net to his investors, and his fund grew to $2.5 billion.

Then in 2001 he was down a little, and in 2002 he lost 15%. Once again, half the money ran home to momma. Can you imagine? After all those good years, half the money left after two loss years that weren't bad, considering what was going on in the markets. Art gritted his teeth, put together big years in 2003 and 2004, and, of course, the wildebeests came running back.

Art has worked very hard on his golf, but he started playing late. He is one of these slow, deliberate golfers who stands over the ball on the fairway and takes five practice swings. He lines up his putts as carefully as if it's the final round at the Augusta National. He enters the statistical details, such as the number of putts of every round he plays, on his PC and plays out every hole no matter how disastrous it has been. Anyway on the round I was with him he was playing fairly well. Then we got to the fourteenth hole, which is a par 3 over a pond. Art swung badly and hit his tee shot into the water. Teeth clenched, he announced he was going to hit another ball. He skied this one high into the steamy Florida air, and it splashed 20 yards short of the green.

Art stared at the spot in the lake where the ball went in. Then he proceeded to take his club and pound it repeatedly into the ground, whack a tree, which bent the shaft, and then threw the damaged club far out into the pond, all without ever saying a word. We, embarrassed at this display of raw emotion, averted our eyes and walked away. On the next tee, Art rejoined us, still saying nothing but looking grim.

After the round was over, we decided to have a late lunch. Art said no thanks, he was going down to the range. It was the white, blazing heat of the Florida noon, but he was going to practice his swing. After I had eaten, I wandered down to the range. It was empty except for Art at the far end. At that moment, Art hit two consecutive woods that never got airborne and rocketed inelegantly along the ground. Art, not seeing me, suddenly had another rage spasm with the same tightlipped, violent club pounding. I snuck away.

I thought about what must have been eating Art. His hedge fund was doing great. His family life seemed fine. He had an abundant supply of the world's goods, including a Net Jets contract on a Gulf Stream Four, a ski house in Utah, and a place in the Hamptons. I remembered that a couple of years before when I was seated next to Art's wife at a dinner, she told me she could always tell when Art's fund was doing poorly because he became unusually grouchy and would grind his teeth in his sleep. Art is very intense and a perfectionist, and that is what makes him such a successful investor, but it was clear that he was now driven to excel at golf.

Maybe it's because degree of excellence in golf, just like investment performance, is so measurable, or maybe it's because hedge-fund guys are so competitive and have such massive egos, but whatever the reason, a lot of them are passionately obsessed with golf and their handicaps. Guys feel playing golf *good* (in sports talk, *good* becomes an adverb), handling pressure with money at stake, sinking that 10-foot putt, or blasting a 280-yard drive dead, solid, perfect on the eighteenth hole is somehow the defining test of their manhood. Remaining composed and playing tough at the tipping point moments when the match is on the line proves they have nerves of steel, guts, and the right stuff.

Besides, who would you rather have running your money, a guy that can coolly birdy the eighteenth hole and curl in a long putt, or a turkey who double bogies the crucial hole when he's the only one with a stroke? "Grace under pressure" is Hemingway's famous description of courage. Apparently a lot of CEOs have the same arrested development mentality. Big-time corporate executives connive and scheme to get into Augusta, Shinecock, and Cypress Point. And then, for the pure-in-heart aficionados, there is Scotland and St. Andrews and those black tie dinners at the Royal and Ancients.

Golf lovers have always stoutly maintained that you learn more about a guy's character and inner soul by playing eighteen holes of golf with him than you would by transacting with him in business contexts for years. Frankly I think it's a bunch of BS, but then I'm a tennis player and not a serious golfer, so I'm not in the fraternity. In any case, my point is that many hedge-fund guys care deeply about their golf. At some point when they get rich enough, golf becomes, except for their families, the most important thing in their lives.

After all, once you are worth half a billion dollars, amassing another half a billion isn't going to make any material difference in your life style and general happiness. Sure you can have more houses, a bigger foundation, and swing for a G-5, but all that extra paraphernalia just complicates your life. You could argue that the next half billion increases the risk that excess riches are going to sap your children's initiative and screw up their family's heads. Of course I know money is the way we keep score, but there is a tipping point out there in the wealth stratosphere where too much is a life-complicating liability what with robberies, jealousy, kidnapping, and so forth.

As a result, for a lot of guys, once you have that first half a billion dollars, the most satisfying, enduring enhancement to your sense of well-being is to improve your golf—which means getting your handicap down. Of course having your daughter get into Harvard or your son make the football team is a thrilling upper, but it's not permanent. It wears off. It's not that hedge fund guys don't love their families. They do, but for them maybe, in the great scheme of everyday life, golf eventually becomes as important as their fund's investment performance.

To understand this, the nongolfing reader has to realize that there is a de facto class system in golf. Having a teen age handicap is respectable, but basically you're not up there with the big guys who are ten and under. When you play with them, glib and full of chatter as you may be, you can't really stand up to them. By the same token, there is a big difference between having a nine handicap and being a two or a three. However, bringing your handicap down, particularly as you get older, is very difficult. A guy can take lessons from famous teaching pros, hit balls for hours on end on the range, buy the best equipment in the world, and it may not make the slightest difference, especially since age inexorably is wearing away at your game. Sometime after 50, you hit the no-improvement wall.

One night, a bunch of us, including Art, were sitting around talking about all this. Someone mentioned that Sam, another well-known hedge-fund guy who was a mediocre golfer, all summer had this famous teaching pro who was Tiger Wood's swing doctor traveling around with him.

"Must cost him at least half a million for the summer," someone said.

"So what," said the first speaker. "Sam would happily pay $10 million to get his handicap down a few strokes."

Respectfully, I pointed out that $10 million was one afternoon's bad trade for Sam, and that the real test of caring about your handicap was whether you would trade performance points on your fund for a reduction in your handicap. "Suppose," I postulated, "the Devil came to you with a Faustian bargain and said: 'I will have you consistently scoring five strokes below what you are now if you will give me five performance points from what your fund would have returned over the same time period.' Would you do it?" I asked.

The guys were intrigued, and because they had had a few drinks and were in a reflective mood, they took the question seriously. Or maybe they didn't. I don't know.

"It's tempting," said Art, "but I wouldn't do it. It would be grossly unfair to my investors."

"Yeah," said another guy who struggles with a 14 handicap and whose net worth is easily halfway to a billion, "and I suppose your investors have always been so loyal to you?"

"Well, I'm a fiduciary, and my record is my legacy and I'm proud of it. I wouldn't want to diminish it."

"Forget your legacy," the guy said. "It's not like the pro football Hall of Fame where kids for all time can go and watch videos of Jim Brown's greatest runs or Johnny Unitas throwing TD passes. My kids are grown up, my wife is distracted, being on charity boards is boring, but golf is golf. I would do it in a flash."

His answer made sense for him. He has all the toys he wants and some that he can't even find the time to use, and he is respected by his peers. However, despite all his work, his golf still verges on the embarrassing, and at his age it's not going to get much better. Without a material enhancement in his game, he is never going to be invited into the big-time member-guest tournaments like "the Hook and Eye," much less be asked to join Augusta. The CEOs that dominate the membership committees don't have much time for filthy-rich hedge-fund guys from Greenwich. A single-digit handicap is about the only thing left in the world he can't buy.

A younger guy, who I have heard is a big hitter, shook his head.

"Not me," he said. "I'd counter the Devil with the opposite. Much as I love golf, I would sign a pact with the Devil that I would never play again if he would add five percentage points a year to my performance." His answer didn't surprise me either. His record is okay but volatile, and he is relatively poor.

Nevertheless, my somewhat supercilious point is that every investor in hedge funds should consider where the fund's managers are in their personal motivation cycle.

CHAPTER
NINE

The Violence of
Secular Market Cycles

W hat makes investing (and the investment business for that matter) so difficult and dislocating is that it has violent, long boom/bust *secular* cycles. Secular cycles occur once in a generation. The booms last at least a decade and often longer, and the busts often are shorter but destroy lives, fortunes, and business models. The word *cyclical* comes from *cycle* which, according to Webster's dictionary, is "a round of years or a recurring period of time in which certain events or phenomena repeat themselves in the same order."

Secular cycles, both in markets and sectors of the market, make a big investment management firm a very conflicting enterprise to manage *if you are a businessperson*, because the rational things to do to maximize short-term profitability are exactly the wrong things from both an investment and a long-term profitability point of view. For example, during 2000, even as the bubble was bursting, Morgan Stanley Investment Management, which has a business-dominated management, acted like businessmen; they heavily promoted the underwriting of technology and aggressive growth stock funds because those were the funds the salespeople could sell and that the public would buy. Management was not evil; they were doing what they thought was right. Large amounts of public money were raised and very quickly lost. Short-term *sales* profits were collected at the expense of, not only the public, but the firm's long-term credibility and profitability.

The firm erred in the other direction in the spring of 2003 when it shut down its Asian Equity Fund, which it had invested exclusively in the Asia ex Japan markets. The fund had shrunk from $350 million 10 years earlier when the Asian Miracle was on everyone's lips, to less than $10 million. At that level of assets, it was a clear money-losing proposition, so it was the right, short-term business decision to close it down. At the time, there didn't seem to be any interest in Asia. However, the smaller Asian markets were then incredibly cheap, the economies of the area were surging, and Asian equities were exactly the right place to be. I argued vociferously to keep the fund open, and maintained that, as the markets rallied, new assets would come. To no avail. No one agreed with me, and the fact that they didn't was a buy signal. If only public investors and the managements of profit-driven investment management companies could understand how important it is to not mindlessly follow the crowd. An Australian oil man, John Masters, expressed it succinctly in one of his annual reports.

> *You have to recognize that every "out-front" maneuver is going to be lonely. But if you feel entirely comfortable, then you're not far enough ahead to do any good. That warm sense of everything going well is usually the body temperature at the center of the herd. Only if you're far enough ahead to be at risk do you have a chance for large rewards.*

PUBLIC MONEY FLOODS IN AND FLOWS OUT AT EXACTLY THE WRONG TIMES

The closing of this fund is an example of what always seems to happen with specialty mutual funds. The big flood of public money comes in *after* instead of *before* the fund has done well, and then redeems *after* it has done poorly and usually just *before* it's about to do really well again. Billions of dollars poured into tech funds in 1999 and 2000 when the Nasdaq was pushing toward 5,000. In fact something like 80% of all the public money that was invested in mutual funds at the height of the bubble in the spring of 2000 went into tech funds. Over the next three years, as the Nasdaq raggedly sank to 1,000, investors lost 60% to 80% of their money. Redemptions were heavy in 2002 and 2003 just before the Nasdaq doubled again.

Jesse Livermore once was asked what his investment strategy was. "Buy low and sell high," he replied. The public instead does just the opposite. It buys high and sells low, partly because the mutual fund industry has an overwhelming incentive to sell (and to hell with the consequences) what is easy to sell, and what is easy to sell is what has just been hot. The public never learns, and the mutual fund industry never can pass up a money-making opportunity. However, in fairness, the people who run the mutual-fund industry and sell the funds are not evil; in the flush of the moment, with stocks soaring, they genuinely believe that maybe it truly is different this time. Of course, it never is!

A couple of years ago, Dalbar, a respected research organization, did a study of the public's returns from investing in mutual funds. The results were something like this. During the great bull market that ended in early 2000, the S&P 500 compounded at 16% per annum. The average U.S. equity mutual fund compounded at 13.8% a year, which is not surprising because the average all-in fee was around 220 basis points. What was truly shocking was Dalbar's discovery that the average investor in mutual funds earned only 7% per annum. Why? Because the average investor was switching (or being switched by a broker) at exactly the wrong time either from one fund to another or into cash. For the public investor, market timing and being fashionable has been a futile and costly activity. The neo-con's idea that the average American should actively run and make asset allocation decisions with a portion of his Social Security account is madness.

During the 1980s and the 1990s the U.S. mutual fund model created great wealth for its purveyors—the investment management companies, the brokers, and the portfolio managers—but utterly failed America's individual investors. After the Battle of Britain, Winston Churchill said that the heroics of "a few squadrons of the Royal Air Force in some cases outnumbered ten to one" by the Luftwaffe averted disaster. Churchill concluded that famous speech: "Never in the history of human endeavor has so much been owed by so many to so few." Chris Davis, president of the Davis Funds and a perceptive thinker, reflecting on the meager returns of mutual funds versus the indexes and the exalted compensation of investment managers, tellingly remarked, "Never in the history of financial commerce has so much been paid to so many for so little." Sad but true. However, the commercial history of the world is that inequities tend to be corrected—eventually and painfully.

Of course, the dismal results for individual investors are partly their own fault as well. They are simply not equipped, either in terms of temperament, research resources, or time commitment, to compete with the professionals. Rational individuals wouldn't dream of competing against professional athletes for money or against professional card players. Why would they in the financial markets? However, the individuals do need to make their own long-term asset allocations decisions. This can be done if they have at least a general concept of secular and cyclical cycles and some sense of contrarian investing. Index funds should be the means of implementation.

THE DIFFERENCE BETWEEN SECULAR
AND CYCLICAL BEAR MARKETS

Let's start with the definitions of *secular* and *cyclical* bear markets. To me, a secular bear market is a decline in the major stock averages of at least 40 percent—and considerably more in secondary stocks—where the decline lasts at least three to five years. The fall is then followed by a long hangover that drags on for a number of years as the excesses are purged. There can be *cyclical* bull markets during this period, but it will be a long time before a new secular bull market begins in which the popular averages exceed the old highs and climb toward new peaks.

By contrast, a *cyclical* bear market is a fall of at least 15% but less than 40% that rarely lasts more than a year. A *panic* is a very short, sharp break. Length is an important part of the secular bear market definition, because time and sustained pain are what alter behavior patterns and change society. By these definitions I count two secular bear markets in the United States in the past century (1929 to 1938 and 1969 to 1974), at least three panics (1916, 1929, 1987), and 25 garden-variety cyclical bear markets.

The long cycles in the U.S. equity market in the last century could be defined like this: 1921 to 1929, secular bull market; 1929 to 1949, secular bear; 1949 to 1966, secular bull; 1966 to 1982, secular bear; 1982 to 2000, secular bull. I think it is obvious that a new secular bear market began in 2000, and that we are now in a cyclical bull market rally in the hangover period. The two big issues are: Have we seen the lows of this secular bear market, and what will be its duration?

I think we have seen the lows, but I keep remembering Japan and the long, cruel, secular bear market that still is grinding on almost 15 years later. As the years went by, the Japanese market kept having short, sharp, cyclical bull market rallies, but each one was a sucker rally that was eventually followed by a further decline to new lows. A number of professionals I respect a lot, such as Jeremy Grantham, David Swensen, and Ned Davis, believe that U.S. equities eventually will break through the lows of the fall of 2002 and the spring of 2003. Before it's over, they look for levels of around 600 on the S&P 500 and maybe 6,000 on the Dow Jones Industrial Average. That's roughly down 45% from today.

The bears argue Nasdaq is impeccably following the classic burst bubble pattern as is shown in Figure 9.1. I agree. Nasdaq won't see its year 2000 summits for years. But so what? The Nifty Fifty, Nasdaq's 1970s lookalike, took a decade to recover, too. That doesn't mean the world equity markets are going to new lows or that other markets can't prosper.

The bears also say they worry most about derivatives and their fat tails. Nobody really knows how dangerous the derivatives overhang is. All anybody knows is that there is a $2 trillion liability out there that is opaque from the outside and probably from the inside as well. Wringing their hands, the doomsayers wail that derivatives are a huge tumor inexorably growing day by day like a cancerous lump in the world's gut. By definition, it is true that derivatives, which are designed to mitigate *specific* risk, at the same time may actually be increasing *systemic* risk because every major financial institution is entwined in the web. The collapse of LTCM gave us a frightening glimpse into the financial devastation that can result from a death spiral of risk taking. It also proved that the greatest mathematicians and geniuses in the world are far from infallible in their ability to compute and manage risk.

But what are you as an investor going to do about the apocalypse risk? As I discussed in the séance with Vince, as an investor, the right thing to do has been always to bet against a return to the Dark Ages and not worry about hedging the unknowable.

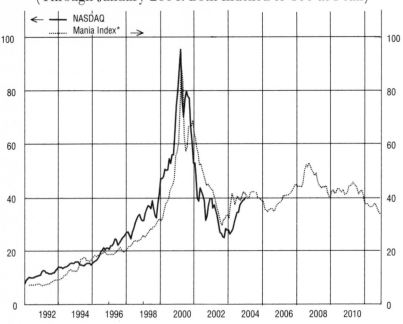

FIGURE 9.1

NASDAQ Bubble versus Composite Mania Index
(Through January 2004: Both Indexed to 100 at Peak)

*Concept courtesy Bank Credit Analyst; Composite index of peaks in Gold & Silver (1980), Nikkei 225 (1989), and Dow Jones (1929)
Source: Global Insight

How long it will be this time before stocks begin a true, new secular bull market is very difficult to guess. The conditions for such a renaissance are that money should be cheap and amply available, the debt structure should be deflated, there should be pent-up demand for goods and services, and, probably most important, stocks should be clearly cheap based on *absolute* valuation measures. Today, money is cheap and available, but the other conditions are not in place. United States equities are far from cheap, but, considering the level of interest rates and inflation, they are not expensive, either. Who knows how long it will be before the Dow and the S&P exceed their 2000 highs, and what about the Nasdaq? The world economy, led by China and India, could grow a lot faster than all the *dirigists* now think. I also recall all too well the agonizing, extended hangover from the secular bear market of the early 1970s. The U.S. equity market wandered up and down in a relatively narrow range for years.

What itches uncomfortably in the back of my mind is that the stock market bubble in the United States and the rest of the world in the 1990s had more pervasive excesses than most of the bubbles that preceded earlier busts. Nevertheless, so far we haven't had anywhere near the distress of the late 1970s or the pain that Japan has experienced. Even after the rally in 2005, Japanese equities are still down 70% from their peak. Japanese real estate prices have declined 50% and have only just begun to stabilize, and the assets of the Japanese equity mutual fund business have fallen by 95% from their peak in 1990. That's what a secular bear market does to the financial services industry. Imagine what would happen to the massive U.S. financial services industry if that happened here! And what would be the impact of a 50% decline in prime commercial real estate?

Secular bear markets in the past have always taken valuations back to the levels at which the preceding bull market started, or even lower. Price to book value is the most stable measure of value, because it is not sensitive to the cyclical swings of the economy as all measures of earnings are. Look at Figure 9.2, a chart of price to book in Japan. The roaring bull market and then the craziness of the bubble took the price to book ratio to over five times; now almost 15 years later, it has fallen to 1.5 times, which is about where it started way back in 1975. At the peak in 2000, the United States also sold at almost five times book. Today it is about 2.9 times.

BULL MARKETS AND BUBBLES IN JAPAN VERSUS THE UNITED STATES

However, there are some important differences between the secular bull markets in the United States and Japan. The United States in 2000 was primarily a stock market bubble bursting, and it wiped out a lot of wealth and caused a recession. The Japanese bubble also involved commercial real estate as well as equities, and the U.S. bubble didn't. Japanese real estate by 1990 had reached utterly ridiculous levels. For example the Imperial Palace grounds alone had a value in excess of all

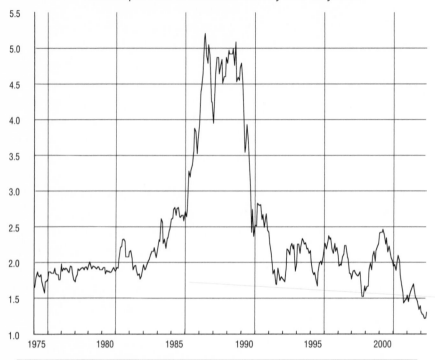

FIGURE 9.2

Price-to-Book Japan Busted Bubbles Are Symmetrical

MSCI Japan Price-to-Book Ratio: January 1975–May 2003

Source: Traxis Partners Quantitative Research, MSCI

the real estate in the state of California. When the Japanese bubble burst, the wealth of the nation was diminished by roughly 50%. In the United States, by contrast, the loss of paper wealth in equities was offset by the continuing rise in home prices. That's a huge difference.

Enormous, sustained price advances in fixed assets always spawn speculation with borrowed money, and the Japanese banks fell all over themselves in their eagerness to make loans to property developers. As a result the bursting of the Japanese real estate bubble and the inevitable bad-loan hangover has crippled the Japanese banking system, which in turn has caused deflation and made the Japanese recession much longer and more painful. Incidentally, now, 15 years later, the Japanese banks are finally recovering but are still feeble and impoverished, and the bad-debt problem has still not been completely resolved.

Another big difference between the U.S. and Japanese bubbles is that the U.S. mania was all about equity money going into technology and the Internet, which were basically productivity-enhancing expenditures. A lot of money was wasted, a lot of money was lost, but, on the other hand, a lot of money funded companies that created new products and inventions. Japan's craziness was focused with a few exceptions primarily on financial engineering, *zaitech* it was called at the time, and it had virtually no saving graces. Again, the Japanese banking system was far more involved. By contrast, today, the U.S. banking system is relatively healthy.

Third, once the bubble had burst, the authorities in Japan made serious errors in both fiscal and monetary policy that caused a vicious circle of recession and deflation, almost an economic death spiral, that has proved incredibly difficult to get out of. The Bank of Japan raised official interest rates even as the bubble was bursting, and the government raised taxes just as the economy began to recover. By contrast, in the United States, the Federal Reserve aggressively cut official rates, and the federal government almost immediately implemented tax cuts on both income and investments. In fact, the U.S. economy was the beneficiary of an unprecedented dose of fiscal and monetary stimulus, and there is no question that these moves averted a more serious recession—for now. Whether they averted or merely delayed the inevitable retribution remains to be seen.

THE SECULAR BEAR MARKET OF 1969–1974

I am trying carefully to point out the differences between the experience of Japan and the United States. None of this is to argue that the United States didn't have a stock market bubble, and that there wasn't massive speculation and fraud. The United States definitely has had a *secular* bear market in equities with three down years in a row. What concerns me is that this bear market doesn't seem as severe or its aftermath as extended as the *secular* bear market this country had from 1969 to 1974, which is why I wonder if this one may be incomplete. Certainly it hasn't been anywhere near as painful as that of the 1930s. The Dow first reached more than 1,000 in 1966 and didn't really breach that level again until 1982. During that period, the cost of living in the

United States expanded by a factor of 8, so a dollar invested in stocks in 1966 could buy only 13 cents worth of goods in 1982.

The anatomy of that bear market was unusual, in that it had three distinct phases. The trouble really began when the Dow and many secondary stocks peaked in December 1968. By May 26, 1970, the Dow was down 35.9% at 631, but the carnage in secondary stocks was much worse. An index of the 30 leading speculative glamour stocks of the 1960s, consisting of 10 leading conglomerates—including Litton, Gulf & Western, and LTV (now defunct); 10 computer stocks, including IBM, Leasco, and Sperry Rand; and 10 technology stocks like Polaroid, Xerox, and Fairchild Camera—was down 81%. Later, LTV was to fall from 170 to 15, Resorts International from 62 to 7, and Data Processing from 92 to 11. By then, some of the real frauds like National Student Marketing, Four Seasons Nursing, and Parvin Dohrmann were virtually worthless.

After the selling climax of May 26, 1970, a powerful, 51% rally ensued, which crested with the Dow at 950 on April 28, 1971. It was a turbulent, emotional time. One of the largest hedge funds was wiped out by the rally after it went heavily net short on May 28, 1970. The Nifty Fifty led the rallies that continued through 1971 and 1972 with the Dow touching a final peak at 1,051 on January 11, 1973. This was a narrow advance that was concentrated in the Nifty Fifty and a few industrial blue chips, while the hot stocks of the late 1960s languished, and some, like Memorex and Equity Funding, fell even further. However, a lot of people got suckered back into this rally, thinking it was the beginning of a new bull market. The same thing could be happening today.

In the monster collapse that followed, the Nifty Fifty as a group were decimated, with an average decline of 60% and some wipeouts like Avon Products (from 135 to 18), Polaroid (70 to 6), and Corning Glass (61 to 13). The American Stock Exchange index fell 56%. The over-the-counter market was much worse, and in the late summer and fall of 1974, it seemed as though every former speculative favorite, regardless of fundamentals, was selling at either 3 or 5. As a measure of the damage, the broadest measure of equities—the Value Line Composite, which had peaked in 1968—six years later was down 75%. Adjusted for inflation, even the major stock indexes fell 70%. In the 1970s, the Yale Endowment lost 45% of its purchasing power, maintenance was deferred, and the university's financial independence was in doubt. An extended bear market would transform the effectiveness of American charities.

Just for the record, if the timetable of the two previous secular bear markets applied this time, we wouldn't get back to a new high in the Dow and the S&P 500 until around 2017. As for the Nifty Fifty, again *on average* it took that group of stocks 10½ years to get back to the previous price highs in nominal terms and 16½ years, adjusted for inflation; in other words don't hold your breath waiting for the NDX Index to touch 5000 again.

What did that secular bear market feel like? It felt like the stocks of companies with good stories that you believed in, that you had visited, going down more than you had ever dreamed, like there was no bottom, no support levels. In the summer and fall of 1974, when the declines were endless day after day, you seriously wondered how you were going to support your family and where you were going to get a job in the real economy, because Wall Street was finished. There were no answers. People you knew in the business—salespeople, money mangers, guys who had started a hedge fund—just disappeared, and years later you heard they had moved to Topeka or Duluth and had bought a hardware store or were teaching seventh grade and coaching basketball. The prices of big houses, the expensive upper crust of the residential real estate markets in Greenwich, Southampton, and Beverly Hills, collapsed.

Then, just as now, scandals wracked the mutual-fund business with the public losing immense amounts of money, Investors Overseas Corporation, and the deline and fall of the Mates and Enterprise Funds. Many of the Wall Street heroes of the 1960s, the so-called gunslingers, the conglomerate magnates such as Jim Ling, and the fund promoters like the lecherous Bernie Cornfeld ("Where are the customers' girls?" asked John Kenneth Galbraith irreverently) became the villains of the 1970s and, one way or another, were run out of town on the proverbial rail. From 1973 to 1979, the number of investment management firms declined by 40%, and the assets in equity mutual funds were cut in half. Professors and consultants wrote articles and books proving investment managers couldn't beat the market, and that professional investing was a loser's game.

Although the hedge funds in the 1970s never reached anywhere near the size and influence they have today, they crashed and burned in that secular bear market. Most failed to preserve their investors' capital in a bear market by having substantial short positions, as they had advertised. In reality, they were just leveraged long funds; in other words, they had borrowed money to buy stocks but had not hedged by selling other stocks short. Many had dabbled in private equity deals, which ended up illiquid and worthless. (Similar madness had occurred in 1929 with the infamous Goldman Sachs Trading Corporation, whose value fell from an issue price of 104 to 2.) By the end of 1974, through a combination of losses and withdrawals, the amount of capital in hedge funds had fallen by 80%.

Over the next five years, many of the most famous hedge funds, including the second largest, went out of business. My old benefactor, A. W. Jones & Company, was the Soros of that era, with a spectacular 30% compound growth record for the 10 years ending 1968. However, the firm was crushed in the 1970s, and although it survived for a while, it never returned to its former preeminence. Instead, a new breed of more professional hedge-fund managers like George Soros, Mike Steinhardt, Louis Bacon, and Julian Robertson rose from the ashes. One big difference between then and now is that the superstars of the late 1960s bull market were all young guys (the kid named Fred, whom Gerry Goodman writing as Adam Smith described so memorably in *The Money Game*), while today the big hitters in the hedge-fund world are mostly (but not all) in their 40s and 50s.

I believe that we have made *the* lows of this secular bear market, but we must remain open-minded.

The Bliss of Starting Fresh

Sometimes I suggest to my partners that we each go home, reflect as though we had nothing but cash, and come in just as we did on that Sunday before we started with a fresh portfolio and a new exposure position. It's a great discipline to pretend that you just got the money and have to build a brand new portfolio. You are unencumbered with stale positions, where the story has deteriorated, has gone down, and is too cheap to sell. An investor, hedge fund or otherwise, with nothing but cash, is forced to focus on fresh opportunities and is compelled to buy the 20 or 30 most attractive positions to be found *as of that moment*. The stale portfolio problem may be the root cause of the so-called *first-year phenomenon*. I am referring to the statistics that show that, a high percentage of the time, new hedge funds *that survive* do best in their first year. This is not the same as saying that new hedge funds do best. Is it because the managers are scared to death and more intense, or is there something else at work? I suspect the latter.

When you are working with an existing portfolio and reshaping it, there are unrecognized, subconscious, emotional hang-ups that block you from impartial, cold-blooded investment actions like selling. Your baggage is what you already own, and it gets in the way of excellence. There are always positions you believe in, but for one reason or another, the market stupidly has not discovered them yet. It's hard to make yourself give up on a position, especially since you suspect, as soon as you do, that the ornery, cussed thing will rally. There is a bias against switching, because subconsciously you know you can be wrong twice. By the same token, it's hard to sell winners because of what they have done for you and because you hope they have more to deliver.

As investors, we often personalize and become emotionally involved with positions when the investment decision-making process should be completely intellectual and rational because, after all, they are just pieces of paper. Remember: "The stock doesn't know you own it." That is so true. There is no reward for being a faithful holder. It is those holds that are too cheap to sell but not attractive enough to buy that make a portfolio stale and retard performance.

I have always done a lot of investment reading. It's interesting that Bernard Baruch and Jesse Livermore, probably the two greatest private investors of the first half of the twentieth century, whenever they felt stale, uncertain, or uneasy, liquidated their holdings and took a vacation. When they returned, it was their practice to start over by buying a completely fresh portfolio. This pattern of reinvesting from scratch is apparent from Baruch's and Livermore's writings, although there is no evidence that either did this as a conscious strategy or on a regular, predetermined basis. In any case, it became almost an instinctive pattern in their operations.

Of course, in those days, when you went away to Florida or to Arizona to get a change of scenery and escape, you really were out of touch. That's obviously not the case today. You can't get away from the babble. However, it can be done. One Christmas, as a family, we went to

Lanzarote, one of the Canary Islands, about a hundred miles off the west coast of Africa. Lanzarote has a volcano that erupted 150 years ago and left it covered with chunks of dried up lava. What a godforsaken spot. The trade winds blew night and day, howling through the ancient hotel, inhabiting my dreams, but there were no newspapers, no CNBC, no e-mail, my cell phone didn't work most of the time—there was nothing. I read the first two volumes of Robert Skidelsky's great biography of John Maynard Keynes, slept marvelously, complained about the weather, played tennis with the children, and came back to New York 12 days later totally refreshed. The hotel had wonderful buffets and the children loved the place.

TEN

The Battle for Investment Survival

*Only Egotists or Fools Try
to Pick Tops and Bottoms*

D ave, another long-time companion in the battle, came by the
office today. Dave, not a fancy or pretentious guy, went to college in the Midwest, and when I first met him in 1974, he
had just been promoted from analyst to portfolio manager at
one of the big Midwestern mutual-fund companies. He is a tough,
smart, hard-working guy, and back then he was very much a fundamental investor. Subsequently he ran a major company's pension fund where
he put up excellent numbers. In 1987, he formed his own investment
management company, which aggressively runs primarily institutional,
benchmark-oriented accounts. At year end of 1987, his assets under
management were a magnificent $72 million.

One interesting thing about Dave is that over the years he has completely changed his investment religion. For a professional investor, this
is a huge, mind-altering event, comparable to a deeply religious person
converting from Catholicism to, say, Judaism. Dave used to be a funda-
mentally driven, value investor, but now, in his maturity, he pays much

less attention to the fundamentals and has evolved into a *momentum* investor. He pays a lot of attention to long-term relative strength patterns of markets around the world, sectors, and individual stocks. As he expresses it, he lets the market tell him what groups and stocks to own rather than trying to tell the market what groups should do well. In other words, he looks for sustained relative strength. If a stock or a group of stocks are going up faster than the market, he will instruct his analysts to investigate them. Unless there is something seriously wrong with the fundamentals, he will buy them, and he will hold them until they start to lose relative strength. He will never buy a stock just because it is cheap. He will never try to be a bottom picker. He thinks that investors who buy underowned, unloved, and undervalued stocks are crazy. Buy and own stocks that are going up; sell and avoid stocks that are going down or sideways.

Dave's performance has always been highly volatile. Hiring Dave is not for the faint-hearted. For example, his U.S. equity accounts were up 56% in 1991 when the S&P 500 (his benchmark) gained 30% and 31% in 1993 when the index rose 10%. On the other hand, he was down 23% in 1994 when the S&P eked out 1.3% and then lagged the index by small amounts in each of the next three years. He did very well in the late 1990s because he stayed with the trend and owned a lot of tech. In 1998, his U.S. equity accounts were up 61% versus 28% for the S&P 500. The next year they soared 90% when the S&P 500 returned 21%. His firm's assets rocketed to $14 billion. His reward for that spectacular performance was that many of his clients took a quarter or half of their money away simply because he had done so well and their accounts had become so large.

As it turned out, they were half right for the wrong reason because, although he got hurt in the bear market that began in 2000, he didn't do much worse than his benchmark. He did not get killed. His system got him out of stocks that were about to collapse.

For example, he had a big position in Nortel, which he had bought at a price of around 16. I visited Nortel in April 2000, and you didn't have to be Benjamin Graham to figure out that this was an accident waiting to happen. The stock was selling at a hundred times exaggerated earnings. Its accounting was a farce. Instead of doing research and product development, the company was paying ridiculous prices to acquire tech startups. It was in commodity, highly competitive businesses. The executive vice president spun me a bunch of baloney about "the innovator's dilemma and disruptive technologies." He told me how "Nortel had a virtuous circle going." It was crazy! Nortel was no growth stock! It was a highly cyclical capital goods company. It reminded me of the new-era crashes of the 1970s.

I came back to New York and called Dave when Nortel was at 62. He listened carefully to my concerns and said, "You may well be right, but I am going to wait for the market to tell me." The stock kept going up and hit 75 in May. Then, that fall, with tech beginning to get hit hard and the stock at 60, one morning Nortel announced that fourth-quarter earnings were going to be down substantially, and that its order backlog was declining. Nortel opened late that morning, down 12 at 48. Dave sold his whole position that day. Over the next two years the stock went to 3.

"Only egotists or fools try to pick tops and bottoms," he said with a smile on this visit. "Which one are you?" Now he likes U.S. tech, Asia, Japan, and the emerging markets. I asked him about the U.S. drug stocks, which have been beaten down, are as cheap as they have been at any time since Hillary Clinton attacked the industry in the early 1990s, and which we own. "No interest whatsoever," said Dave. "They look weak and weaker. Why would you want to buy stocks like that? You are just guessing that they have stopped going down. Wait until the market tells you."

Cyril and Madhav came in, and Dave talked some more. He got on my Bloomberg and showed us the charts of Hong Kong, China H shares, the German Dax index, and Tokyo. In each case, when the market broke through to a new high, it immediately thereafter surged about 10%. "It's like smoke going up a chimney," said Dave. (At the time he thought the S&P 500 was going to do the same in the next month or so, and he was right.) He recognizes that U.S. stocks, in general, are expensive, and he is unsure about the strength of the economy. But he refuses to make judgments. "The market is smarter than I am or you guys are," he says. "Right now the markets are telling me that they are going higher, that Asia is a tiger again, and that the U.S. economy is coming on, so I want to own stocks. Maybe the markets know something about the world economy we don't. I want to own stocks with strong cyclical earnings streams."

Listening to Dave, I couldn't help but think of similar comments in *Reminiscences of a Stock Operator*, which I wrote about in Chapter 3. The protagonist, the Old Turkey, who describes himself as a momentum trader and a student of greed, at one point in the narrative, gave this advice when suddenly stocks stop responding to good news:

> *When the market leaders begin to lose relative strength even though the news is still very good, and buying strength and selling weakness no longer works, get out of stocks in general because the game is over.*
>
> *It is enough for the experienced trader to perceive that something is wrong. He must not expect the tape to become a lecturer. His job is to listen for it to say "Get out!" and not wait for it to submit a legal brief for his approval.*

As I said before, Dave's extreme, momentum-following style results in huge swings in his performance versus the benchmarks. When he is hot, he is very hot, and when he is cold, he is ice. During the growth stock era in the late 1990s he literally shot the lights out. Then, when the worm turned from growth to value, he underperformed. His volatility has scared the daylights out of the prudent plan sponsors, even though his results, over the 10 years that ended June 30, 2005, are 600 basis points a year better than the S&P 500 and 800 basis points better than the Russell 1000 Growth Index. However, his assets under management fell to $6 billion at the end of 2002 and have been static at around $8.5 billion for the last four years. Institutional investors apparently can't tolerate his volatility, which is crazy because what they should care about is long-term performance. In any case, I love and admire Dave. He is no cowardly, cringing benchmark clinger, no closet indexer. He also admits he follows momentum, which most of us do, too, but won't admit to. Dave is a real investor man.

Dave's style is not my style, which is value, contrarian, and distrustful of momentum. In fact, my investment religion is almost the exact antithesis of his. However, I have deep respect for Dave's judgment and intuitive feel for markets. There are periods when momentum investing works wonderfully, and we need to keep in touch with the best practitioners. I talk to Dave every couple of weeks.

GREAT EXPECTATIONS FOR EUROPEAN
PRIVATE EQUITY (BUT THAT'S NOT THE
WAY THE WORLD WORKS)

After Dave's visit, I went to Paris to attend the board meeting of a European foundation that is an important investor. It was very worthwhile. The investment staff of this foundation is convinced, like everyone else, that publicly traded stocks and bonds in both the United States and Europe will produce only mid to high single-digit annual returns over the next five years. They have greater expectations and want 10% nominal and 7% to 8% *real* after inflation. I told them that this is a very ambitious target for a large portfolio. They believe it can be attained by migrating to more fertile asset classes such as hedge funds, timberland, venture capital, and private equity.

The staff of the foundation argues that good European private equity funds can deliver 20% to 22% annual returns *after fees*, but they feel that they lack both the processing capability and the qualifications to make the selections. The very best private equity funds are now closed to new investors, and there are so many new European private equity firms that they are swamped with offering memorandums. Therefore, the staff is proposing employing a fund of funds. The board listened to a rather haughty presentation from two immaculately dressed Swiss from one of the large private banks in Geneva. Their pitch went like this:

> *As the postwar generation reaches retirement age in Europe, there are a large number of excellent private companies coming up for sale. European private equity is a relatively new enterprise, so there are very few firms with audited records. Our background is account management, but we have studied private equity for years. Our model portfolio for our fund of funds has appreciated at an internal rate of return (IRR) of 21% per annum after all fees over the last three years. It is estimated that there are 400 private equity funds in Europe, so you couldn't possibly cull through them to find the 10 or 15 best.*
>
> *Admittedly, we have not done this before, and the returns mentioned are projections, but our perch in a private bank and our experience gives us unique vision and access. Through our contacts, we can get you into*

the best private equity funds that would otherwise be closed to you. We
project an IRR for our fund of 18% to 20% net over the next decade.
After we make the initial investment in a fund, we usually go on its
board. We hold our fund investments for the full 10-year life of the
fund. We charge a fee of 2% on both committed and uncommitted cap-
ital and 10% of the profits. Our fund is already fully subscribed, but
we can find a place for you if you act quickly.

"Can you achieve 18% to 20% annual returns if the European equity markets only do 8%?" I ask.

"We anticipate gross returns from the funds we invest in of 1,500
to 2,000 basis points above that of the European equity markets," was
the answer.

I was dazzled or should I say incredulous? Fifteen to twenty percentage points a year before fees above that of the equity markets! If the
European markets do 8% a year, they expect to do in the mid to high
20s. Amazing! I have never heard of any asset class that has achieved
consistent returns of this magnitude with huge amounts of money. That
simply is not the way the world works, but even more astounding are
the underlying returns their fund will need to achieve this target. I
roughly calculate that the double fee structure is so onerous that, for the
foundation to get 14% per annum, the underlying private equity firms
would have to earn a gross return of about 24% a year. For the foundation to get 18%, the firms will have to do close to 30%. Maybe such returns were possible 20 years ago when the use of leverage and the
importance of cash flow weren't understood and there were only a
handful of LBO firms. Now, there are hundreds of LBO firms with
hundreds of billions of committed but uninvested capital, and courses in
how to start and run an LBO firm are part of the curriculum of virtually every major business school. Currently, working for an LBO firm is
the most desirable career choice at the Harvard Business School. An
ominous sign!

The reaction of the board to the fund of funds' pitch was enthusiastic. Private equity is fashionable, and they want to be involved. It's a
complex area, and they think using a fund of funds makes sense. I am
totally, utterly skeptical. Success in private equity investing is not only
about the entry; it's also about the exit. If there are 400 funds competing

for buyouts, won't that drive up prices and lower returns? The average life of an LBO fund is about 10 years. How can the LBO fund of funds charge a 2% annual fixed fee and 10% of the profits for the one-time selection process and then do nothing but just sit on the board of their portfolio companies? What a sinecure! What a business!

I remarked that the fund of funds' fees are way too high for the service and the value they provide. If private equity really makes sense, the trust should invest directly. The staff was doubtful. It was a tricky area, they said. The fund of funds was hired. So be it. In the years to come, it is probably bullish for European economic growth and equity markets that there is so much money going into private equity, but somehow, something doesn't solve. It's the old story: If a deal sounds too good to be true, it probably is too good to be true.

TRACKING U.S. PRIVATE EQUITY AND WONDERING

There are many private equity databases, but the most accurate may be that of Thomson Venture Economics. It's fascinating to study. The IRR for all private equity firms for the 20 years that ended in 2002 was 13.7%, which is good but not exactly spectacular for a totally nonliquid, highly volatile asset class, particularly considering that public equities returned about the same. There is a big spread between the top quartile and the median with the fifteenth percentile firm earning 24%. I calculate that buyouts returned 16.2% per annum from 1983 to 1992, but then, as the big money poured in, only 8.2% a year from 1993 to 2002 and only 1.6% for the five years that ended in 2004. Discovery and success always kill the goose that lays those golden eggs. (See Table 10.1.)

The allure of private equity and venture capital has not been diminished. For example, pension funds and fiduciaries are still scrambling to get more money into venture capital even though at the end of 2004 there was an overhang of $54 billion of allocated but uninvested money in the hands of venture capitalists. I have a couple of friends in venture, and they say that there is so much money looking for deals that valuations are once again ridiculous. This is good for the United States and great for innovation because entrepreneurs will get

TABLE 10.1

U.S. Private Equity Returns
(Pooled IRR Net to Investors as of 09/30/04
All Funds Formed 1969–2002)

Fund Type	1Yr	3Yr	5Yr	10Yr	20Yr
Seed Stage VC	10.3	11.0	−1.4	16.8	10.7
Early Stage VC	−19.1	−26.9	57.0	37.1	20.7
Balanced VC	−0.6	−18.0	19.6	20.5	13.5
Later Stage VC	−36.1	−23.3	8.0	17.8	14.0
All Venture	−17.2	−22.7	26.0	25.5	15.8
Small Buyouts	−1.9	−2.6	1.0	11.3	26.8
Medium Buyouts	12.2	−6.7	4.6	12.5	17.8
Large Buyouts	9.5	−6.5	2.8	10.6	13.4
Mega Buyouts	14.1	−4.9	0.8	5.9	7.7
All Buyouts	12.5	−5.3	1.6	8.2	12.2
Mezzanine	9.1	1.2	6.5	7.9	9.8
All Private Equity	3.4	−10.4	6.9	13.4	13.7

Database source: VentureXpert database from Thomson Venture Economics
Investment data source: The MoneyTree Survey by PricewaterhouseCoopers/Thomson Venture Economics/NVCA
All other data sources: Thomson Venture Economics
Note: Venture capital commits money to start-ups and nonpublic companies. In a way, it is really just early stage private equity, but venture capital does not use leverage.

funded, but bad for the investors because high entry valuations mean low exit returns.

As for private equity, the boom is even more dazzling. UBS estimates that global private equity firms in 2005 will raise $200 billion, four times what they took in last year. This is not an unrealistic number. For example Goldman Sachs and the Carlyle Group have both raised $10 billion funds. Because LBO firms traditionally leverage up five times, the $200 billion becomes $1 trillion that will need to be invested. The UBS report babbles away about 15% to 20% annual returns stretching endlessly into the future. Why would any fiduciary do anything else with their money? Why would any smart young guy go into any other business? Good luck!

David Swensen of the Yale Endowment (more about him later), in his wonderful book, *Pioneering Portfolio Management: An Unconventional Approach to Institutional Investing,* points out that even in the very favorable environment of the past 20 years, most private equity firms performed poorly, risk adjusted. The best firms, however, did very well, and, furthermore, they continued to do well even after they got big. In fact, a study issued in mid-2005 of 4,000 private equity funds by Private Equity Intelligence found that the top 25% of funds by size raised each year between 1998 and 2003 beat the industry's performance by six percentage points in Europe and two percentage points in the United States. Two-thirds of the 24 European jumbo funds in the sample beat the average.

Swensen maintains that in private equity the poor and mediocre performers stay that way. Just being in the asset class won't do it. It's very important to be with the real pros. He emphasizes that the difference between the twenty-fifth and seventy-fifth percentiles among U.S. fixed income managers is minimal, and even among equity managers it's only three percentage points a year. But in the universe of private equity funds, this same performance differential exceeds 20 percentage points per annum.

The Yale Endowment's numbers are proof of this view. Its large private equity portfolio earned 37.6% over the 10 years that ended June 30, 2004, outperforming the return of a pool of private equity managers, compiled by the consulting firm Cambridge Associates, by 14.7% a year. Since its inception in 1973, Yale has earned an astounding 30.6% per annum from its private equity program, but as noted, there has been immense volatility in both the one- and five-year returns. When there were years of red ink and the conventional wisdom was that private equity was caput as a high-return asset class, that was the time to double commitments. In other words staying power is absolutely essential.

Swensen argues convincingly that LBO firms that concentrate on improving the operating performance of their portfolio companies consistently do far better than those that just leverage up troubled businesses. Using a lot of debt to buy mediocre or poor businesses cheap doesn't work, mostly because it's hard to sell them and you are very vulnerable to cyclical swings in the economy. Even though the practitioners are loath to admit it, for the LBO business as a whole, the environment has to be much tougher in the future than it was in the glory days. In fact, even in the glory days, Swensen demonstrates that if you had leveraged up the S&P 500 by the amount of the average leverage used by LBO firms, the return on the S&P fund would have been 45% higher than that of the relatively small number of LBO funds that then existed. His point is that the investor in LBO firms in general is not compensated for the extreme risk of leverage and the immense nonliquidity.

Carol Loomis, in the June 2005 issue of *Fortune*, has a superb piece on Kohlberg Kravis Roberts & Company (KKR). Were they brilliant or just early? The answer seems to be the latter. From 1976 to September 2004, KKR raised 10 funds and invested $21 billion of investors' money into 93 companies. It borrowed $109 billion so it leveraged up five times and committed $130 billion. Its profits are $34.7 billion or a 185% return on the equity but only 26% on the total money invested. In other words, the story is leverage. The hit ratio is 62 winners, 22 losers, and 9 squares. Hardly spectacular! A stock picker would not survive for long with that ratio, and private equity is getting tougher as new nobodies flood in. Including all the leverage, KKR's weighted average of returns on its last four funds has fallen to 16%.

Meanwhile, today, back in the good old United States of America you might think private equity firms would be suffering because the IPO market has been slow and selective. They need to book gains to get paid their fees. However, the private equity guys are ingenious, and they have found a new escape hatch. The investment world is desperate for yield because interest rates on Treasury bonds are so meager. As a result, fixed income investors are reaching for yield by buying heavily into high yield, or in the parlance, junk bonds. The spread between the yield on junk and Treasuries is close to an all-time low. Everyone seems to have forgotten that from time to time, just when the buyers are frothing at the mouth about a new era, junk lives up to its name and defaults soar. Reaching for yield over time has proved to be extremely hazardous to your financial health. As one wag put it, "More money has been lost reaching for yield than at the point of a gun."

What the private equity guys are forcing their portfolio companies to do now is finance by issuing bonds in the high-yield market in which there is plenty of demand for paper. They then use the proceeds to pay big special dividends. Of course, this loads more debt onto companies that are already highly leveraged. Here is the way it works.

In December 2003, Thomas H. Lee Partners (THL), an LBO fund, bought the mattress maker Simmons Company, investing $388 million of equity and using debt for the rest. In the summer of 2004 THL attempted to do an IPO of Simmons, but the deal flopped. So that December, Simmons sold $165 million of bonds and paid out the entire amount to THL as a dividend, giving THL a return of more than 40% on its investment. And incidentally, THL still owns 100% of Simmons. In 2004, 77 dividends worth $13.5 billion were financed by junk-bond deals, and highly leveraged loans from banks paid for another $9.4 billion of dividends. Somehow this doesn't seem like sound corporate finance!

The other method of exiting is for one LBO firm to sell a position to another LBO firm at a profit, thus booking the gain and charging their investors 20%. These transactions are called "secondary buyouts." I'm puzzled about how they are going to work out for the buyer. Theoretically, the seller has already done everything possible to improve the company, and presumably the seller is better informed about the company's prospects. The unfortunate limited partner invested in both firms in such a transaction ends up owning a share of the same company minus the fees paid to the seller's general partners. Some cynics even wonder if mutual backscratching is occurring sometimes.

THE CROWD IS ALWAYS WRONG DURING MARKET EXTREMES

Here, in the summer of 2005, my sense is that many hedge-fund investors believe that the equity markets have rallied a bridge too far, are scared, and have done some selling. The complacency everyone was talking about seems to have been only skin deep. They all recite the same mantra that almost all of the sentiment indicators show a dangerously high level of bullishness. Therefore, they are contrary to the consensus and are bearish. Being a contrarian is very chic. The only trouble is that now everyone is a contrarian. Even Wall Street economists are now contrarians. Goldman Sachs recently published a paper on inflation that began, "Our new forecast for inflation is out of consensus." In other words, the writer thought the most important aspect of his forecast was not his economic analysis but rather that it was out of consensus. Therefore, instead of being contrarians, perhaps we should be contracontrarians.

The sentiment indicators are not easy to decipher. Ned Davis of Ned Davis Research has studied them for years, and he points out that the *crowd* is always wrong at market turning points and that they are always wrong at extremes in sentiment. He says: "If one knew for certain *the* peak or trough in sentiment, then one could go contrary and be correct nearly all the time." However, because one cannot know exact extremes for certain except in hindsight, one can be weeks or months early, which can be very painful. The Ned Davis Sentiment Composite began showing extreme optimism in January 1999, then really extreme optimism in December, but the bubble didn't burst until the late spring 2000. That was an eternity for those who sold in January 1999 and very painful for people like me who reduced allocations to technology in December 1999. However, in 1987, the Ned Davis Composite spiked to an all-time high just a month before the Crash. It's the same with bottoms. In August 1990 the Composite reached extreme pessimism, but that was 47 days and 12% on the S&P 500 before the low.

Ned's advice is to use stop losses. Easier said than done. Most stop-loss orders are put in at 10% limits. Admittedly in the bubble run-up, speculators who went short or sold too early would have been stopped out or gone back as prices soared, but when would they have known to sell again? And in the 1990 example, they would have bought in August, and then, when the market fell more than 10%, they would have had their stop-loss order activated just as the turn was finally about to occur. The timing of the execution is crucial. Often when you leave a stop-loss order with a dealer or when it is on the specialist's books, you get picked off by the market maker. In other words, you get an execution just before the asset in question rallies.

Obviously you can't just be contrary because the crowd is nearly always right in the vast middle of moves when the sentiment measures are not particularly extended. Be patient! Don't react to them until they are at historical extremes. They are easily charted. Ned Davis says, "Go with the flow until it reaches an extreme and begins to reverse; it is at that point where it often pays to be contrary." Merrill Lynch did a fascinating study that back-tested the four main sentiment indicators and found that they had virtually no predictive powers at market peaks, although they were decent at bottoms. Morgan Stanley did a similar analysis of the VIX Index and came to a similar conclusion. This index, which measures complacency and which everyone tracks on a daily basis, currently has fallen to a very low level. That suggests a high degree of complacency and is, therefore, a bearish sign. However, when Morgan Stanley back-tested its predictive ability, it found VIX virtually useless in signaling tops. So much for the popular wisdom. It's the old story. The character of markets is continually changing, and there is no single timing system that will consistently, indefinitely work.

Another sentiment indicator is the media because they are invariably focused on what just has spectacularly happened (because that is what makes a good story) rather than what is *about* to happen. For years *BusinessWeek* cover stories have been wonderful contrary indicators, and, in fact, one friend of mine subscribes to the magazine for just that reason and has a cover collection. The rest of the print and TV business press also are notorious pilers on. A classic case was during 1979 to 1981 as oil prices and inflation surged. Numerous books were published by experts forecasting hyperinflation, depression, and a collapse of the dollar. At one point, 7 out of the top 10 books on the bestseller list were about inflation and how to survive it. Even wise investors like John Templeton gave speeches saying 7% to 8% inflation was inevitable. Of course, decades of disinflation, not inflation, were about to occur, during which both stocks and bonds would soar.

The most recent example was in December 2004 when the dollar was at its low. *The Economist*, probably the most respected business magazine in the world, ran a cover titled "The Disappearing Dollar." Shortly thereafter, *Newsweek* had a cover, "The Incredible Shrinking Dollar." There were numerous articles about how Warren Buffett was short the dollar in huge size, and another famous investor said being short was "a slam dunk." Wall Street economists ranted and raved about the twin deficits, a bearish book by the highly regarded Pete Petersen entitled *Running on Empty* was a best seller, and hedge funds were a record short the greenback.

I confess I succumbed to the madness and was short the dollar as well. So what happened? The dollar bottomed in the midst of the frenzy and began a powerful rally that elevated the DXY index almost 10%. Leveraged speculators were crushed. Of course, now that the dollar is up, everyone has figured out all the reasons it should stay strong. Euroland is splintering politically, U.S. short rates are higher than euro bloc and Japanese short rates, U.S. growth is stronger, the Fed is still tightening, and the twin deficits are beginning to shrink. In late spring 2005, the new media craze is the alleged housing bubble and how soon it will bust with God-awful consequences. All the same, suspects are warning of imminent disaster because real estate is a gold rush and a gigantic bubble. The cover story of the April 11, 2005, issue of good old reliable *BusinessWeek* was "After the Housing Boom: What the Coming Slowdown Means for the Economy and You." *Fortune, Worth, The Economist,* and the *New York Times* have all joined the chorus. I wonder.

THE MOTHER-IN-LAW FACTOR— AND OTHER CONTRARIAN INDICATORS

There is another sentiment measure to which I pay attention. It's the personal one, the people one. Some people have an uncanny instinct for joining a stock market trend just as it is close to ending. My partner Cyril's mother-in-law may have this incredibly valuable characteristic. She is an attractive, intelligent woman but not a stock market person. However, she circulates with people who have a general connection to the market, so she hears the chatter. She is reluctant to interfere in Cyril's business because she knows she is ill-informed, so only when she has the conviction that she could be missing something really big, a trend that is vitally important, does she speak up to him about it. Three times in the past couple of years she has talked to him about an investment idea just as it is in the process of peaking.

It happened most recently in December 2004. It was a Sunday night. She and Cyril were feeding Cyril's two young children. As a spoonful of porridge is inserted into the baby's mouth and rejected, she says something like, "It looks to me as though the dollar is going to fall much further. How are we ever going to be able to afford to go to Europe again? Shouldn't I buy some euros?"

Cyril's wife, Olivia, who is there, too, is trying to keep from laughing. "Oh," says Cyril. "Why do you think so?"

"Because absolutely everybody says so."

The next day, Cyril told us about it, and, sure enough, the next week the euro peaked and began a precipitate decline. "Well," I said, "I guess our new sentiment measure is using your mother-in-law as a contrary indicator, but if she is really that good, you have to cherish her. Tell Olivia she can't smile. Contrary indicators can be easily broken. If your mother-in-law discovers you are using her as a contrary indicator, it will screw up her head and ruin her usefulness. She has to remain totally spontaneous and unselfconscious." Of course by writing about her, I have shattered the magic.

I was serious. Certain people are very valid contrary indicators. Years ago, there was a salesman from Goldman Sachs whom I talked with a lot. I really liked the guy, and he was very conscientious. He knew his job was to pass on what Goldman's analysts and strategists were saying, not to venture his own opinions on investing. However, once in a while the consensus, the momentum behind a theme, would become so powerful that he would be confident enough to really push me, backing his story up with anecdotes about how big money was moving in that direction. Almost invariably he did this at or close to tops or bottoms. As this pattern emerged, I always took his calls and paid close attention.

Then one night at a Goldman Sachs conference, probably after a few drinks, I told him why he was so important to us. As soon as I did it, I knew it was a mistake. I could see in his eyes that he was hurt and offended. He didn't want to be a contrary indicator. He also knew I was serious. Afterward, he tried to fulfill his old role, but I could tell the magic was gone. He was continually thinking about whether he was falling into the momentum trap, and sometimes he would even mention it. In the end, both our heads were screwed up. I was trying to out-think him, and he was trying to unravel himself. It was the end of a beautiful and symbiotic relationship.

Another sentiment indicator that has become almost an investment legend is that almost by definition a secular bear market can't be over until there is true and utter *capitulation*. Capitulation is the despair of unconditional surrender. Capitulation is Germany or Japan in 1945. The gloomers today argue that in this secular bear market there has not yet been enough pain and suffering, and there have not yet been sufficient manifestations of distress in living patterns. They seem to want an angry and vengeful financial god who punishes the greed of his subjects. Others have this strong but repressed Puritan streak that requires retribution by subjecting malefactors to public floggings before life and the good times can resume. Fear must gain total ascendancy over greed. Of course, the trouble with wanting blood flowing in the streets is that some of it is apt to be your own. However, it certainly is hard to maintain that the aftermath of this 1990s bubble has been anywhere near as painful as what happened in the 1930s and again in the second half of the 1970s.

The problem with the capitulation theory is identifying whether there truly has been capitulation. A lot of entrepreneurs and investors certainly think they *got* capitulated in the first three years of the new century when their personal bubbles burst. But was it enough? Some of the villains have been flogged and some have even gone to jail, but a lot of the old games are still being played. My dictionary's definition of capitulation is "unconditional surrender," but my thesaurus mentions synonyms like *renunciation, abandonment, cession, relinquishment, giving up.* . . . Investment literature has very little to say about capitulation. In his classic *Manias, Panics, and Crashes,* Charles Kindelberger says virtually nothing about it. In the very detailed *Panic on Wall Street,* Robert Sobel extensively studies the time it takes for a market to recover from a panic or a bear market, but he doesn't discuss any of the so-called sociological signs.

Sobel's historical studies on the duration of recoveries also are inconclusive. He finds that after the Panic of 1837 it took until 1844 for the market to recover its composure, and it required six years after the Panic of 1873. The conventional wisdom is that following the Crash in 1929, it was 20 years before a new bull market began, yet several huge bear market rallies that lasted a couple of years could be called "new bull markets." That was not the case after the 1970s bear. Things were back to normal almost immediately after the sharp breaks in 1792, 1869, and the epic Northern Pacific Panic.

So here we are now more than five years after the bull market top. Is this just a sucker rally or are we in a new bull market? My guess is that it is the latter.

CHAPTER
ELEVEN

From One
Generation to Another
Bismarck and the Yale Endowment

I'm on the board of a family trust and of a foundation. The meetings I go to get me thinking about what kind of expectations are reasonable for long-term, *real* returns for family money, and the problems of planning for good investment management generations ahead. An interesting book in this regard is Fritz Stern's *Gold and Iron: Bismarck, Bleichröder, and the Building of the German Empire*. It's a book I first read maybe 20 years ago, and it's about power, money, real returns, and how to protect future generations from themselves.

TIMBERLAND FOR CHILDREN
WITH INHERITED MONEY

Gerson Bleichröder was a nineteenth-century German Jew who had a life filled with immense financial triumph, persecution, and personal sadness. Otto von Bismarck represented the Old Prussia—aristocratic, agrarian, hierarchic—and it was his ambition and vision that welded the First Reich into an empire. In 1859, when he was 37, Bleichröder

became the banker and investment adviser for the rising Junker diplo-
mat, and for 30 years the two leveraged their insights and power to
achieve great wealth and prominence. In nineteenth-century Germany,
it was the custom of the Prussian aristocracy to employ a Jew as "a
more or less occult instrument," as Bismarck so exquisitely put it. Incidentally, that's the ultimate compliment for an investment adviser.

In addition to being Bismarck's occult instrument, Bleichröder was
his investment adviser, financial markets interpreter, and a crucial intelligence source. He was the *éminence grise* of the Bismarck government,
and he made sure everyone knew it. He used his position for both commercial purposes (getting stock in hot deals) and social purposes (his
daughter's marriage), and over the years he built a great firm and became the richest man in Germany.

It's fortunate there was no SEC in those days, because Bleichröder
traded for his own account and for his illustrious client on the basis of
highly privileged inside information. There was every conceivable conflict of interest, and Bleichröder's judgment of how the financial markets would react to international developments was consistently superb.
For example, at one crucial moment the German chancellor's portfolio
was 70% in Russian securities because his investment adviser determined that the moves he was about to make would benefit Russian railroad equities. Sometimes they bought the cheap shares of good
companies first, and then Bismarck caused events to happen that made
them appreciate.

Both Bismarck and Bleichröder were profoundly complex people.
Both were, in Bismarck's own words, cursed with a brutal sensuality, and
both were lecherous men who seemed incapable of developing truly
intimate relationships with women. Bleichröder was obsessed with penetrating the shallow but glittering world of Berlin society. Even though
he was a ubiquitous presence on the political and financial scene, above
all else, he thirsted for respectability and acceptance. He entertained lav-
ishly at his magnificent house, but the guests snickered at his ostentatious pretensions. His dumpy wife sat alone, laden with jewels, and his
romances were shadowed by lawsuits and blackmail.

Bismarck, the Prince, worked hard at projecting a magnificent exte-
rior and omnipotence. He was the Iron Chancellor who was creating
the new German industrial and political empire. Henry Kissinger calls
him "the white revolutionary," whatever that means. However, he was

also a Byzantine personality: greedy, arrogant, and a hypochondriac. He suffered frequent bouts of nervous exhaustion and irritation. In private, he often remarked on his troubled spirit and was plagued by his sexuality. His principal obsession, other than ruling Germany, was with making money in the stock market so he could buy more and more timberland. He treated everyone around him abominably.

However, both men must have had that mystical "seeing eye," which enabled them to perceive the future chain of events that would be triggered by an action in the present. This is what successful investing still is all about. While suspended in the midst of times that were full of mystery, uncertainty, and doubts, they had the capacity to maintain their poise and world view and never to impatiently or irritably reach for a fact or conclusion.

Bleichröder exploited the insights that Bismarck provided to make both his patron and himself very rich. But he also had what Bismarck once referred to as "a certain timidity in investing." He told his clients he would attempt to get them over the long run a *real* return (after inflation) of 4% per annum, which would mean that the purchasing power of their wealth would double every 17 or 18 years. His timidity kept him from becoming engulfed in the new-issues market of the 1870s or in the mania for colonial investing that later wiped out so many men and German banking houses. In other words, he became very rich because he endured. I calculate that Bismarck's account with him compounded at about 10% per annum over 25 years and that inflation averaged less than one percent. Bismarck was perfectly satisfied with this return, but always withdrew his profits and invested them in land and trees. He was convinced that investing in paper securities was a fine and quick way to get richer, but that the repository of true wealth should be land on which you could grow trees.

Bismarck's appetite for timberland was insatiable. His theory was that the price of land would gradually appreciate in line with population growth, or about two percentage points annually. His studies had convinced him that German forests would grow 2.75% a year, so that his real return from timberland would be around 4.75% per annum, because inflation at the time was virtually zero. If there was inflation, he was sure timberland and log prices would appreciate in line with the inflation. He thought that with very little risk, this was a spectacular compounding of wealth. As it turned out, Bismarck was absolutely right.

Over the next half century in Germany of war, inflation, surrender, and depression, timberland held value far better than anything else.

Reading about the modest but realistic return expectations of German investors, I couldn't help thinking about David Swensen and the very sensible way he is trying to lower expectations for the returns from the Yale Endowment. Swensen is convinced expectations are still excessive, and that the university and its alumni have to accept the reality that the high teens annual returns the Endowment earned in the 1980s and 1990s were an aberration. Unfortunately, the average U.S. investor has similar exalted expectations and is also certain to experience disappointments.

There is a story about Winston Churchill and excessive expectations that may or may not be apocryphal.

In the 1930s, out of power and financially strapped, Churchill taught a lecture course at Cambridge on human sociology. One afternoon standing at the lectern and, always prone to the dramatic, he turned to the large class and demanded, "What part of the human body expands to 12 times its normal size when subjected to external stimulation?"

The class gasped. Churchill, obviously relishing the moment, pointed at a young woman in the tenth row. "What's the answer?" he demanded.

The woman flushed and replied, "Well, obviously it's the male sexual organ."

Wrong!" said Churchill. "Who knows the correct answer?"

Another woman raised her hand. "The right answer is that it's the pupil of the human eye, which expands to twelve times its normal size when exposed to darkness."

"Of course!" exclaimed Churchill, and he turned back to the unfortunate first woman. "Young lady," he said, "I have three things to say to you. First, you didn't do the homework. Second, you have a dirty mind, and third, you are doomed to a life of excessive expectations."

And so, also doomed to a life of excessive expectations is the U.S. equity investor, who surveys show still expects over the next 10 years to earn 15% a year nominal from stocks and 12% to 13% adjusting for inflation.

Bismarck also worried that his descendants would not know what to do with an inherited investment portfolio composed of stocks and bonds that required informed buying and selling decisions. He was very skeptical about investment advisers, and he thought it was highly unlikely his descendants could find another Bleichröder. Therefore, he liked the immutable, stable characteristics of owning timberland. Land and timber didn't require his descendants to find investment geniuses to manage their money. All they had to do was hold the timberland forever and collect the income from the controlled harvesting of logs. Besides, when it rained, they could rejoice because their trees were being nourished.

There is a lot to this simple theory. Today, when you leave your children financial assets, if they are not in the investment business, how are they going to manage them? Even the greatest growth stocks get old and die. No trust has ever been devised that effectively mandates investment policy over more than one generation. Most brokers are hopeless, large fiduciary organizations are populated with mediocrities, and even the most dynamic investment firms are unlikely to survive beyond the lifespan of their founders. All things considered, leaving your descendants timberland with the proviso that they can't sell it makes some sense. However, single asset trusts can be dangerous. In retrospect, the one in 1920 stipulating the shares of the New York, New Haven, & Hartford Railroad or later the ones that permitted only holdings of American Telephone & Telegraph—failed to account for change. Timberland doesn't seem to have the same vulnerability, but it is hard to get big money to work because there simply aren't enough properties to buy.

YALE'S ENDOWMENT: FROM BANKRUPT TO NEGLECTED TO THE BEST

I was still thinking about the board meeting and the difficulty of achieving investment management succession and superior returns over a long period of time when I had lunch in New York with David Swensen, who, as I've mentioned earlier, runs the Yale Endowment. I am convinced David has done more for Yale than anyone since old Elihu himself. Instead of giving honorary degrees to elderly politicians and brilliant but irrelevant academics, Yale should honor David with one. Since he took over in 1985 as the chief investment officer, Yale's endowment has compounded at 16.1% per annum, the best record of any university or college endowment. Harvard at 14.9% is a close second. Yale's record places it in the top 1% of all large institutional investors. Yale uses a moving average long-term target spending rate, and over the years that rate has been raised from 4.5% to 5%. The endowment now provides 30% of the university's operating budget, up from 14% in fiscal 1993! Thus, Yale has benefited from the strength of its investment program, both from the much larger size of the endowment and from the justified increase in the spending rate.

The performance of its endowments is vital to the fortunes (and even survival) of a university. It is very difficult for a premier private university to finance itself on tuition alone, and it cannot rely indefinitely on alumni contributions to meet the shortfall. Prior to David's arrival, Yale was a case study of what not to do in managing an endowment. Now it's an actual Harvard Business School case (*Yale University Investment Office,* June 2003) on highly successful, unconventional portfolio management.

Very little data exists about the perils and pitfalls of managing a pool of money over a long period of time, so the Yale Endowment is a fascinating historical study.

Yale was founded in 1701, but the endowment wasn't created until the early 1800s when, as the result of a fund drive to establish the independence of the college, numerous alumni made gifts. In 1811 the treasurer of Yale College, James Hillhouse, and two prominent trustees who were highly successful businessmen and respected community leaders, Eli Whitney and William Woolsey, founded the Eagle Bank of New Haven. They were so convinced of the inevitable success of this new bank and the growth of its service area that, along with their own money, they invested most of the endowment in the shares of the bank. Not only that, they leveraged the investment with a loan, even though Yale's finances at the time were perilous and the college had substantial unpaid debts.

By 1820 the entire endowment (with the exception of a few small holdings) was committed to Eagle bank shares. Suddenly in 1825 out of the proverbial clear blue sky, as a result of inadequately collateralized loans, the bank declared bankruptcy, plunging the New Haven economy into depression, reducing the value of the Endowment to a mere $1,200, and jeopardizing the future of Yale.

I recount this episode for its educational value. First, the primary rule of an endowment or foundation always must be diversification and avoidance of concentration. Second, just because trustees are illustrious men doesn't mean they know anything about investing. Third, avoid conflicts of interest. Hillhouse, Whitney, and Woolsey were founders and investors in the bank, side by side with the endowment. With the best of intentions, they did great damage to their beloved college. Think of what the compounded value of Yale's endowment would be today if the Eagle Bank had not gone bust. Ironically, despite this tragedy, a major avenue in New Haven is named after Mr. Hillhouse, Yale's gym is Payne Whitney, and one of Yale's great, historic buildings is Woolsey Hall.

Yale survived the trustees' bungling, and by 1900 the endowment was $5 million and still supervised informally and casually by the treasurer and the trustees. Yale is governed by a small board of prominent trustees that are expected to spend a good deal of time (six to eight two-day meetings a year) on the affairs of the university. Because of a major commitment in equities, the endowment prospered during the 1920s. By 1929 Yale had 42% of its portfolio in equities versus 11% for the average university, and, as a result, its endowment was bigger than Harvard's or Princeton's. However, it was hit harder by the Crash and the great secular bear market of the 1930s.

The treasurer of Yale in the late 1930s, Laurence Tighe, was a fine, upstanding, prudent man but a retrospective thinker. He reacted to the losses in the endowment from the bear market by decreeing that Yale should be at least two-thirds in bonds and no more than one-third in equities. He further believed that the treasurer and trustees, as famous and powerful men, were best qualified to select the securities to be owned by the endowment. For the next 30 years, the endowment was basically run by the trustees who came and went, and, as a result, it suffered from what you might call *benign neglect*. With 70% of its portfolio still in high-grade fixed income, Yale missed out on the great postwar bull market in stocks but fully participated in the equally great bear market in bonds.

By the late 1960s, after a 20-year bull market in stocks, the trustees belatedly decided they should substantially increase the endowment's exposure to equities. They were greatly influenced by the report of a task force sponsored by the then president of the Ford Foundation, the legendary and aristocratic McGeorge Bundy, who had graduated from Yale. This report argued that most endowments had been too conservatively managed because of the fear of another Crash. It went on to maintain that "this concern did not survive dispassionate analysis," and that equities, particularly growth stocks, should be the major portion of an endowment's corpus.

Nevertheless, in 1968, because of how well stocks had done in the previous 20 years and because of Bundy's reputation as a genius, the report's conclusion soon became the prevailing wisdom. Since prep school at St. Paul's, McGeorge Bundy had been known as "the great brain." He was thought to be the American Keynes. At St. Paul's, each quarter the academic averages and historic percentile rankings by form were posted, and Bundy was always in the ninety-ninth percentile. The year he took the College Boards, an essay was required on one of two subjects: "What I Did Last Summer" or "My Favorite Pet."

Bundy instead wrote a scathing paper attacking the test's designers for posing such inane topics and arguing that both were meaningless and irrelevant to a world in turmoil. Because he hadn't answered the question and annoyed with his arrogance, the first grader gave him a zero. The second grader, intrigued, gave him 100. The head grader was called over and, after having read too many essays on pets and vacations, he also gave Bundy a perfect score. Since Bundy had blitzed the other two parts of the exam, he became the first applicant ever to get a perfect score on the College Boards. Shortly after graduating from Yale, he was hired by Harvard, inspiring this piece of doggerel:

A proper young prig, McGeorge Bundy
Graduated from Yale on a Monday
But he shortly was seen
As establishment Dean
Up at Harvard the following Sunday

Later, as one of the best and the brightest on Vietnam, Bundy's judgments eventually came to be even more seriously questioned, but in 1969 he was still riding high. The Yale trustees, desperately worried about the performance of the endowment, decided on a dramatic step. They not only increased equities in a major way, but they decided to help found a new investment management company in Boston to be called Endowment Management & Research (EMR). They stocked the new firm with the most aggressive growth and emerging growth stock investors (called *gunslingers* in those days) who had done best recently. The theory was that Yale would own part of EMR and be the firm's biggest and preferred client.

The results of this venture into the heart of the consensus were disastrous. Growth stocks, particularly the new, smaller ones, were making a secular peak. The gunslingers were about to become extinct. The timing was exquisite. The U.S. equity market was peaking, growth stocks were at exorbitant multiples, and a secular bear market was beginning that would take the S&P 500 down 45% and crush growth stocks in particular.

Over the next 10 years, the value of the endowment, adjusted for inflation, was cut in half, Yale's finances were plunged into disarray, and maintenance on the physical plant of the university was deferred. Fortunately, the alumni remained generous, but the abysmal performance of the endowment became a detriment to fund-raising. In 1979, EMR was terminated by Yale and subsequently went out of business. Once again, by following the dictums of a supposedly great man, who was a dominating intellect but not an investment professional, and by not diversifying, Yale had suffered grievous wounds.

Admittedly, during the 1970s, McGeorge Bundy had a lot on his mind besides asset allocation. Nevertheless, his unfortunate advocacy of momentum investing influenced institutional investment strategy elsewhere. One of the most damaged was the prestigious Ford Foundation where he had been so influential. Groupthink and committee paralysis must have been at work. In 1980 the *Bawl Street Journal*, with its tongue firmly in its cheek, ran a wonderful ad. (See following page.)

For the next five years, the Yale Endowment was managed in a fairly haphazard manner. However, in 1985 Swensen, who had earned his Ph.D. at Yale, was recruited by the provost and by the economist

PROFIT FROM OUR MISTAKES!!

Investing money is a zero-sum game. For every winner, there is a loser. We've been losers! If you had sold what we bought, and if you had bought what we sold, you would be rich!

In 1968, we went heavily into stocks and by 1974 were down almost 50%! In 1973–75, we invested over $150 million in real estate, and not just any real estate—we concentrated in Atlanta; We lost our ass! In 1978, we hired a bright theoretical consultant from Harvard who had a "yield tilt" model which told us that energy stocks were overpriced and auto stocks cheap. This seemed to make sense, so we sold Texas Oil and Gas at $8 and bought General Motors at $60. We lost 33% of our money. If you had gone the other way, you'd be up 430%!

All investors make some bad decisions. But we make a lot—and with consistency. Now for the first time, you can profit from our mistakes. For $10,000 a year, you can receive copies of the minutes of our quarterly Finance Committee meetings in which we establish our investment philosophy. For an additional $25,000 a year, we will give you a monthly update over the telephone of our current market outlook. And for only $100,000 a year you will receive copies of our trade confirmations so you will know on a daily basis what not to do. It's part of our Contrarian Theory.

This may seem like a very unusual offer, but look at it this way: we can't seem to get on the right side of markets, so if we let you pay to profit from our mistakes, we will have finally found a way to profit from our mistakes as well.

Subscribe now. Time is limited. We are about to undertake a major restructuring of the portfolio, and we'd hate to see you get caught going the same way.

THE FORD FOUNDATION
Not eleemosynary on purpose

James Tobin. What a brilliant selection, especially since Swensen, then 31, had never been a professional investor and had spent the previous six years working as an investment banker. However Tobin had taught Swensen and knew he was smart, analytical, and willing to challenge the conventional wisdom. Swensen later hired Dean Takahashi, whom he had known as a student at Yale, as his alter ego, and the two have worked as a team. Incidentally, both today could easily go to any number of much more lucrative positions, but both enjoy the intellectual atmosphere and the challenge, and both teach at Yale. Swensen, according to the *Yale Alumni Magazine* in the July–August 2005 issue, was paid about $1 million in 2003, making him Yale's highest paid employee.

The Harvard endowment, which is now $22.6 billion, has also been superbly managed in the past 20 years and was up 21.1% in the year ending June 30, 2004. Harvard also has very little invested in domestic equities and a lot in real estate, foreign equities, absolute return strategies, and timber (including $600 million in a forest in New Zealand). Harvard Management runs a substantial amount of the absolute return money in-house, and, in order to keep superior investors, offered a rich but competitive incentive compensation program. This model resulted in some huge paychecks ($35 million), which aroused fierce complaining from some incredibly foolish alumni. As a result, Harvard Management has blown apart, with Jack Meyer, who was the mastermind, and most of the stars leaving to set up their own hedge funds. It is not clear how Harvard Management will be put back together again. Yale is incredibly fortunate.

David and Dean stick to five basic principles. First, they strongly believe in equities. As investors, they want to be owners, not lenders. Second, they want to hold a diversified portfolio. Their conviction is that Yale can more effectively reduce risk by limiting aggregate exposure to any single asset class rather than by attempting to time markets. Despite the professionalism of the Yale staff, no attempt is made to fine-tune allocations until valuations become very extreme. The third principle is that greater incremental returns are achievable in selecting superior managers in nonpublic markets that are characterized by incomplete information and illiquidity. This is where Yale's staff expends its energy.

Fourth, at our lunch, Swensen mentioned that he is convinced Yale should use outside managers for all but the most routine or indexed investments. The staff prides itself on knowing its investment managers extremely well. Finally, Swensen in particular has always focused on the explicit and implicit incentives facing outside managers. He believes most asset management firms are organized for the primary purpose of growing assets rather than delivering investment performance. He is particularly disinclined to use investment management firms associated with investment banks and mutual funds because of the potential conflicts. He wants his investment firms to be owned and managed by the people who are doing the actual investing, not by businesspeople, who, he says, invariably care about growing assets under management, not about fostering a culture that creates excellence and performance. Businesspeople eventually wreck investment management firms.

David doesn't believe that the lows of this bear market have been made. He thinks the principal asset classes, ranging from domestic marketable securities (both equity and fixed income) to private equity, are still overvalued, that the public hasn't learned its lesson, and that the returns from stocks and bonds, particularly in the United States, will be paltry over the next 5 to 10 years. As a result, Yale's allocation to domestic marketable securities has fallen from more than 75% in 1984 to 22.5% today. By contrast, the average U.S. educational institution has 54.3%. Instead, Yale uses diversifying asset classes like absolute-return-oriented hedge funds, capable of grinding out consistent 8% to 9% returns. Timberland and emerging market equities are the asset classes he is emphasizing now. He is convinced that alternative assets, by their very nature, tend to be less efficiently priced, providing an opportunity for active management.

The official results aren't in for the year ending June 2005, but Swensen indicates they will be around 20%. Over the 10 years that ended June 30, 2004, the Yale Endowment compounded at 16.8% per annum, which works out to be about 13% *real*. Over the past 20 years, the compound return has been 16.1%, which means that the value of the endowment has increased more than tenfold. Swensen is very doubtful that the next decade will be as bountiful. His current asset allocation and asset class return expectations solve for a real return of 6.2% per annum, with a risk or volatility of 11.1%. The present asset allocation emphasizes alternative asset classes, which tend to have much wider return dispersions between managers. Thus, he is hopeful that good manager selection will enable Yale to achieve a better real return than the 6%. In his annual reports and speeches, he preaches reversion to the mean, and emphasizes that the endowment's recent returns are unsustainable. There are 20 people including secretaries in the Yale Endowment office, and Yale has about 100 outside managers.

For me the travails and triumphs of the Yale endowment vividly demonstrate how hard it is to structure an investment organization that can adapt to the ebb and flow of investment talent over even a couple of generations, much less centuries. The message I derive is that the main individual (or perhaps individuals) who run the portfolio is the absolutely crucial choice. A committee can't do it. A committee can be instrumental in picking the individual, and hopefully it will make a wise choice, but it can't get involved in actually managing the asset allocation of the portfolio. Their consensus wisdom is bound to be wrong. How you identify another David Swensen is beyond me.

CHAPTER
TWELVE

Nature's Mysticism
and Groupthink Stinks

In a weak moment, I agreed to see a guy who has a very expensive technical market service. Let's call him Maine, because that's where he lives. One of our big investors has been imploring me to listen to this technician, who is heavily into the Fibonacci numbers. The investor sent me Maine's weekly letters for October 14, 2002, and March 8, 2003. Using the Fibonacci numbers, lo and behold, Maine did call the market bottoms both times.

Basically, I believe that technical analysis is a tool best used in conjunction with fundamental research. I look at charts all the time, but I use them as though they were roadmaps of where an asset price has been. I think support and resistance levels are worth considering in timing a purchase or a sale because so many other people pay attention to them. Because a lot of investors, some of whom are just too lazy to do the fundamental work, do believe in the predictive value of technical analysis, even someone like me, who thinks they're non-sense, has to be at least aware of technical patterns, because they affect behavior and prices.

The Fibonacci numbers are a different matter. It's hard not to be intrigued with them. I don't believe in the occult or the supernatural, but there are forces in nature and life that are far beyond our understanding, our ken. There is the stock market, for example, a dark, mysterious beast that reflects not just economic and business fundamentals but the most basic human emotions of greed and fear. Another is the Fibonacci numbers. Many casual investors don't know about the Fibonacci numbers, and maybe they should.

Nicolas Fibonacci was born in Italy in 1175. He was obsessed with numbers and must have been a mathematical genius. In 1202 he published a book, *Liber Abaci*, which introduced Arabic numerals to Europe, and in it he wrote of his discovery of a series of mystical numerical patterns that had their basis in the nature of the construction of the universe. He began by posing a question:

> *Someone placed a pair of rabbits in a certain place, enclosed on all sides by a wall, to find out how many pairs of rabbits will be born here in the course of one year, it being assumed that every month a pair of rabbits produces another pair, and that rabbits begin to bear young two months after their birth. The answer is 1, 1, 2, 3, 5, 8, 13, 21, 34, 55, 89, 144, 233. The hundredth number in the sequences is 354,224,848,179,261,915,075.*

Fibonacci went on to analyze this series of numbers and found they had many strange and intriguing characteristics. Among them are the following:

- The sum of any two consecutive numbers forms the next number in the sequence.
- The ratio of each number (after the first four) to the second below it is always 261.8 to 100, and the ratio to the next below is 161.8.
- Each number divided into the second above it goes twice with a remainder of the exact number below it.
- The square of a number less the square of the second number below it in the series is always a Fibonacci number.
- The sum of the squares of any consecutive series of numbers from 1 will always equal the last in the series chosen times the next higher number.

The most cosmic discovery was that if you divide a Fibonacci number (after the first four) by the next higher number, you will always find that it is approximately .618 times as large as the number that follows (the higher the number in the series, the closer it is to .618). And .618 is the magic number. The so-called *golden proportion* of .618 to 1 is the mathematical equation for perfect beauty. It is the mathematical basis for the shape of the Parthenon, sunflowers, snail shells, Greek vases, the great spiral galaxies of outer space, and playing cards. It is the most pleasing shape in the universe to the human eye, whether in rectangular or in spiral form.

The golden proportion or *phi*, the so-called *logarithmic spiral*, is everywhere and has fascinated humanity for thousands of years. The ancient Egyptians were a highly sophisticated and learned society of astronomers and mathematicians, but as mystics they were also comfortable with concepts of infinite time and space and the afterlife. The enduring monument of their civilization is the Great Pyramid of Gizeh, whose majestic design was planned both inside and out with golden proportions. It has an elevation to its base of 61.8 percent. The height of the pyramid is the square root of 161.8 times half its base. The Egyptians used inches as their standard of measure, and the height of the Great Pyramid is 5,813 inches (5, 8, and 13 are Fib numbers), and the circumference of a circle inscribing that pyramid is 36,524.2 inches. How could the Egyptians have calculated that the exact length of a year is 365.242 days? All the proportions of the Great Pyramid are consistent with phi, which they viewed as the symbol of the creative function, that is, of reproduction in an endless series. The angle of the famous Ascending Passage in the pyramid is 26 by 18 degrees.

The Greeks also were aware of .618 and called it the *golden mean*. They based much of their art and architecture on its dynamic symmetry and whirling squares that seemed to vibrate with intense energy. They were convinced that the golden mean was so pleasing to the eye because humans could see the image of life in designs that were based on it. They believed the navel was the golden mean of the perfect body, with golden proportions at the neck, eyes, legs, and arms. The secret of the numbers was lost with the fall of Greece, until Fibonacci discovered it again. And in the seventeenth century, Jakob Bernoulli transposed the *golden rectangle* into a *golden spiral*, which he likened to the pattern of nature. Leonardo da Vinci used the golden rectangle (1.618 to 1) to enhance the design of many of his paintings, as described in the recent best seller *The Da Vinci Code*.

Fibonacci numbers, the golden rectangle, and the golden spiral are broadcast throughout nature. *Science* magazine has published several scholarly articles on the subject, showing the numbers in everything from daisy petals and sunflower spirals (55 counterclockwise and 89 clockwise) to phyllotaxis, which is the arrangement of leaves on the stalks of plants. The golden spiral appears in horns, claws, teeth, shells, and even the web of a spider. Bacteria multiply in a Fibonacci sequence, and the examples go on and on, as documented in *Science*. The human body has five extremities, five fingers, and five toes, and in music the octave has 13 keys with 8 white and 5 black. The musical chord that gives the greatest satisfaction is the major sixth, and the note E vibrates at a ratio of .625 to the note C. The ear itself is a golden spiral.

There are no really good explanations of why the Fibonacci sequence exists. One response is that God is a mathematician; others say it is pure coincidence and the humbug of fevered minds. Some scientists argue that the Fibonacci sequence and the golden spiral are so widespread that they must be part of some recurring growth pattern. Others speculate that it is nature's way of building quantity without sacrificing beauty, whatever that means.

As you would expect, attempts have been made to apply Fibonacci to the stock market, most notably by R.N. Elliott in the early 1930s. He argued that the growth and decay pattern of humankind's path through history is not random but a supercycle of three steps forward, two steps back. He also maintained that this sequence was mirrored with exquisite precision by the stock market's ebb and flows. In the 1960s, Hamilton Bolton, the editor of the *Bank Credit Analyst*, wrote extensively on the Elliott wave theory; Bob Prechter, who writes a market letter, is another prominent disciple. Using Elliott wave theory analysis, Prechter correctly forecast the bull market of the early 1980s and identified 1987 as a pivotal year. Markets obligingly crashed in 1987, and Prechter became an investment diety with a huge following. In 1990 he wrote a book about impending tidal waves, doom, and gloom, and as far as I know he has been bearish ever since. Supposedly, his problem has been that he got the supercycle wave count wrong.

In Japan, during the latter stages of that great bull market, Morgan Stanley had a market strategist who relied on an old Osaka rice trader's timing strategy that was essentially a version of the Fib numbers. Like so many other systems, it worked well retrospectively but failed in real time. The guy was one wave too late and got drowned when the Japanese market collapsed in 1990. The trick with the Fibonacci numbers and the stock market has always been in getting the starting point and the wave count right. There are waves within waves, so many Fibonacci disciples try to market themselves as short-term timers. I am skeptical. The record of the Fibonacci–Elliott wave counters is not good, and I think they can get you into serious trouble with their dogma.

FIBONACCI NUMBERS ARE POWERFUL— BUT TOO MYSTERIOUS FOR ANALYZING MARKETS

Thus, with some unhappiness I met with the Fibonacci guy from Maine. He was young, clean-cut, enthusiastic, and incredibly sincere. Obviously, he passionately believed. "God must be a mathematician," he told me as he unfolded from a plastic tube a long chart that was the length of our conference table. Entitled *Fibonacci Durations in Years at Supercycle Degree*, it showed the U.S. stock market back to 1789, heavily annotated with thin blue lines and delicate, handwritten notations. He then launched breathlessly into his spiel, arguing that, based on the Fibonacci numbers, the fourth wave of a giant, once-in-a-millennium supercycle ran from 1966 to 1982. It was then followed by a fifth wave that ended in the spring of 2000. He believes we are now in a three-wave "killer" down cycle, although he admits there is disagreement among the other disciples as to exactly where we are in the wave count. The current interim "minuette" [sic] wave we are in counts to 1052 on the S&P 500. Maine passionately believes the next killer down wave bottoms at 650 (.618 of 1,050).

Maine also is not shy about using the Fib numbers to time the market short term. He can count corrections and rallies on a week-to-week basis. A number of other technicians also use the Fib numbers, but often each comes to completely different conclusions. It all depends on where they start counting from. Counting is also a convenient excuse. If a Fib technician is wrong, he blames it on not getting the count right. Fib isn't broke, and he, the technician, will get it right next time, so you should keep using him.

I tried to be polite. The guy was so sincere, such a true believer, but I could tell that he sensed my disdain. He was hurt, but then I was just another skeptical old barbarian who eventually would be carried out. What do I think? I don't think God is either a *mathematician* or a *technician*. He is inscrutable, and the stock market is inscrutable. The creed of the Fibonacci numbers is powerful and mysterious, but I am doubtful that anyone has ever been able to effectively and consistently apply them to the stock market.

In the end, my reaction is that all this Fibonacci, supercycle theory is too long term to be of much use to us day-to-day investors. It's interesting stuff and good cocktail party conversation, but don't bet your portfolio on it. Nevertheless, human nature doesn't change, history tends to repeat itself, and the stock market is all about human nature, so keep an open mind as events unfold.

The idea of long cycles in human economic history goes back to biblical times. The Old Testament tells of 50-year jubilees, in which slaves were freed and debts were forgiven. Gibbons's *Decline and Fall of the Roman Empire* gives evidence of a 50-year cycle of war and inflation, and a 54-year cycle can be found in the history of agricultural prices going as far back as the Mayans in Central America in 1260. Even primitive economies seemed to become overextended in a regular, more or less half-century cycle. Wealth in land, slaves, and debt would be concentrated, and a purge, a depression to rebalance and revitalize, was almost part of the order of nature.

All investors by nature are conditioned by their memories. If they have only been investing for a short period of time and don't have a lot of combat experience, they are particularly vulnerable to what has just happened to them. It is very important not to fall into the attractive trap of extrapolating the most recent past into the future. If you do, it is like steering a sports car up a mountain road, with a steep drop on one side, by peering through the rear-view mirror.

ADAM SMITH HAD IT FIGURED OUT

One of the great books about investing is Adam Smith's *The Money Game*, which was published in 1967, which was another time when stocks were rising after a bear market that had grievously wounded many investors. One of Adam Smith's protagonists is the Great Winfield, who runs a high-performance mutual fund. He is the epitome of the gunslinger of that era, jaded, cynical, but perceptive.

> *The time is the late 1960s, and the prices of story stocks like conglomerates and computer leasing companies are going to the moon. But the Great Winfield can't bring himself to buy junk stories, and his performance is lagging. You see, the Great Winfield was badly, in fact almost fatally, wounded, destroyed in the tech bear market of the early 1960s when the story stocks collapsed. He remembers too well that terrible day "when the orchestra stopped playing" and the wind rattled through the broken windowpanes of his portfolio. The memory, the anticipation of this utterly inevitable moment, freezes him. As a result, he can't bring himself to buy tech stocks because of his past, even though he senses for now tech is the place to be.*
>
> *So the Great Winfield finds a solution by hiring three twenty-nine-year-old kids "for the duration." "Kids," he says, "this is a kids' market." The kids have no accumulated investment baggage, and they believe in and buy garbage stories as though they were new and forever. "The strength of my kids is that they are too young to remember anything bad, and they are making so much money they feel invincible," says the Great Winfield.*

He names them Billy the Kid, Johnny the Kid, and Sheldon the Kid, and when Adam Smith visits the Great Winfield's office, they enthusiastically tell him about the computer leasing, shale oil, and conglomerates they own. They call the Great Winfield "sir" and come to attention when addressed. "Aren't they cute?" says the Great Winfield proudly. "Aren't they fuzzy? Look at them, like teddy bears. It's their market!" He orders them to tell the computer-leasing concept story.

"Computer-leasing stocks, sir," said Sheldon the Kid, like a West Point plebe being quizzed by an upperclassman. "I buy the convertibles, bank them, and buy some more. The need for computers is practically infinite, sir."

The Great Winfield beams with pride. "See? See? The flow of the seasons: Life begins again. It's marvelous! It's like having a son! My boys! My kids!" He then berates Adam Smith as a "middle-aged fogey" and says, "Look at the skepticism on the face of this dirty, old man."

The opposite of this is happening today. The kids, the golden children of the late 1990s, were the true believers in tech, and they were so devastated when the bubble burst, that now they can't pull the trigger on tech. They are paralyzed, emasculated, traumatized by what happened to them. But there will be times in the next few years when tech will be the place to be, because orders and earnings will be much better than expected. So instead of a kid, you may have to get an old man— like me.

GROUPTHINK = GROUPSTINK AND SOLOTHINK: INVESTOR MEETINGS NEED A LITTLE AGITATION AND CONTENTION

Recently as a favor to a friend I attended an investment committee meeting at a big foundation. It is almost always frustrating to observe such a meeting because with the best of intentions they are implementing wrong judgments about equity ratios, the role of alternative asset classes, spending levels, and manager hiring and firing. Groups of highly intelligent, sincere people are reaching bad decisions that reflect the easy, prevailing current consensus of what has worked recently, despite compelling evidence that there is a mean to revert to.

The most important investment judgments at most big institutions and for most large portfolios are made by committees, but few realize the negative dynamics of group interaction. I think that, in most instances, groups of intelligent people have so many inherent liabilities that a lone individual has a far better chance of making good decisions. The collective intelligence of the group is surely less than the sum of its parts, and the more people on a committee, the less chance it has to be wise and crisp in its decision making. It's a throwaway line, but Nietzsche was onto something when he said madness was the exception in individuals but the rule in crowds.

Groupthink (or maybe it should be called *groupstink*) is the disease that plagues every committee, and most don't even know it. In fact, most inadvertently luxuriate in it. The more compatible the group, the more its members respect and like each other. The bigger the committee and the more important a place in the group becomes, the likelier it is to make bad decisions. Years ago Irving Janis, a Yale psychologist, wrote a wonderful little book called *Groupthink*, which compellingly highlights its dangers. It is full of fascinating case studies of the phenomenon, but the book never sold and is now out of print.

Janis describes groupthink as "a mode of thinking that people engage in when they are deeply involved in a cohesive in-group, when the members' striving for unanimity overrides their motivation to realistically appraise alternatives . . . a marked distortion in information processing, reality testing, and mental efficiency that result from in-group pressures." He is not talking about a noncohesive, politically oriented group or a leader/dictator-manipulated group. Groupthink occurs even when the leader does not try to hear only what he or she wants to hear but sincerely asks for opinions. It happens even when the group members are intelligent, motivated, and are not sycophants afraid to speak their minds.

Investment teams and committees, when they disagree about the proper course of action, can become paralyzed by respect and politeness. This happens most often when the groups are compatible and there is no overriding leader. They discuss the alternatives and then do nothing. I have been on small investment teams where this happens. Controversy, passionate disagreement, and even anger are healthy.

The more the group socializes, and the more important a place in the group becomes, the likelier it is you will see groupthink. Individual members are unwilling to risk ostracism or excommunication by expressing dissent, because remaining a member means so much. Another point is that as more spectators attend a meeting, the less uninhibited discussion and decision making is likely to be. Janis cites as classic examples "the best and the brightest" advisers to presidents Kennedy and Johnson who stumbled into catastrophically bad decisions about Cuba and Vietnam.

In his classic *Instincts of the Herd in War and Peace*, Wilfred Trotter argues that men and women are gregarious or "herding" animals. The cardinal qualities of the herd are homogeneity and conformity. Society teaches us from childhood that it pays to be part of the group and not be too different. Trotter points out "the fearful repressing force which society has always exercised on new forms of opinion and how constantly the dungeon, the scaffold, and the cross have been the reward of the contrarian." If you are on an investment committee, unfortunately it appears it is almost better to be wrong with the group than to express a contrary view, even if it is right, because if, by any chance, you are both wrong and a dissident, you are finished as a functioning member of the committee. And if you are right, many will conveniently forget.

Although there are some *groupthink* countermeasures, the only real defense against this intellectual cancer is awareness. Without going into a lot of detail, here are some manifestations of the disease from Janis (the parenthetic comments are mine):

- *Collective rationalizations of shared illusions generally believed.* (It's just another correction in a bull market.)
- *Crude, negative stereotypes of out-groups.* (The bears are a bunch of losers and idiots. Valuation models are for impractical academics.)
- *Shared belief in the group's inherent morality.* (Applies more to government and corporate policy decision making.)
- *Illusions of invulnerability to a risky course of action.* (We've hung in there before when things looked bad, and it's worked. No guts, no glory. Combat units and athletic teams may benefit from shared illusions about power and luck; policy-making committees do not.)
- *Illusions of unanimity and suppression of personal doubts.* (Everyone else on the committee thinks it's just a correction, so I must be wrong to be worried, and besides, if I spoke up, they'd think I had no guts.)
- *Subtle group pressure on dissenters.* (I used to think Joe was a good, smart investor, but now it looks like he's losing his nerve.)
- *Self-appointed* mindguards *who protect the group from thoughts that might damage their confidence.* (There is no point in listening to that crazy bear technician.)
- *Docility fostered by charismatic, previously successful leadership.* (The Bay of Pigs decision was a classic example: The group believed John F. Kennedy was a born winner, and he managed the meetings to encourage this viewpoint.)
- *Free-floating conversation in group meetings.* (This is a sign of a disorganized decision-making process and is characterized by general, unstructured discussion of issues.)
- *Lack of standard risk analysis using methodical procedures.* (The group should have some kind of formal risk model and pay attention to it.)

Janis argues that the group leader must establish an atmosphere in meetings that fosters "intellectual suspicion amidst personal trust," which is easier said than done. Members must feel confident of their acceptance in the group and be sure that their standing and compensation won't be jeopardized by critical or contrary arguments. The leader, he says, must be impartial, encourage debate, and praise critical evaluators who disagree with him or her. Sometimes, the leader should let the group meet by itself to foster freer talk. At every meeting, at least one member should be assigned to play the devil's advocate to challenge the consensus. After reaching a preliminary decision, there should be a second-chance meeting at which members are expected to express their residual doubts and the group has the chance to rethink its decision.

Harmonious, happy meetings may be a warning of groupthink and complacency, whereas agitation, passionate arguments, and some stress are good signs. Some of the most successful investment management firms have contentious, agitated meetings, but the committee members are secure in their standing as investors and with each other. Janis says members of the group should be encouraged to periodically discuss the process of deliberations with trusted associates outside the group and report their reactions. This a remedy for groupthink that to me seems a little far-fetched and impractical.

In a big investment management firm that has to function through an investment policy committee, I think the chances for good decisions are best with a leader who meets regularly but informally with a small group of trusted advisers (I think three to five is the right number). The small group chews over the issues and the leader may poll it, but, in the end, the leader makes the decisions and is responsible. A large group that votes democratically sounds good because it encourages participation, but in investing, democracies don't work. In fact, they invariably fail. Decision making and responsibility has to be located in an individual.

Janis is more bureaucratic, and if you must labor in a big investment management organization, what he has to say makes sense. He maintains that the core decision-making group should include people with varying tenures, social backgrounds, and beliefs. If possible, a few contentious, contrary, even slightly obnoxious members who are nonetheless respected and secure, should be included. Everyone in the group should have a stake in the outcome of the decisions. Neither clients nor internal spectators should attend, although this will cause unhappiness. At Traxis, the three of us are certainly from different backgrounds, but, although we may be contentious, we don't have an obnoxious member (as far as I know). We certainly have a stake in the outcome of the decisions. Each of us has specific position responsibilities that we are held accountable for by the other two.

Organizations like foundations and endowments, which must operate through investment committees, should try very hard to get a strong, experienced chairperson. They should also keep the investment committee small and make sure that only experienced, involved people are members. Meetings should have time limits, so decisions have to be reached without interminable soliloquies. Many foundations do almost everything wrong. They have a weak chairman, rambling meetings, large committees that have sloppy attendance, operate on hearsay, and vote on decisions. These flaws were not seriously debilitating during the run of the great bull market, but in the years to come, when there is no one-way bull market in bonds or stocks, effective decision making may matter much more. Just remember, search the parks in the world's cities; there are no statues to committees.

BUT *SOLOTHINK* IS DANGEROUS, TOO

Solothink where one very strong, very successful individual dominates the investment decision making can be just as dangerous as groupthink. Solothink can easily become authoritarian and tyrannical. A firm is particularly vulnerable to solothink when the predominate investor is also the rainmaker and the boss, but even committees can be dominated by a strong individual who others are reluctant to challenge. The people who have built the big hedge-fund empires have always been domineering, self-confident, blood-and-biceps personalities. Julian Robertson, George Soros, and Louis Bacon didn't get very rich by lacking self-confidence and being lazy or wrong. It was Jimmy Hoffa who modestly said, "I may have my faults, but being wrong ain't one of them."

As business organizations, investment management firms and hedge funds are particularly vulnerable to solothink, because a run of poor performance quickly affects assets and revenues and can bring to the surface all the detritus of human interpersonal relationships. As long as the investment messiah can keep walking on water, everything is fine, but if the messiah loses his touch, performance is so measurable that he can lose his halo very quickly. Recently, a young analyst I know was telling me what happened at Circuits, a big tech hedge fund that was created and built by Sid. Sid is very bright, opinionated, confident, and hardworking. In the 1990s he put up big numbers in the glory years, and in 2001 he reacted quickly, went short tech, and avoided the worst of the carnage. However, he has stayed bearish, arguing that tech is still expensive and that there is no new product cycle. As a result, Circuits' performance is limited to the fourth quartile when half the firm's assets have left.

The young analyst (who has now departed) says that Sid suppressed dissent at the weekly portfolio managers meeting. He told me: "There are four matrixes at Circuits. You agree with Sid, good; you agree with Sid and make money, great; you disagree with Sid and make money, maybe not so good; you disagree and lose money, you're fired." Apparently, at the meetings in 2003, no one really challenged Sid on his pessimism on the fundamentals or on his bearish market view. He was such a strong personality, it was his firm, the portfolio managers were so in awe of him, and his record had been so impressive that dissent was quashed. In fact, the participants had a tendency to echo whatever Sid's bearish views were. If you didn't, you were a heretic and risked excommunication.

So the meetings at Circuits were not groupthink, but solothink, which, to my way of thinking, is always fragile and dangerous, just as dictatorships are. As long as the dictator is benevolent and right, it's efficient and works fine. Some people would argue that even if it's not ideal, who would you rather have making the decisions? The guy who has made a fortune over the years or a group of unproven young people? However, it does sound to me as though Sid can be faulted for not being open-minded and for creating an atmosphere where his cohorts are afraid to disagree with him. That's totally counterproductive and quickly will destroy an investment team. It's a very bad sign when the group leader talks all the time and lectures the group on his opinions while everyone else sits there mute. The original thinkers, the best investors, will exit the firm leaving only sycophants. Sid should clearly have done less dominating and talking and more listening.

THERE IS NO SUCH THING AS A COLLECTIVE BRAIN

Speaking of groupstink and of how rooms full of smart people usually get it wrong, *The Economist* had a piece in its 2003 year-end issue about a dinner the magazine sponsors at the Federal Reserve's annual symposium in Jackson Hole. This is the most prestigious gathering of economists in the world, and it is a prized invitation that goes only to the cream of the economist crop. Alan Greenspan and the chairmen of most of the major central banks in the world are there to give arcane speeches and hobnob with each other.

The story relates wryly how each year the editors of *The Economist* host a dinner to which they invite the conference's elite, otherwise known as The Jackson Hole Gang. A poll is conducted. (The results confirm my belief that rooms full of smart people are self-reinforcing and come to wrong conclusions. Thus they are powerful contrary indicators.) At the peak of the stock market boom, the Jackson Hole Gang is asked, "Is this a bubble?" They confidently vote no. In August 2000 they rule out a recession in the United States, and in 2002 they predict that short-term interest rates will not fall to 1 percent. In August of 2003 with the euro at $1.10, they are asked, "Will the dollar fall to $1.25 against the euro anytime in the next year?" They respond with another resounding no! with only one dissenter. Four months later the dollar falls to $1.26 and then in 2004 to $1.37. The point is that a consensus of the best and the brightest is usually wrong.

As for me, I think there is a strong case to be made for running money solo, totally by yourself, with full and total responsibility for a specific hunk of capital. The downside is that there is heavy emotional stress and loneliness in doing it this way, but ultimately making decisions is an individual act. In certain cases, where the chemistry is right, two individuals can function as one. One and one can make three. My experience is that more than two becomes cumbersome, and gridlock can result. In *The Fountainhead* Ayn Rand wrote:

> . . . the mind is an attribute of the individual. There is no such thing as a collective brain. . . . An agreement reached by a group of men is only a compromise or an average drawn upon many individual thoughts. . . . The primary act—the process of reason—must be performed by each man alone. . . . This creative faculty cannot be given or received, shared or borrowed. It belongs to single, individual men.

Some hedge funds with three or more principals divide their capital into separate portfolios and then keep score. This system can work very well, as long as there is total trust and confidence between the principals. The decision-making principals should meet daily and discuss their positions and share thoughts. This modus operandi can be very synergistic, as long as the atmosphere does not become competitive or antagonistic about performance. Everyone in the firm has to be oriented for total firm, not individual, performance. The firm's analysts should not even know the segments' performance differentials.

There should be an understanding among the partners that, if partner A is a laggard for a long spell and another partner C is the best performer, C's capital is reduced and A's is increased. It's the old reversion to the mean and cold theory. Of course, it has to be implicitly understood that if A underperforms for a very long period, an agonizing reappraisal of A's role in the firm has to take place. I don't think this system will work if the partners' interests in the firm are reallocated each year based on each individual's performance. Firms that have done it this way argue it's cleaner and purer. From what I've seen, it usually eventually results in a splintering of the partnership.

In the end, I believe a cohesive team is always stronger and more enduring than a single individual, no matter how brilliant. No one is always right. Of course, a lot depends on who the people are you are working with and what their level of commitment is. Obviously, an investment committee that meets six times a year can't be organized to operate the same way a hedge fund is. However, in general, all investment organizations work best when they are relatively small, and when the principals like and trust each other. If you don't have affection and trust, the best-organized firm will never realize its potential. Decision making is the most important part of the investment process. Groupthink and solothink are elements to consider when organizing a group for effective decision making. It's not easy.

CHAPTER
THIRTEEN

The Internet Bubble
I'd Still Rather Have Air-Conditioning

This is a self-serving chapter about the tech bubble and me. I took a lot of grief in late 1999 and spring 2000 because I became bearish on technology stocks too early. In December 1999, I went to a 15% weighting in technology, which was then less than half of its weight in the S&P 500 and the EAFE index. This was a good move *eventually*, but not as technology stocks soared in the excitement about the Year 2000 effect and as the tech bubble got even bigger in the first six months of 2000.

It was a very painful spring. You couldn't be half the index weight in the biggest sector that was going up the fastest and expect to keep up with the indexes, much less the pack. Some of my clients became upset as their portfolios lagged, and I was subjected to considerable abuse. Some of it was well-meaning advice. A Japanese friend told me of an old and famous Japanese proverb about manias. It goes, "Only fools are dancing, but the bigger fools are watching." Someone else unkindly quoted Nietzsche: "And those who were seen dancing were thought to be insane by those who could not hear the music." Those pithy sayings made me feel like an idiot for not participating at the Great Tech Ball. The young, swaggering tech types at the office rolled their eyes.

What really got me negative about tech back then was a gala conference I went to in late August 1999 in a fancy western town. The conference was sponsored by a prestigious Washington think tank, and the attendees were mostly the West Coast technology and Internet glitterati and other assorted elites. There also were a fair number of technology investment bankers present, and a famous professor from M.I.T. who had just written a best-selling book about the innovator's dilemma.

That summer, tech stocks were on a rocket trip to the moon, and the technology entrepreneurs at the conference were real dudes. Frank Quattrone and Mary Meeker were their heroes. Mary actually cautioned the crowd that things were getting crazy, but the herd thought she was kidding. As executives and entrepreneurs, they oozed optimism and confidence. Their chatter was all about sustaining and disruptive technologies, growth trajectories, Gulfstreams (it's an airplane), and units. In case you don't know, a unit is $100 million of net worth, so a guy would say, "Yeah, he's worth five units." One thing you could say for them was that they totally believed their own BS.

I found the sociology of the wives in attendance interesting, too. They attended the meetings, took notes, and wore designer blue jeans and high heels. They didn't talk about children or nannies like the normal Greenwich young and beautiful; instead, they swapped gossip about stocks. At the cocktail parties, they babbled endlessly about the size of the IPO allocations they were getting and bragged loudly to each other or to anyone else who would listen about the huge profits they were making trading Internet stocks.

JIM GLASSMAN'S DOW 36,000: INFLAMMATORY FOOLISHNESS

As part of the program, one night after dinner, I debated a guy named Jim Glassman, who, at the time, was stridently maintaining in print and on TV that the Dow was worth 36,000—not five years out, but right then. I got slaughtered in the debate. The crowd embraced Glassman and his theory and all but carried him off in a sedan chair. I said tech and the Internet stocks were a mania like tulips in 1650, and that, when investors began to realize that the emperor had no clothes, there would be a panic. The crowd thought I was either crazy or senile. When I spoke of equity markets that had run too far, extreme overvaluation in tech stocks, risk, and how all bubbles eventually burst, they looked at me incredulously. They wondered why I didn't grasp that technology in general and the Internet in particular had created a new economy in which the old rules no longer applied. Reversion to the mean was a concept for the History Channel. Two and two did not make four; with technology, two and two could make five or six or ten. At the end of my comments, I quoted what Bernard Baruch had written in 1931 as the introduction of a reprint of Charles Mackay's great classic, *Extraordinary Popular Delusions and the Madness of Crowds.*

> *Although there be no scientific cure, yet, as in all primitive, unknown (and therefore diabolic) spells, there may be potent incantations. I have always thought that if, in the lamentable era of the "New Economics," culminating in 1929, even in the very presence of dizzily spiraling prices, we had all continuously repeated "two and two still make four," much of the evil might have been averted. Similarly, even in the general moment of gloom in which this is written, when many begin to wonder if declines will never halt, the appropriate abracadabra may be: "They always did."*

The famous West-Coast tech investment banker in whose mammoth mansion the dinner party was being given, who was sitting next to my wife, told her in a kindly, sympathetic way that I had lost it. He hoped I would come to my senses before it was too late. The Glassman vision was the future. Incidentally, three years later, with his firm faltering, he had to auction his art collection.

Who is Jim Glassman? He and Kevin Hassett wrote a long article that was the cover story in the June 1999 issue of the *Atlantic Monthly,* entitled simply "Dow 36,000." There was not even the decency of a question mark. A book from Random House followed with the modest title *Dow 36,000: The New Strategy for Profiting from the Coming Rise in the Stock Market.* It became a best seller, and Glassman went on the lecture circuit for big money.

Actually, Glassman and Hassett are considered to be serious academics, which made them even more dangerous. As the *Atlantic* cover put it, "They bring an extraordinary amount of expertise to their investigation." Both are scholars at the American Enterprise Institute, a highly respected, conservative think tank. Hassett has been a professor at the Columbia University Business School and a senior economist for the Fed. Glassman is an engaging man who clearly believed (at least at that time) what he preached. He has been a syndicated columnist for the *Washington Post*, and host of CNN's *Capital Gang*. Glassman and Hassett were not charlatans, but they should have been (and should be) ashamed of themselves, because what they were arguing was so patently ridiculous. They provided academic respectability to the bubble when they should have known better. To this day, they remain at large in the press, and the world seems to have forgotten their previous inflammatory foolishness. It seems as though the longer a bubble lasts and the bigger it gets, the larger, the more respected the intellects that are sucked into it. But that's still no excuse!

Maybe I shouldn't be so hard on them. The historian Charles Kindelberger relates how the chronicle of manias and panics is full of cases of rational men who sensed an engulfing madness, sold out, and then were sucked back in and ruined by the speculative atmosphere. The great Master of the Mint and the epitome of the rational scientist, Isaac Newton, said, in the spring of 1720, in the midst of the South Sea Company bubble, "I can calculate the motions of the heavenly bodies but not the madness of people" and sold his shares in the South Sea Company at a solid 100% profit. However, as the stock continued to climb, the infectious speculative enthusiasm overcame him, he bought back at a much higher price even more stock, and was wiped out in the crash. So bitter was his loss that for the rest of his life he could never bear to hear the name South Sea Company.

The Glassman-Hassett thesis at the time was that U.S. stocks were not overvalued but instead were currently "in the midst of a one-time-only rise to much higher ground, to the neighborhood of 36,000 for the Dow Jones Industrial Average. After they complete[d] this historic ascent, owning them [would] still be profitable, but the returns [would] decline." In our debate, however, Glassman said he thought that because of the technology and Internet revolutions, even from that new elevated point of 36,000 on the Dow Jones Industrial Average, equity returns in the years to come would still be higher than the 10% per annum rate realized over the past century. It was a new era. Glassman and Hasslet, serious academics, were proclaiming that, despite the huge advance that had already occurred in equities, fair value for the Dow was three times its level at that time, or 36,000. Unbelievable! but it was believed!

Glassman went on to argue that investors "have begun to realize—especially during the past four years—that stocks are not particularly volatile." As a result, he said, the risk premium, which had averaged about 7% in recent history, had fallen to about 3%. He believed it was headed to a proper level of zero, which means stocks should rise accordingly. Glassman-Hassett's exhortation to the U.S. public was in essence that, historically, stocks have outperformed bonds and, therefore, you should own them. Forget bonds! Stocks as an asset class should sell at a valuation that provides the same return as bonds, they asserted, which happens to be roughly 100 times earnings, because over the long run, they insisted, equities are as safe as short- or long-term government paper.

Traditional valuation methods had predicted trouble throughout the last years of the bull market and had been wrong, Glassman emphasized, and, therefore, his methodology was better. The professionals, particularly the older ones (like me, he gently implied, to laughter) with their slavish adherence to outdated valuation methods, have been too bearish. (Alan Greenspan spoke of "irrational exuberance" in 1996, but the public has been right to be "rationally exuberant." The people instinctively understand that the risks of investing in stocks, "never so great as imagined, really have declined.")

THE CROWD HOOTED

My reply to Glassman was that although it is true that, over very long periods, equities have delivered vastly superior returns to bonds or cash, it is also a fact that for short periods of 5, 10, or even 15 years, stocks have underperformed dramatically. If you need the money in the meantime, it can be very painful. It took 15 years for stocks to regain their 1929 highs, and 21 years to outperform bonds. The Dow Jones Average was at the same level in 1982 as it had been in 1965 and had lost more than half its purchasing power. Returns depend a lot on when you invest. As for volatility, to suggest that stocks are no more volatile than bonds in the long run is simply not true. As Keynes said, "In the long run, we are all dead."

In fact, since 1926, the annualized volatility of stocks is about 20%, versus 8% for bonds and 1% for cash. The only way to ignore this volatility is to lock up your money for 30 years and make yourself very illiquid. If you change your mind and want or need to sell after 10 years, you will suffer from the high volatility. Obviously, you should demand a risk premium for that illiquidity or for stomaching the volatility.

Supporting the case for a risk premium, I continued, is the fact that stocks are obviously less secure than corporate bonds, not to mention government bonds, because they are a junior and levered claim on a company's assets and earnings. Equity holders get paid only if there is money left after the bondholders get paid, and they, therefore, require a risk premium. To assume a zero premium is to ignore the fact that corporate bonds do default (unlike the U.S. Treasury). Discounting uncertain and cyclical corporate cash flows at a risk-free rate just does not make sense.

During our debate, Jim Glassman said that it was different this time and emphasized the power of the new era in which "fresh, unfettered thinking and new rules apply." However, it absolutely overwhelmed my imagination that the new world could be so different that fair value for U.S. stocks would be 100 times earnings when, for almost two centuries as a young country exploded with fantastic progress and growth, the multiple of the S&P 500 had averaged 14 times. At one point Glassman conceded that the real earnings of the S&P 500 have only compounded at 3.5% per annum, but that didn't trouble him. It didn't seem to trouble anyone else in the crowd, either.

Yet the human emotions of fear and greed that drive the stock market to excesses, I argued, have not changed over the course of human history and remain as valid today as in the past. Busts are busts, booms are still booms, and bubbles always burst, but this was boring stuff, and the crowd stirred restlessly. The glitterati understandably had no interest in hearing about busts or bursting bubbles. On to the next IPO and salacious stock idea.

Glassman ended his talk by saying that the Internet was the most important invention since the printing press. He asked if I agreed. I said no. The Internet was a breakthrough technology, but there had been other inventions in the past hundred years that were at least as important.

"Like what?" he asked incredulously.

"Like electricity, the airplane, the telephone, the computer . . . even air-conditioning," I added, perhaps unwisely.

The crowd hooted. He challenged me on the air-conditioning point, so, feeling a little cornered, I went on to say that air-conditioning had hugely transformed for the better the working and living conditions of hundreds of millions of people around the world. After all, without air-conditioning the hot cities of the world would have remained uninhabitable in high-rise form. There would be no Houston, Miami, Hong Kong, or Singapore. The Southeast and Southwest would still be hot, humid backwaters. Without air-conditioning, New York would be a sweatshop in the summer and fall. Air-conditioning was a transforming invention, just as important as the Internet for our daily lives.

"What would have the most impact on your daily life? No air-conditioning or no Internet?" I asked.

The master of ceremonies, an Internet mogul from San Francisco, gleefully called for a vote on the question: "Was air-conditioning as important an invention as the Internet?" It was a debacle! I lost in a landslide 80 to 2, and one of the two was my wife, who voted for me only out of loyalty. I remember as I sat down how the investment banker from Morgan Stanley at my table regarded me with pity and embarrassment. At another table I heard someone remark, "The world has passed him by."

As it turned out, I was early: Tech stocks and the Dow did rise for another six months. In the grip of a mania, markets always go to unimaginable extremes. However, I recount the exchange at this conference as a benchmark of the time. It shows how manic things became in the frenzy of the bubble, and how allegedly respectable and scholarly academics twisted and stretched analysis to justify the excesses. It's the nature of the beast. There is an old Russian proverb that goes:

Dwell on the past, and you will lose an eye.
Ignore the past, and you will lose both of them.

The Japanese have another proverb that is applicable to the aftermath of the tech debacle: "Fallen blossoms do not return to branches; a broken mirror does not again reflect."

THE NEXT BULL MARKET: AFRICA AND
THE MIDDLE EAST

My guess is that in the next bull market, the hot, concept group that the speculative money flows to, the inheritor of the craziness, the successor to technology that eventually becomes the next big bubble, will be emerging markets equities. Every bull market has its signature sector, and emerging markets could be it next time. In fact, I would argue the movement is already under way, but what has happened so far is just the beginning. The emerging markets have the potential to get as crazy as tech. Remember that they have been through a true secular bear market that really began in 1993 and that included huge declines in their currencies.

I am a lover of emerging markets. Back in the early 1980s, purely by chance and with a big assist from David Fisher of the Capital Group and the World Bank, I stumbled into emerging market investing. When I first went to Thailand as an investor in 1983, the total market capitalization was a few billion dollars, and stocks traded at six to seven times earnings. The great bull market was just beginning in the developed world, and virtually nobody was interested in investing in emerging markets. In the next seven years, with the help of the World Bank, I promoted and then Morgan Stanley underwrote the first New York Stock Exchange–listed closed-end funds for Thailand, Malaysia, India, Africa, Turkey, Russia, and a diversified emerging-markets fund. These funds were very successful for us and their investors because we were early, they had an edge of one type or another granted by the host government, and they went to premiums—for a while. A Pakistan fund that Morgan Stanley underwrote in the ebbing days of the emerging-markets bull run was another story.

The bank robber, Willie Sutton, appearing in court, was asked by the judge why he robbed banks. He replied simply, "Because that's where the money is." I love emerging markets because they are where the money is, which causes me to think of Miles Moreland, the ultimate, heroic emerging-markets investor. Rather than regurgitate all the conventional babble about emerging markets, let me tell you about a man and his firm, Blakeney Management, both of whom are the real thing.

Miles' specialty is investing in Africa and the Middle East, not areas of the world anyone would think of as fertile ground (at least until recently), which probably is exactly why it is fertile ground. In fact, his markets remind me of Thailand and India when I first went there. Miles disdainfully refers to Europe and Japan as the "wheelchair economies," with stagnant, elderly populations, capable only of delivering periodic *cyclical* growth. The youthful economies of the developing world are the places that can produce *secular* growth. His theory is that the undiscovered, truly raw developing countries are those with the greatest growth potential in both their economies and their stock markets.

Incidentally, this is why buying an emerging-markets index fund doesn't work as a way of getting full exposure to the essence of the developing-country concept. By definition, the index itself is capitalization weighted, so it is always skewed toward the developing markets that already *have* been discovered and already *have* gone up, not the disliked, undiscovered basket cases. There is far less risk in this neglected, unloved group than there is in the markets that are loved and have levitated. Miles comments that, when he talks with people, their immediate reaction is that investing in African markets is an investment version of Russian roulette. He tells them it's more like going to Grandma's tea party and even better, if pressed, he can prove that the volatility of the African markets is considerably less than that of the so-called civilized world. Furthermore, the Blakeney African portfolio currently sells at less than nine times earnings, yields more than 5.7%, and its median price to book is 1.3 times.

Miles Moreland is an Englishman who is probably in his mid-50s. He has the horsey, aristocratic good looks and speech of someone who went to Cambridge, as he did. I first knew him when once, long ago, he labored gracefully as an institutional salesman for Morgan Stanley in New York. Rejecting this as an inferior cultural experience, he matriculated to write a charming book about walking across Europe. Subsequently he founded Blakeney Management, an investment company that focuses exclusively on Africa. Miles is a charming, very bright, unconventional man. His firm is located in London, where he lives in a houseboat on the Thames and drives a motorcycle.

Miles' theory is that the African and Middle Eastern emerging markets are the last undiscovered investment frontier, and that, if you know a great deal about what everyone else ignores, you should be able to find some amazing values. In other words, he is addicted to investing in *inefficient* markets. As he likes to point out, the African markets (in which stocks are held for yield, more or less regardless of the earnings outlook) are inherently mispriced and present unusual opportunities. He argues that African companies sell at basket-case valuations because of where they are located, not because they are basket cases.

Among the investors in Blakeney is David Swensen and the Yale Endowment. In his book, *Pioneering Portfolio Management*, Swensen extols the firm as "the essence of an entrepreneurial investment management organization." Miles himself describes Blakeney as "a small group of investment guerrillas that fights and forages in places too small and too risky for people with more to lose." Some years ago, a large firm wanted to buy Blakeney. Swensen quotes a wonderful letter that Miles wrote declining the offer. In it, Miles said that "guerrillas cannot be integrated into the regular army without losing what it is that makes them effective." Swensen went on to say:

> *By selecting investment managers with an entrepreneurial orientation, fiduciaries improve the chances for investment success. Large, multi-product, process-driven financial services entities face the daunting hurdle of overcoming bureaucratic obstacles to creative decision making. Small independent firms with excellent people focused on a well-defined market segment provide the highest likelihood of identifying the intelligent contrarian path necessary to achieving excellent investment results.*

This is a succinct summary of what people with money should be looking for in their investment manager. With all their bureaucratic trappings, like endless meetings, human resources departments, and large marketing organizations, big investment management firms are unlikely to attract and keep many original thinkers and good investors. Because these firms are run by businesspeople, not investors, their primary objective is not investment performance but rather, by hook or by crook,

to increase their assets under management. Their sales forces can sell
only investment products that are hot, what has just done well, not what
will do well. That is why billions of dollars of technology funds were
sold to the naive and unsuspecting public at the top of the tech bubble
in 1999 and 2000.

Blakeney's performance historically has had virtually no correlation to the raucous bourses of the world or even to emerging markets
in general. However, it has correlated with the African and Middle
Eastern markets, and some years have been great and others not so
great. Lately, Blakeney's results have been fabulous! Emerging markets
as an asset class over the past 10 years have had a 76% correlation with
the S&P 500 and 81% with EAFE. Blakeney, by contrast, has correla-
tions of 31% and 46%, respectively. Over the long term, Blakeney has
prospered mightily from investing in companies you have never heard
of, in some highly unlikely places you would never dream of visiting,
much less investing in. But if you are going to give money to Miles,
you have to be patient.

That said, Blakeney in the spring of 2005 is up 28% for the year and
is returning 10% of the money invested with it to its clients. Celtel, a
pan-Africa cell phone company and one of their largest positions, was
purchased by a Kuwaiti company at a big premium, so his accounts are
flush with cash, and Blakeney is finding African stocks popular and no
longer cheap. Miles senses growing enthusiasm about investing in Africa
and in Egypt in particular, a country where the firm has major holdings
and one that has been the best market in the world so far in 2005. For
years, Miles says, the occasional African investment conference has been
populated by salesmen selling to other salesmen and perhaps 20 or so
seedy, old-time investors. The agenda is usually allegedly important men
from the IFC and the local securities regulator, none of whom would
recognize an undervalued stock if it flew in through the window and
perched on their breakfast table.

However, this year he was horrified and frightened when, at the
annual conference, there were hordes of eager young analysts from
U.S. and English institutions. Suddenly stocks in Cairo, Abu Dhabi,
Dubai, and the United Arab Emirates began to spike up. Appalled,
Miles has been reducing his positions until he can find some truly
sleepy places that nobody is interested in. In the most recent Blak-

eney quarterly letter, he explained why he had sold out of the United Arab Emirates:

> *If we were cynical people we would say that the peak in the UAE will coincide either with the IPO for the new $1 billion UAE telecoms company in July or in September with the opening of the much-touted Dubai International Financial Market, a shiny new exchange whose purpose is not immediately obvious: Dubai already has a perfectly good stock market. Still we are not cynics and Dubai is an amazing place; perhaps the market will keep on going up forever. A pity that your money will not be invested in it.*

I suspect Miles is right to pull back from certain of his markets. Fueled by excess liquidity created by higher oil revenues plus some tentative signs of reform and better macroeconomic management, the Middle Eastern and North African markets have boomed to crazy levels. Saudi Arabia, whose stock market is off limits to foreign institutional investors, now has a market capitalization of $450 billion—bigger than India's or China's. Bank stocks sell at 30 times earnings. It's a classic case of a liquidity driven market. But note the difference. His markets are expensive and popular, so Blakeney, a firm run by investors, returns money to their clients. The big American investment management companies, firms run by businesspeople, even as the bubble was on the verge of bursting sold every tech fund it could to the public.

Of course, Miles and his cohorts are sometimes lied to and cheated (as we are in the civilized markets), but Blakeney is a true strategic investor, and combined with Miles's reputation across Africa, this makes managements reluctant to diddle him. Currently Miles feels that Nigeria (our kind of basket case), Kenya (somewhere over the rainbow), and eventually Iran, three countries that no self-respecting fiduciary would dream of investing in, are both cheap and attractive. All are countries with big populations (Nigeria has 150 million people) and immense natural resources.

Change at the margin is what Miles is looking for, and Nigeria, for example, is a place where things are going from truly horrible to just plain bad. He points out that you can't let your psyche be influenced by the BBC, *The Economist*, or the *New York Times*. For example, Miles says the widespread publicity about a woman sentenced to be stoned to death for adultery in Nigeria was merely a jiggle in the direction the country is moving. Franchise companies there growing at 35% a year, such as Guinness Nigeria or Nigerian Foods, can be bought at 10 times earnings. Nigerian Breweries, whose earnings are doubling every two and a half years, sells at seven times profits.

Miles and his colleagues are now searching for new investment orphans in such markets as Cyprus, Lebanon, and Tunisia. These are countries where Miles says the brokers are driving taxi cabs, and where there are companies with good businesses and real growth that no one is interested in because they are quoted on the wrong stock exchange.

Blakeney's list of brave companions (i.e., clients) is short but elite. His erudite commentaries about remote parts of the world alone may be worth the price of admission. In the colonial tradition, Miles loves to travel to exotic places; he doesn't mind staying in rundown hotels in the flea belt and risking contracting strange diseases if he can find local companies growing at 20% a year and selling at five times earnings. No one knows his way around the Middle East and Africa the way Miles does, and I pay close attention to what he says. Like Rudyard Kipling's proverbial adventurer, "his tongue is twisted by strange dialects and his face is bronzed by unknown suns."

As noted, Miles is very bullish on Iran, which, he argues, is the only country in the Middle East that actually has Western-style elections with all citizens, male and female, having equal voting rights. He is bullish on Iran as a country, as an economy, and eventually as a stock market. He points out that the country has a population of 60 million people and is growing rapidly. It actually has an elected parliament, a rarity in the Middle East. In fact, more women are elected to office in Iran than in the United States, and the population is young, dynamic, and very interested in Western culture. They clearly are chafing under the harsh dictums of the mullahs. There is even a rudimentary stock exchange. It is possible that a prosperous, progressive, democratic Shiite bloc of 100 million people that includes Iran, Iraq, and Afghanistan could become a counterbalance to the smaller Sunni gulf states. Given an opportunity, Miles would buy shares of Iranian companies even though Iran is part of George W. Bush's axis of evil.

In short, Iran is a dream situation in Miles's universe: big country, aggressive people, evolving toward democratic capitalism. Being a maverick, Miles relishes that it's totally politically incorrect. He maintains that, in the long run, the United States and the United Kingdom are going to have to figure out a way to reach an *entente cordiale* with Iran. The country is simply too important to dismiss out of hand. Positive change is occurring. Iran belongs in the axis of opportunity, not the axis of evil.

I think Blakeney's seed capital approach to emerging markets makes good investment sense and is a great thing for Africa and the world. However, discovering new markets requires a lot of patience and is not for me. In selecting investments for here and now, I prefer *recognition* to *discovery*. That said, I do believe emerging markets over the next five years are going to be the best asset class in the investment universe.

CHAPTER

FOURTEEN

Great Investment Managers Are Intense, Disciplined Maniacs

I t's a couple of years ago and I'm having lunch with one of my favorite people, Greg, who runs Mega, a $2.5 billion long-short eq-
uity hedge fund. Greg is the best! He is about 60 years old, worth
at least half a billion dollars, with a formidable reputation, but he is
just as driven as he was when I first met him 30 years ago when he was
just another attractive, compulsive, young guy on the make. Now, a third
of a century and a fortune later, four nights a week he sleeps in a small
room off his New York office. Greg remains one of the most intense
players of the money game, and part of his charm is that he wears his
heart on his sleeve. If Mega is doing well, he tells you about it. If it is
doing badly, he moans and groans. If one of his people has screwed up
and lost him money, he doesn't keep it a secret. He is totally transparent.
He is a charming, loquacious maniac.

Greg has a reputation of being difficult to work for and a screamer.
A screamer is a hedge-fund guy who yells at the people who work for
him when they are wrong or careless. I suppose that Greg actually is a
screamer. He needs to be. All the people who are the founders of big,
successful hedge funds are rigorous and demanding with their investment staff. They can be charming and charismatic, but if an analyst does

shoddy work, he or she gets screamed at. Above all, Greg doesn't like to be wrong or lose money anytime, anywhere, anyhow, and when he does, he goes nuts.

Running a big hedge-fund complex is like being the coach of an NFL team. The smartest, best-organized, hardest-working team with the most talent and the most cold-blooded management wins. Nice, relaxed, friendly guys who are tolerant about mistakes finish last and go out of business. Julian Robertson of Tiger was and is a demanding examiner of investment ideas and intolerant of incomplete knowledge and mouth bets. In his presence, the brilliant young analysts he employed quaked with fear, but in the end they loved his relentless search for investment truth. Julian, too, was generous in sharing the goodies at year end, and he cared deeply about his employees. They care just as deeply about him.

I have known Greg from the time he was a hot stock picker and portfolio manager at Fidelity. Fidelity Investments identifies and rewards winners, and Greg was a bright, glowing, albeit chubby, star. Before Fidelity, as he likes to say, he was just a fat Jewish kid from Brooklyn. Greg has always been a great stock picker because his analysis is so rigorous and his logic so compelling. He is also usually right, and when he is not, to hear him tell it, it's invariably because some management guy has lied to him. Greg is maybe five-foot-seven inches tall, and weighs 270. He is truly spacious. "I go to a fancy weight loss spa every year," he says wryly, "and in the past 15 years I've lost 300 pounds but gained 350."

Once, at a conference, we left lunch together. "Where are you going?" I asked him. "I'm going back to my room to make some calls and curl up with my mini bar," says he with a sly grin. At lunch today he sits there wielding a fork and, with a quick flick of his wrist, spearing meatballs, which he then plops into his mouth, meanwhile philosophizing about markets, the ingratitude of the young guys who work for him, and life in general.

"Five years ago this kid comes to me and tells me I am his hero and he will be happy to work for free," Greg says. "He has no money, he loves the business, and he just wants to learn. He tells me that on weekends he reads my old Fidelity reports and quotes things I said in them. He worships me. In spite of myself, I'm flattered. The first couple of years I pay him a pittance because that's all he's worth. Then we have some big years. He helps me find some major hits. I pay him a couple of million dollars. Two years ago he says he likes the money, but above all he wants to be a partner, his life objective is to be a partner with me. So I make him a partner. He makes big money the first year. At our year-end partners' dinner, he is all choked up and he thanks me for all I've done for him with tears in his eyes. His wife takes pictures of us. Then she kisses me and she is crying. They both hug me. I'm like a sandwich between them. I cry, too. It's the rags-to-riches story, the American dream come true. I felt really good about it.

"Then last year we are down 20% and nobody gets paid anything to speak of because there's no money. Late last year, the kid comes to me very serious and tells me he's going to leave in January and join another fund. He hangs his head and looks sad. He says he's lost faith in me as an investor, and because of the high-water mark, the fund will have to earn back what we lost the previous year before he gets paid again, and he needs to make money. Their children are in private school now, he bought into a Net Jets contract, they bought a condo in Palm Beach. So he's leaving to join a fund that's not under water."

Greg is so disgusted he can barely speak. "The kid bought a Net Jets contract? You know I flew commercial until I was 55 years old and worth half a billion dollars. It's unbelievable! I have made this kid, who came from nowhere and knew nothing, rich. Now, after one bad year, which he was partially responsible for, he's walking out on me. I've been raving about this kid to my investors, and so, along with every-thing else, his leaving is a major embarrassment. It makes me look re-ally bad at a lousy time. So I am pissed. I tell him you're not leaving in January, you ungrateful little piece of crap, you're packing up today and leaving tonight, and would you believe it, he was offended. Told people I wasn't gracious."

Greg shakes his head and plops in another meatball to soothe his psyche. "I'm up 50% this year," he says. "The kid would have made $10 million bucks easy. Instead, he went to a market-neutral hedge fund that has been long quality and short junk all year long and is up a pitiful 3%." He snorts with disgust. "Kids," he says, "if they're good, they are restless, ungrateful, and greedy, and you're lucky if you get three years from them before they're gone. If they are no good, all they do is cost you money and aggravation, and you have to fire them and give them a generous separation package or they'll bad-mouth you. It's a no-win game. New smiling faces every year telling you how wonderful you are and then will eventually screw you."

We talked about how the potential for making big money in hedge funds distorts young guys' minds. There is a whole legion of young hedge-fund wannabes who drift from one big hedge fund to another as analysts or traders, always waiting for the break that will get them a spot where they can actually pull the trigger and run some capital. In their hearts, Greg and I agreed, what they all really want is their own fund. The problem with having your own fund is that you have to raise the capital first. If you can do that, then you can control the allocation of the profits, the *carry*. If you can't do it, then you have to give up a lot of the carry to the money raisers. A smart young guy with a good record can probably get a firm or an individual to fund him with $20 million to $50 million of capital, but in return he will have to surrender 30% to 40% of the carry.

There is also a soft, almost sweet side to Greg. He has endowed everything in sight in the Brooklyn neighborhood he grew up in— the community center, the synagogue, the high school, the library et al. The same in the Westchester community where he lives now. So many hedgehogs are charitable. George Soros, Louis Bacon, Julian Robertson, Stan Druckenmiller, and Paul Tudor Jones in particular. It's their money, not corporate money that they give, and they're not in it for publicity and self importance like so many corporate CEOs seem to be.

Greg is the consummate stock picker. No one has a keener mind for identifying companies whose stocks are incorrectly priced. He has four or five analysts who do the legwork, but Greg himself visits every company he has a position in, talks with—no, interrogates, grills—every CEO, and puts each company under his personal analytical microscope. If he buys the stock, he is an activist shareholder, and his letters to management, when they fail to deliver, are constructive but severe. If management doesn't respond, the letters become threatening. God forbid that management lies to Greg about a material event. One company did, and he reported it to Spitzer and testified against them. Conversely, if he is short a stock, he is not silent about telling one and all the flaws and foibles.

Greg may have changed his mind by now, but that day he wasn't pushing anything. "I can't find many cheap stocks," he grumbles. He is bearish about the U.S. market over the next few years. "We are eating our seed corn," he says. "The Bushies for political purposes have pushed through two huge tax incentives for depreciation that have encouraged current capital spending at the expense of future spending. Meanwhile, Greenspan's easy-money policies have promoted the borrowing of consumption from the future. Those two have front-loaded the stimulus, and I'm afraid eventually we're headed for slumpflation and another bear market."

DON'T HOLD ON BLINDLY:
GREAT INVESTORS CUT THEIR LOSSES

Greg is very tough about cold-bloodedly reviewing his losses. Like many traders, he does it automatically, usually at the 10% loss level. Roy Neuberger, Gerald Loeb, Bernard Baruch, and Jesse Livermore all did it. Baruch had an ego that would have fit comfortably into the Temple of Dendur, but he was an astute investor. In his book *My Own Story* he tells how he learned the hard way to cut his losses by selling when a position went against him. He wrote:

> In the stock market the first loss is usually the smallest. One of the worst mistakes anyone can make is to hold on blindly and refuse to admit that his judgment has been wrong. Occasionally one is too close to a stock. In such cases the more one knows about a subject, the more likely one is to believe he can outwit the workings of supply and demand. Experts will step in where even fools fear to tread.

Baruch argues one should always buy on a scales-up.

> Many a novice will sell something he has a profit in to protect something in which he has a loss. Since the good position has usually gone down the least, or may even show a profit, it is psychologically easy to let it go. With a bad stock the loss is likely to be heavy, and the impulse is to hold on to it in order to recover what has been lost. Actually the procedure one should follow is to sell the bad position and keep the good position.

Baruch wrote that one of his most important rules of investing was to "learn how to take your losses quickly and cleanly."

In *Reminiscences of a Stock Operator* by Edwin Lefevre, Jesse Livermore says over and over again that you should buy on a scale-up and sell on a scale-down. "Never make a second transaction in a stock," he writes, "unless the first shows you a profit. Always sell what shows you a loss. Only suckers buy on declines."

Livermore did not have a hard-and-fast rule on when to eliminate a losing position, arguing instead that the timing depends on the feel of the stock and the market. However, he was an unusually gifted, intuitive trader, and he was not burdened by much knowledge of the fundamentals of the positions he took. Thus Livermore was more flexible in his thinking than most of us who probably overintellectualize our stocks, and he was a dedicated believer in owning strong stocks that were in clearly defined, long-term up-trends. As soon as a stock he was long faltered, he got rid of it. His rule was that when a stock that had been strong failed to rally after a reaction, that was the first sign of trouble and time to get out.

Of course, buying strength and selling weakness is pure momentum investing, and as a value investor and believer in the inherent efficacy of fundamental analysis, I disdain that style. So does Warren Buffett. He has said that he doesn't believe in stop-loss disciplines. Nevertheless, you have to be respectful of the knowledge of the market. If a position goes against you by 10%, maybe somebody has understood something you have missed. When a position declines by 10%, we force ourselves to do an extensive and systematic review of the fundamentals with both internal and external resources. We have to be sure nothing has changed. After the review, if nothing has changed except the price of the stock, we have to buy more. If we lack that conviction, we have to sell at least half of the position.

> *A trend is a trend is a trend*
> *But the question is, will it bend?*
> *Will it alter its course*
> *Through some unforeseen force*
> *And come to a premature end . . . ?*
> —*Sir Alec Cairncross, Chief Economic Adviser*
> *to the British Government in the 1960s*

VISILES AND AUDILES AND DISCIPLINED READING

Recently I read an interview with Charlie Munger, Warren Buffett's alter ego. Munger is a great investor and a really smart, wise old guy:

> *I have said that in my whole life, I have known no wise person over a broad subject matter area who didn't read all the time—none, zero. Now I know all kinds of shrewd people who by staying within a narrow area can do very well without reading. But investment is a broad area. So if you think you're going to be good at it and not read all the time, you have a different idea than I do. . . . You'd be amazed at how much Warren [Buffett] reads. You'd be amazed at how much I read.*
>
> —*Charlie Munger at the Berkshire Hathaway*
> *2003 Annual Meeting*

Reading is definitely my thing, too, and I think you have to read not just business stuff but also history, novels, and even some poetry. Investing is about glimpsing, however dimly, the ebb and flow of human events. It's very much about breasting the tides of emotion, too, which is where the novels and poetry come in. Besides, sometimes you have to refresh your mind and soul by consuming some crafted, eloquent writing. When I get home at the end of a business day, after being absorbed in investment babble and dull, plodding writing, replete with trite phrases such as *make no mistake*, which is my pet peeve, I am stuffed with babble. My gorge rises at the thought of more business carbohydrates. So I sit down with a nice big glass of wine and immerse myself in something I want to read. I always have at least one book going, and my taste is eclectic, but the *sine qua non* is that it has to be well written. At this moment, I am rereading William Blake's great biography of Disraeli, a complex and intriguing figure.

I am a *visile*. A visile primarily absorbs information through the eyes by reading. An *audile* ingests information mostly through the ears, through talking and social interaction. Charlie Munger, too, is a visile. Of course, we all do some of both, but I share Munger's skepticism that someone who doesn't read much can be a really successful investor. I do know a number of people who are very successful traders and speculators who don't read anything but the sports page.

One of the biggest, most difficult issues I have is time management. Receiving and processing information and data in order to have the knowledge to make wise investment decisions is what the professional investor does all day and night. For example, one friend of mine, a visile who has been in the business a long time and has a fabulous record, is a truly compulsive but very disciplined reader. By disciplined, I mean that he has a keen eye for junk research and wastes no time on it, but he is continually looking for the pearl of knowledge, the flash of insight that makes the pieces in an investment puzzle fall into place.

Not only does this fanatic read all week long, but every weekend, to his wife's dismay, he comes home with several heavy satchels full of research reports and magazines. He gets up early and spends six to seven hours each weekend scanning this mass of material and scrawling notes on it to his analysts and portfolio managers. Perhaps 10% of it he reads and studies carefully. Of course, he also talks and listens, but nevertheless, this visile gets most of his information by reading. "You get less lies and BS this way," he says.

Another friend, who also has a brilliant investment record and is equally obsessive but very different, an audile, used to read a lot, but now he doesn't read much at all, although he carries around a briefcase full of research, which he paws and shuffles. Yet he still wants to be on every mailing list and becomes very insecure when he thinks you have a piece of research he doesn't. There is research all over the floor of his office, and once last summer, when he opened the trunk of his car to get his golf clubs, I saw great mounds of moldy old research reports that had been there for God-only-knows how long.

Instead of reading, this guy obsessively works the phone. All day long, including weekends and evenings, he makes calls that usually begin, "Big guy, what's going on?" Yet in his own way, he is very disciplined, too, because each conversation is short and to the point, and once he has pumped dry the person on the other end of the phone, he terminates the call with, "I gotta fly." There is no idle chatting. In effect, he has decided that after 30 years of reading research reports, the return on his investment is low, and that the best stuff isn't on paper. So he spends his time gathering information from talking and listening to an eclectic variety of sources.

As for me, although, Lord knows, I spend a lot of time every day chattering with my investment buddies, I am a compulsive reader. Sometimes, getting through my in-box so dominates me that I sacrifice thinking time. Processing the pile and having a tidy desk and a clean in-box can be compulsions that hurt rather than help. The objective is not to prove how much you can read but rather to unearth insights that lead to money-making decisions.

I find it's almost impossible to do serious reading in the office because there are so many interruptions, so I spend a lot of time nights and weekends reading. Often I wonder if it's all worthwhile or just an addiction. Although I know there is no direct correlation on a day-to-day basis between reading and making money, somehow I feel less guilty if I read everything in my in-box. As investment managers, we must control our reading by being disciplined and ruthlessly selective rather than let it rule us. I want original information or analysis about the state of the world, an industry, or a company that is going to help me make money. Change at the margin is what moves markets. Of the written material I receive each day, 90% is worthless to me because it either repeats what I already know or is irrelevant. The odds are almost zero of my finding anything new in one more 20-page report on GE. The problem is that I can't winnow out the 10% without glancing at the rest, and no secretary, no matter how smart, can do it for me. When I do find a report or an article that has truly fresh, at-the-margin thinking, I try to take the time to read it carefully. I find underlining helps.

So here is what I read, for better or worse. Obviously, a lot of topical, random stuff comes up, but what follows is my regular fare. Every day on the train going to work I read the *New York Times* and the *Financial Times*. I always read Thomas Friedman's columns. The *FT* is excellent for corporate news. Later in the day, I try to scan the *Wall Street Journal*. When I am traveling in Asia or Europe, it's *The International Herald Tribune*, which, in my opinion, is the best single newspaper in the world. The Asian and European editions of the *Wall Street Journal* in some ways are even better than the one in the United States. I am beginning to think I should spend more time reading corporate news in newspapers, which at least doesn't pretend to be anything but reporting, and less on brokerage research, which often is just biased reporting of what has already happened. A good read for out-of-consensus content is Kiril Sokoloff's *What I Learned This Week*. It has to be taken with a grain of salt because Kiril has a tendency to present only one side of whatever view he is taking. However, he is an original thinker.

Each weekend I try to read *The Economist* carefully. It is unquestionably the best magazine in the world, and nothing else has close to its global reach. I review *Time*, *The New Yorker*, and *Newsweek* (Fareed Zakaria is excellent) by looking at the table of contents to see what sounds interesting. All three used to be better, and they still have some good pieces, but they have been junked up. I usually look at *Fortune*. It has been junked up, too, but it has some of the very best, most incisive long articles. Carole Loomis is great. *Institutional Investor*, *Absolute Return*, and David Smick's *International Economics* are on my reading list, too. However, you can go through only so many magazines, because there is so much promotional babble in them. I must confess I am a huge *Sports Illustrated* fan because the writing is so superb and because I like sports.

We get massive amounts of research and market letters every day, mostly by e-mail. My way of dealing with the sheer volume each week is to focus on about 25 different sources, ranging from Ed Hyman, Jim Paulsen, and Jim Walker to Byron Wien, Steve Roach, and Chris Woods. There is meat to be found in scanning the company summaries issued by serious research firms. I don't disdain by any means Wall Street research or Wall Street analysts. They are still valuable to check out ideas with, and sometimes a conversation with them can be very instructive. Our primary research sources are Morgan Stanley, J.P. Morgan (for economics), Goldman Sachs, Credit Lyonaisse, ISI, Bernstein, Credit Suisse, The Bank Credit Analyst, Merrill Lynch, Intregal Associates, and Bear Stearns. My assistant erases everything else. From time to time I add sources to and delete from the primary list. Otherwise, I would get overwhelmed with stuff I really don't pay any attention to.

I do this because I used to lug around a heavy briefcase full of research. I had the bad habit of wanting to reduce the load by discarding paper. I would end up putting aside the really good stuff to read later while I compulsively worked through the junk. I found I was reducing the weight I was lugging, but ending up carrying around, not reading, the meat, which, after a week or so, I would throw away because it was stale. Obviously, not a best practice.

I don't bother to read most economists (particularly those who insist on being called Dr. Sam or Dr. Eric) and strategists because they tell you only about what has happened, not what will happen. They don't forecast; they just extrapolate recent trends into the future. They are mostly followers, who revise their forecasts of the future based on the direction of the latest economic numbers or what markets have done recently. As a result, they are always behind the curve instead of in front of it. They always underestimate the dimensions of the swings that economies are capable of. Of course, there are a few exceptions. Dr. Copper is still the best economist I know. Some of my best sources are businesspeople because they give me a flavor of what's going on. And then, of course, there are always those people who are contrary indicators.

It is very hard to read in the office, what with interruptions from phone calls and the inevitable seduction of the screens. E-mails and the Bloomberg are huge distractions and time wasters. Staring at Bloomberg screens is not productive for thinking. Cleaning up your e-mail in-box can easily become another compulsive activity. I find myself responding to trivia e-mail messages instead of thinking. The same applies to voice mails. We have a reading room, almost a library, in our office. Good light, reasonably comfortable chairs, no phones, no chatting of any kind allowed. Without interruptions, you can go through an incredible amount of research in an hour. Nevertheless, the most productive reading time in my day is the 85 minutes on the commuter train.

As an investor, you have to dominate your intellectual intake environment and not let the outside world control you. You have to be adamant that you make the choice of who accesses you and not be at the mercy of others. The conventional wisdom now believes that the Internet and e-mailing are brilliant, time-saving inventions. They can be, but as noted earlier they can also be huge distractions. We all tend to cite studies that confirm our prejudices, so here's mine. A recent study of 1,000 adults by the University of London found that habitual e-mailing and text messaging reduces intelligence and intellectual productivity more than being a regular pot smoker. Most office workers, the study found, are seriously e-mail addicted. A third of them are so totally plugged into their screens that they respond to an e-mail immediately or within 10 minutes. One in five routinely interrupt a meeting to answer an e-mail.

The study found that the average reduction of intelligence from e-mail interruptions was 10 IQ points compared to 4 points from smoking cannabis in the office. A loss of 10 points is associated with missing a night's sleep. Of course all three are temporary. The other fascinating finding was that women are less affected than men. The average IQ decline for women from e-mail addiction was 5 points whereas for men it was 15. In other words, women are much better than men at multitasking.

It's not just reading but reading smart.

CHAPTER

FIFTEEN

You're Only as Beloved as Your Most Recent Performance

anaging mutual fund money in a big firm is a hard, traumatic job. Every day the change in the NAV of your fund for the previous day and the gain or loss for the year to date is right there for everyone to see. You feel as though the whole world knows whether you're a hero or a bum. At a big investment management firm with a sales force and a retail client base that is intensely focused on short-term performance, having that daily NAV on display generates violent mood swings in even the most secure and stable portfolio manager. Running institutional money is stressful, too, but at least your worth as an investor isn't being assessed on a daily basis.

When your investing is going well, you feel immortal, you have conquered the beast, and finally solved the riddle of the performance game. But when you are lagging the competition, and the sales force and the clients are restless, it's a bummer. It's hard to figure out what you are doing wrong because a portfolio is a combination of perhaps 30 or 40 different decisions or bets. When you are in a slump, the right decisions are being overwhelmed by wrong ones. It's incredibly frustrating, and before long you begin to second-guess yourself. Slumps can last for 6 months, for 18 months, or even a couple of years.

THE TRAUMA OF RUNNING MONEY IS NOT FOR EVERYONE *OR* TRAUMA WHEN YOU BITE THE DUST

This intoxicating (or maybe toxic is a better adjective) performance cocktail encompassing the thrill of victory and the agony of defeat is very difficult for the portfolio manager to deal with. A hot run swells the ego and breeds confidence and even a touch of hubris. A cold spell is devastating. Once, at Morgan Stanley, I promoted a guy to be the sole portfolio manager of a fund. This guy was maybe 40 years old, very smart, his record as an analyst and as a co-portfolio manager had been excellent, and he very much wanted his own fund. By background and experience, he seemed fully qualified. Furthermore, he was well adjusted, happily married, and a confident and secure person, which are personal characteristics that are always reassuring. It's not that manic-depressive dyspeptics can't be successful, even great money managers; it's just that, given the choice, I'd prefer a Huckleberry Finn.

Anyway, this guy I had so fastidiously selected either got off to an unlucky start or wasn't as talented as I thought, once he was running his own fund. In any case, during his first year he was in the bottom third of comparable managers and 400 basis points behind the benchmark. He then began to press and trade more as though activity counted. Of course, it doesn't. In fact, trading is often counterproductive because it adds to costs and risks being wrong twice—in other words, on either the sale or the new buy decisions or both. After 18 months at the helm, he was even further in the hole, and the sales force had tuned out. He confided to me he wasn't sleeping well. I told him to relax. He was running a marathon, not a sprint. We would give him time.

However, a few months later he came to me and said he was going to resign. He couldn't take it anymore. It was affecting his family life. He was going to leave the business, move his family to Wyoming, and be a ski instructor. I tried to talk him out of it. Human Resources suggested counseling. All to no avail. He worked with us on the transition to a new portfolio manager, and at the end of the year, he left. A couple of years later he moved back to Chicago and took a job as the research director at a bank. But as far as I know, he never ran money again.

EVEN SUPERSTARS GET PUSHED OUT

An even more dramatic story sticks in my mind like a splinter. I still remember how shocked I was that January day a couple of years ago when I heard that Big Firm Investment Management had let Sandy Andrews go. She had been one of their superstars, and then, suddenly, they fired her. It was hard to believe. I'm sure they gave her a very generous separation package but still. . . . Her story is *sic transit gloria*. But don't get me wrong; I'm not suggesting Big Firm made a bad or unfair decision. It's just the ebb and flow of the human side of a cold-blooded performance business.

Sandy is about 50 years old. She is a tall, good-looking woman with long black hair. She dresses well and speaks slowly with a faint, southern accent, and sometimes she has a slightly spaced-out look in her eyes as though she were deep in thought. Sandy isn't fancy. She grew up in Florida, went to high school in Tampa, and then to the University of Miami, not Andover, Yale, and the Harvard Business School.

I got to know Sandy after Big Firm merged with Wean Ditter in 1997. With relentless hard work and by delivering good performance numbers on the funds she managed, Sandy had pushed and shoved her way up through the old Wean Ditter investment management company. I am sure it was not easy for a woman like Sandy, or for that matter, any woman, to get the opportunity to have her own fund in an investment management world where the superstars and, in fact, most of the portfolio managers are men. The fact is that all investment worlds were (and probably still are) male-dominated. She had to be both good and aggressive even to get a platform to stand on to show what she could do, and I'm sure she ruffled more than a few rooster feathers on her way up. The odds were stacked against women investors 10 or 20 years ago, and to some extent they still are.

The truth is that, in the investment management business, there is an unspoken, inherent bias against women in the portfolio manager role. There are some but not many women running large, long-only money, but I can't think of a big-time woman hedge-fund manager. The vast majority of male investors, both young and old, accept that women are just as smart as men. However, they don't believe women are capable of playing the money game for two reasons: first, they are too emotional, and second, and most important, if they are also mothers, men believe women simply don't have the inclination or the time. There are elements of intellectual snobbery, gender bias, and professional envy in this attitude.

Most investment men appear to believe that women with young children have too many distractions at home to do the reading homework and put in the office and travel time required to be a winning investor. They think the proper and basic instinct for women is to be good mothers, and that being obsessed at the same time with investment work is an irreconcilable conflict. Maybe when they are 50 and their children are off at college, they can be investors, but by then they will be so far behind and out of date that they will no longer be qualified to run money.

When I was there, some of the young investment studs at Big Firm argued that the firm shouldn't have any illusions about the staying power of women and their ability in the long run to perform as portfolio managers. They thought the right role for women was in the more menial support jobs such as client service, marketing, and administration, where the intellectual and time burden wasn't as high. The firm, however, was adamant that the playing field had to be level and that women, just like men, could balance the requirements of work and family, and the young studs mostly kept their opinions to themselves.

But Sandy navigated her way up through the labyrinth. She is smart, she worked very hard, and above all she has a good nose for markets and a stock story. As a momentum investor, the second half of the 1990s were a fertile time for her. She cultivated sources on the sell side, and paid them well when they gave her an edge. She has a disarming softness about her, but those in the firm who tried to crowd her learned she had sharp elbows. How did she balance work and family? I don't know.

However, like many other good investors, she is not always easy to get along with. I never had any trouble with her, but her staff said she was very demanding of herself and of the people who worked for her.

As I have said before, almost all of the really good investors I know are both temperamental and tough, and most have a reputation as occasionally being screamers. Their obsession with winning is what makes them that way. Their obsession with winning is also what makes them good investors.

By 1998, Sandy was running one of the firm's best-performing funds that was attracting huge inflows from retail investors. She was managing $20 billion, and even in the exuberant atmosphere of the times her numbers were spectacular. I liked Sandy. We talked and had dinner a couple of times. She is a real investor, but I also was glad I was not directly managing her because I could sense that she could be a handful.

After the merger of Big Firm and Wean Ditter, the first big meeting I went to was the 1998 Insights Conference at The Phoenician in Phoenix. Insights is the feature conference of the Big Firm retail system, where the 600 top producers (out of 10,000) are wined and dined and educated about the firm's mutual funds. The brokers who get invited to Insights are the smartest, most successful of the lot; entrepreneurs who have built their own businesses. With some justification, they view senior management, portfolio managers, and mutual funds with a jaundiced eye. They are friendly people but very interested in making money. Nobody is going to BS them.

That year the meetings were in a huge auditorium, and there were lights, music, and special effects. The speeches by the portfolio managers were rehearsed in front of teleprompters and carefully scripted. The crowd of brokers was mildly interested in the canned presentations, but in general they were cynical, restless, and impatient to use their cell phones, call customers, or get to the golf course. During the sessions, a lot of the brokers would be wandering around outside reading newspapers, making phone calls, or chatting. I made a presentation, and they were a tough audience, although I managed to get a few laughs. By the fifth canned presentation from portfolio managers trying to promote their own products, I sensed the crowd was bored.

Sandy was the next speaker. Now suddenly I noticed groups of brokers wandering in from the corridors. The auditorium hushed expectantly, and following the introduction, when she came on stage and stepped to the podium, a number of brokers around the room stood and began to applaud. Suddenly and spontaneously, the whole crowd was on its feet, giving her a loud, standing ovation. I was stunned, dazzled. The tribute was genuine and reflected the fact that her fund had provided the brokers and their clients with excellent performance. They deeply appreciated her numbers, because it made them look good. She was their shining star. They loved her. They listened intently, respectfully to her speech like it was The Investment Gospel straight from the enchanted lips of the mystic woman Oracle.

When she had finished her speech, and walked up the main aisle, brokers bowed to her and shouted things like, "We love you!" and "Keep knocking 'em dead, Sandy!" Outside the auditorium, they flocked around her, wanting to ask her about stocks and have their pictures taken with her.

Sandy loved it all. She stood there at the podium soaking up the adulation and applause with a demure, half smile on her face. She liked the attention afterward. Who wouldn't have? I assume standing ovations are heady stuff, although I have never had one. As an investor, when you are performing well, it can be very intoxicating, and you begin to feel invulnerable. Sandy was the prima ballerina of the investment management division. The money came pouring into her fund. She demanded and got precedence and prime billing with the retail system. Sandy felt that for years she had been underpaid, and now she got very tough with senior management, demanding big increases in compensation and privileges. They didn't like it, but they had no choice. She was their star.

In the following years, Sandy continued to be as obsessive as ever. She had good but not spectacular results in 1998, 1999, and in the first half of 2000. However, as a momentum-oriented investor, she went headfirst over the cliff with tech, and then played 2001 as if it were still a bull market. She finally gave up in 2002 and raised a lot of cash. Unfortunately she stayed bearish as markets made a double bottom in the fall of 2002 and in March 2003. As a result she carried 20% cash throughout 2003. In other words one misstep—remaining bullish too long—led to another—staying bearish too long—and the result was a streak of abysmal performance.

As an investor managing competitive money, when you get wrong-footed, so to speak, it is very easy once you are out of phase to get the next turn wrong as well. That doesn't mean you won't get back into phase thereafter; it just suggests that cold spells tend to feed on themselves and persist for a couple of years. Also being wrong and having the world know it, as was the case with Sandy, really gets into your head. We talked from time to time, and it seemed to me she was being stubborn and inflexible *and not listening to the market.* In support of her high cash position, she often would cite to me market technicians who were bearish. But as I have said before, everyone, and I mean everyone, gets turns wrong from time to time.

As her fund's performance slipped, Sandy reacted by trading more and driving her people even harder. In any case, at the end of 2003, the combination of poor performance, abusing people, and being difficult to manage caused senior management to ask her to leave the firm, presumably with a generous separation package.

I was shocked. Sandy is a good investor. All good investors have cold spells. Sandy was hard on her staff, but managing a large mutual fund is not supposed to be a popularity contest. It's a life-or-death struggle with the markets. The newspapers report how you do every day, and the brokers and their clients don't care whether your secretary and junior analysts think you're insufferable. You can't afford to tolerate mediocre people working for you. Unintentionally, their inefficiency undermines your performance and jeopardizes you and themselves.

I feel very bad about Sandy. Being a star investor is a big part of her psyche, and it must have hurt to be the topic of negative gossip. I respect her judgment about markets. I talked with her right after she had left the firm, and she told me that she had not been able to raise money on her own for a hedge fund because her recent run of poor performance made attracting investors difficult. She said she was finding it hard to get located.

Months later, a guy who runs a good sized hedge fund called me. He was thinking of hiring Sandy as an analyst with a line of capital. What did I think of her as an investor? I told him I thought she was a winner. He said he agreed, but his only reservation was that she didn't seem tough enough, intense enough. I had to laugh. I assured him she had plenty of both those qualities. I hear she is doing well, and that her line has been increased.

Incidentally, Sandy's saga is not a totally unusual event. A few years earlier, the same thing happened with a guy from the firm who ran a growth and income fund. Great numbers for a couple of years, standing ovation at Insights, brokers bowing to him in the hallways, then a cold spell, and a few years later a not-so-fond farewell. It's a tough business!

So what is the moral of this bleak vignette? The first and everlasting truth is that in the investment business you are only as beloved as your most recent performance. *Sic transit gloria*; in other words, fame and glory are transitory events. It's a numbers game. Clients' loyalty, salesmen's admiration, management's love are all totally fickle, so don't get cocky. Smooth investment sailing inevitably is followed by vicious storms. Winter comes after summer. The second truth is that if you work in a big, political investment management firm where everyone is *empowered* by Human Resources and you are a screamer, you had better have consistently good performance. If you have good performance, management will figure out a way to tolerate even the most abusive screamer. But when you are in a slump, you should mind your manners.

Third, the senior business management in most firms don't understand that investment performance is cyclical, and that they need to be tolerant of the foibles of their handful of *real* investors. A big investment management firm may have 200 portfolio managers across 100 product lines, but only 10 or 15 *real* investors. Sandy, in my opinion, is a real investor. You don't want to lose your real investors.

EVEN CONSERVATIVE CYNICS LOSE CLIENTS

Steve came by the office today wearing his trademark big grin, and we had a long talk. That smile goes with him everywhere; he sleeps in it and even hand-washes it for freshness on weekends because sometimes it gets a little ragged, like right now, since his performance is lousy, and a number of his clients are closing their accounts.

Steve is a guy whom I have known for years. He lives in Greenwich, as I do, but doesn't play the country club sports or belong to the fancy clubs. Hidden behind that big smile is a sardonic view of the world in general and Greenwich in particular. A couple of years ago he sent out a Christmas letter, which I reproduce here for its social value. In our neck of the woods, Christmas letters attached to Christmas cards have become a not-so-subtle bragging thing in which upwardly mobile families advertise how absolutely nifty cool their perfect, blemish-free lives are and recount all the brilliant things their wonderful children have achieved. Even family pictures have become polluted. Last Christmas one family picture included with each name the prestigious college attended, like the father was Amherst 1979; mother, Amherst 1981; Lisa, Harvard 2002; Colin, Yale 2004. God forbid that 14-year-old Cricket ends up at Southeastern Nevada State!

Both Steve and I cringe at and then mock these ghastly epistles, but he did something about it. Two years ago he cranked out a Christmas letter of his own. I must confess he showed it to me first, and I made a few suggestions. I loved the letter! Probably just a coincidence, but since his letter was circulated, the ones you do get have become less gushy! I saved his.

Dear Friends,

In this our annual Christmas letter, we want to share with you all the special things that happened to our talented family in this glowing year of 1998 which just dripped and drooled with happiness for us all.

In February, Jane came back from her third trip to the Betty Ford Clinic—radiant from all the new friends made and old companionships renewed. This truly is a warm and wonderful place, and by now it has a special spot in all our hearts. Always upbeat and honest, Jane says the clinic is marvelous for social climbing; an even better way to get to know and bond with rich and famous people than getting onto the boards of prestigious charities—and cheaper too.

March was very exciting. After a brief engagement, our lovely daughter Nancy married Antonio Miguel de la Figuerosa whom she met last year in Geneva. He's from Panama and comes with an instant family of four. This will be Nancy's third trip up the proverbial aisle, and we sure hope that Antonio's sense of humor and impressive connections mean he is Mr. Right for her. Antonio chartered a Concorde for the flight to Panama (makes our G-5 look a little shabby) for the wedding party, and we were really wowed by the three spectacular homes he owns in Panama City and his vast hacienda in the countryside.

Antonio is a lieutenant in the Panamanian police force and also runs a small export business in his free time. It's obviously a very successful little hobby—although Antonio is quite diffident about it—because apparently he comes from a very modest background and now is one of the wealthiest men in Panama—a real go-getter. Our beautiful daughter Julie was quite taken with one of his bodyguards (there must be six of them at least!). This one was a strapping young fellow from Libya.

Our whole family went to the wedding celebration with the exception of Billy whose parole officer in Michigan is extremely small minded. We had a super time! It was fascinating to meet so many politicians and businessmen from all over Central America. Once you get accustomed to it, everyone wearing a gun is really quite erotic. And the wedding gifts were so generous. The happy couple received among other things an armored Mercedes and a power boat with its own 50-caliber machine gun mounted on it—really neat stuff. They will be honeymooning in Colombia where Antonio has some business associates. Our little girl has turned into quite the jet-setter! She now travels with her own hair dresser!!

A little rain must fall into all lives and besides the moisture nourishes fortitude. We trust that none of you believed those scurrilous insider trading allegations made about Steve by that corrupt and politically ambitious district attorney in Hartford. It was scandalous the way the press played them up. And incidentally, as a family we never did any late trading or market timing in Steve's mutual funds, despite what the *Wall Street Journal* says.

We have just returned from Thanksgiving in the Bahamas on our shiny new rowboat *The Indefensible,* which is a mere 165 feet long and cruises at 30 knots. The sojourn was a little longer than we planned because, in a bizarre case of mistaken identity, the whole family was put under boat arrest for a week in San Oroda for suspected trafficking in illegal substances. We were released only after we gave a lavish reception for the entire police department, their wives, girlfriends, and children, complete with what they called party envelopes for everyone.

> We hope all of you will drop in for a drink or a meal at our new digs on Round Hill Road. The Olympic-sized swimming pool will be finished by early spring so by all means bring your bathing suits. Jacques, lately of Caravelle, will be doing the cooking. . . .

The letter ended with a few additional jabs that were specific to life in Greenwich, Connecticut.

Steve's cynical cast of mind has served him well as an investor, and he has a fine long-term record. He has his own firm, which runs long-only money for wealthy individuals, small foundations, and endowments. In other words he doesn't run a hedge fund. He was at Fidelity in the 1980s where he was a big star, and then started his own firm in 1991. The firm has grown because, until the past few years, he has posted solid numbers. He is a careful, intense investor whose style is to own the shares of 30 to 40 growth companies that he really knows and believes in and that are reasonably priced by classic, old-time valuation criteria. Steve's strong adherence to growth at a reasonable price caused him to miss the surging bull market of the late 1990s, but that fastidious adherence to value, which should have helped in the bust, was offset by a big position in Enron.

Steve's accounts got killed in Enron. He likes to buy growth at a reasonable price, which is precisely what Enron appeared to be. Steve had studied Enron from top to bottom, visited the company on numerous occasions, and was convinced it was for real. When the rumors started to fly and the price began to fall, he bought into the declines just as Buffett preaches. Unlike my friend Dave, he doesn't believe in momentum investing or that market action tells you anything. Personally I'm convinced an Enron could happen to anyone. Security analysis and research don't work when there is fraud involved. Buffett points out that Henry Kaufman and Marty Liebowitz, two of the smartest guys he knows, are on the board of Freddie Mac and they missed a $6 billion misstatement of earnings. Al Harrison of Alliance Capital, one of the best investors I have ever known, also took a hit in Enron. But Steve's clients have not been understanding.

Then in 2003 Steve continued to have a lot of cash in his accounts, because he still couldn't find really cheap stocks and he had a cautious view of the world. As a result, even though his accounts were up 12%

in 2003, he lagged the S&P 500, which was up 28.7%. In 2004, he did about 5%. In other words, he hasn't really made anybody money for five years, and everyone remembers Enron. Now, his natives are becoming restless, and he is losing assets. In fact, the buzz is that he has lost his touch.

Although Steve has heard the whispers, the smile is as big and wide as ever. Deep down, though, I can tell he is hurt that some of his longtime clients weren't more steadfast and didn't really believe in him and his methods. However, he also knows that disloyalty and losing clients when you are at the bottom of a performance cycle are part of the business. In fact, often the best sign that the worst of a performance slump is over is when an important client closes his or her account with you.

If you think your investment manager truly has gone batty, is no longer paying attention, or was just a flash in the pan to begin with, then obviously you should terminate the relationship pronto. If your manager has had a long record, although like everyone else has experienced occasional rough spots, it's unlikely he is a flash in the pan. If your manager doesn't seem as committed or intense, or if he or she has panicked in the face of adversity and changed their style, then that is another matter, and you are justified in terminating. But if he or she is just having a cold spell, resist the urge. If you believe in reversion to the mean as a golden rule of investing (as I do), and if you believe that smart managers over the long run can beat the indexes (as I do), then closing your account after below-benchmark performance makes no sense and, in fact, is asking for a double hit. You have absorbed the pain of the underperformance cycle, and now you are going to miss the ecstasy of the performance rebound.

If your investment manager has had a good record in the past but is doing badly now, be patient. Good investment managers are hard to find, so once you have one, don't give up quickly. It will be agonizingly difficult to find a replacement. Swings in performance are cyclical, and even the best investors have episodes, sometimes long episodes, of underperformance. You pay a fee to an investment manager to obtain over time annual returns that, on average, are at least a couple of hundred basis points higher than those provided by an index fund. Compounding this extra return over the years results in staggering wealth enhancements, even after paying considerably higher fees than index fees. For example, over 30 years of good times and bad when John Templeton was at the helm, the shareholders in his fund saw an investment of $10,000 grow into $632,469; a comparable commitment in the Dow would have been worth only $35,400. John had several three-year bouts of underperformance, but he also had a run of nine straight years of beating the index.

EVEN GREAT INVESTORS HAVE COLD SPELLS

Some years ago, Warren Buffett gave a speech at the Columbia Business School entitled "The Great Investors of Graham-and-Doddsville," on the anniversary of the publication of Benjamin Graham and David Dodd's great classic, *Security Analysis*. In that speech he attacked the professors who maintain that the stock market is efficient, that prices reflect everything that is known, that there are no undervalued stocks, and that investors who beat the market are just lucky. He then went on to elaborate on the records of 10 investment management firms who were committed value investors.

All 10 firms had exceptional records and had produced returns, again over long periods, far above those of the major indexes. For example, Pacific Partners over 19 years achieved an average annual return of 32.9% overall—23.6% to the limited partners—versus 7.8% per annum for the S&P 500. Over 16 years Tweedy Browne's limited partners enjoyed a gain of 936% versus 238.5% for the S&P. Buffett's own record, of course, speaks for itself.

The surprising discovery, however, is that all of these superstars, with the exception of Buffett himself, underperformed the S&P 500 in 30% to 40% of the years studied. Templeton, who was not in Buffett's group, also lagged about 40% of the time. None in the group always beat the S&P, probably because no one thought that was the primary objective. However, the underperformance in the down years was generally (but not always) small, and the positive differentials were large and, in some cases, huge. Most of the lag occurred in years when the averages made big advances.

Furthermore, with only two exceptions, all of the great investors cited by Buffett had long cycles (defined as three or three out of four consecutive years) of underperformance. Almost invariably, sustained bursts of spectacular returns either preceded and/or followed those bad periods. Obviously, to close your account after a cold spell would have been a spectacularly costly mistake. By contrast, it would have been a better tactic to lighten up after four or five vintage years. Relative performance runs in three- to five-year cycles, probably related to the manager's style and the dominant themes of a particular market. See what I mean by reversion to the mean?

Some of the history is fascinating. An extreme example is Pacific Partners, which, after five straight years of beating the S&P 500 by big margins (the last three providing its investors gains of 120%, 114%, and 65%), then had returns below those of the S&P 500 for the next four years and in five out of six years. Pacific then got back on track with a 127.8% rise followed by three more years of solid albeit less spectacular gains. Now, you might say that as a client you just can't tolerate that kind of volatility, which is understandable. However, for those 19 years the S&P 500 provided an increase of 316% (7.9% per annum), and the limited partners of Pacific after fees had a gain of 5,530% or 23.6% per annum. Returns of that magnitude are worth some heartburn.

Other examples include Charlie Munger, the man who reads, who later became Buffett's partner. Munger once had a slump in which he lagged the S&P 500 in 4 out of 5 years, but over a 13-year span, which included the bad patch, achieved a compound return of 19.8% versus 5% for the index. Tweedy Browne has had a superb long-term record, but the firm has suffered bad spells in which it underperformed the S&P 500 in three out of four years. The Sequoia Fund lagged the S&P 500 for the first three and a half years of its existence, somehow survived, and then went on to glory.

The point that Buffett didn't make is that two or three straight years (much less four) of performance worse than the S&P 500 today would result in most investment managers getting fired—certainly by the consultants who dominate the business and probably by most of their institutional clients. People have short memories, and the money management business is big on statistics and consultants who need to advocate change to justify their fees.

So it's no wonder Steve is feeling beleaguered. He just can't find stocks that look cheap enough to buy, what he does own languishes, and he is wondering if the world has passed him by and he needs to change his investment standards. I told him to hang in there and not bend. He said he was having a lot of trouble sleeping, and sometimes, before and after a painful client meeting, he has experienced severe stomach cramps, which his doctor tells him are really anxiety attacks. He mentioned that he is even wondering whether he shouldn't quit, play more golf, and just run his own money. Steve is about 50 years old, and he is a very competitive guy with an active mind. I think for him to pack it in would be a big mistake because I don't think he would be happy on the sidelines. I am confident he will emerge, but at the bottom of a performance cycle, it's a hard, unforgiving business.

CHAPTER

SIXTEEN

Once You Have a Fortune, How Can You Hang On to It?

P reserving and enhancing your fortune is a demanding task that most people fail at. The standard approach of an age gone by was to hire U.S. Trust, Morgan Guaranty, Scudder Stevens & Clark, or some other prestigious investment counseling firm to manage your affairs as the legendary prudent man would have. Unfortunately those institutions are mere shadows of their former selves. Sorry, but my view is that the general level of investment (as opposed to sales) competency in what is now called private wealth management is low. Good people are being driven out by the bureaucrats. This chapter is a stroll through some unconventional storehouses for wealth.

IN AN APOCALYPSE, JEWELRY WORKS

When I was in Hong Kong some years ago, I visited the elderly patriarch of a very wealthy Chinese family for whom I have run money. At the time, he must have been in his mid-90s, but he still went by the title General. As a general in the Nationalist Army, he had fought the Japanese and then the Communists. After World War II, he was on the long retreat across China. The General is very old and frail and a little inclined to gloomy reminiscences, but who wouldn't be if you had seen what he has seen? Somehow we got talking about the difficulties of preserving wealth in Asia over a century of wars, depressions, inflation, and revolutions.

The family has a large portfolio run by three major investment management firms, but the General on this occasion was philosophizing about the uses of wealth in an apocalypse, which, he pointed out, is when you *really* need it. Paper assets are fine and wonderful things in normal times, he said, but they are useless when anarchy reigns. And once every half century or so, anarchy does reign. It reigned in Asia, Russia, and Europe in the past century, and the Four Horsemen of the Apocalypse will ride again. War, Famine, Pestilence, and Death periodically are part of the human condition.

In the old man's opinion, quality jewelry was as good a storehouse of value, disaster hedge, as anything he knew, and in fact was better than gold. Wealthy families should have disaster hedges just as they carry insurance or set up irrevocable trusts. Disaster hedges, he pointed out, must be highly portable, easily hidden, and very marketable. Both Marie Antoinette and the czarina of Russia stuffed jewels into the bodices of their garments when revolutions forced them to flee their palaces.

He said that when the Japanese took Hong Kong in 1941, his family was transformed overnight from being very rich to the brink of starvation. The men were away in the army, but the family had a compound on The Peak inhabited by his grandparents, mother, and the wives and children of his three brothers and himself. There were a lot of mouths to feed. With the occupation, the British economic system disintegrated, and all bank deposits were frozen. The local people believed that the Japanese, with their military might and the Greater Asia Co-Prosperity Sphere, would rule for the foreseeable future—maybe even forever. Singapore had fallen, 200,000 British soldiers had surrendered, and the HMS *Repulse* and the HMS *Prince of Wales*, the two mightiest battleships in Asia, had been sunk by Japanese naval aircraft. His family owned large amounts of rental property in Hong Kong, but the tenants simply had stopped paying rent. The family's overseas assets were intact, but there was no way of getting cash from them. All their sources of income had dried up as the local economy reverted to barter.

As it turned out, the family survived the next couple of years because the women traded their jewelry for food and protection. In Hong Kong in 1942, jewelry had great purchasing power value because the Chinese girlfriends of the Japanese military wanted it. The street prostitutes got money and goods from the Japanese soldiers, but the most beautiful courtesans wanted to accumulate jewelry, both to wear and as a store of value. As a result, the Japanese officers acquired jewelry to court their favor. "Dumb jewels often in their silent kind/More than quick words do move a woman's mind," wrote Shakespeare. Neither the Japanese nor their girlfriends apparently cared much for gold. It wasn't decorative. Bartering their jewelry was what enabled the family to survive in the dark days of 1942 and 1943.

Throughout history, conquering armies seek sex from the women of the occupied country. Women naturally want something of value in return, the old General said, so what happened was not unique to Hong Kong. Jewelry has always been used to beautify and to display one's rank and wealth. Jewelry also works as wealth in an environment of runaway inflation. The studies show that gold and silver are excellent inflation hedges, and since they are so much a part of jewelry, the record indicates that jewelry at least maintains purchasing power during inflationary episodes. This was certainly the case in Germany during the Weimar Republic and in the early 1930s. But the song has it slightly wrong; jewelry, not diamonds, are a girl's best friend. Diamonds are a commodity with a manipulated price.

The old General's theory about jewelry went further. He argued that in a world with a complex computerized banking system that is vulnerable to both social and technological terrorism, conditions similar to 1941 in Hong Kong could occur again. If a power failure persisted, and the banking and transportation systems in the United States were knocked out, living conditions could become desperate, and paper money could lose value as a medium of exchange for essentials. A barter economy would probably spring up. Jewelry might well become a preferred currency.

It is an intriguing concept. I can't find any price/performance record for what might be called collectible jewelry. One expert describes collectible antique jewelry as items that are pre-1950s; another said it had to be at least from the 1930s. Signed pieces by recognized designers, such as Art Deco jewelry produced by Cartier, sell at a premium, and fine costume jewelry is also collectible. "The more a piece is a work of art, the better," the expert remarked. Modern jewelry must be designed and in fashion to offer value. At recent auctions in Geneva, unique pieces uniformly exceeded reserve prices. Diamonds and big rock jewelry, however, did not sell particularly well.

It's hard for me to conceive of jewelry as a major asset class for serious money. However, as a repository for some wealth, like art, it makes sense for reasons beyond the aesthetic. For one thing, it can be easily given to daughters and daughters-in-law, skipping gift taxes, and when the matriarch dies, it can be quickly scooped up by the heirs, avoiding inheritance taxes. Jewelry is highly portable and easily concealed, so refugees fleeing pogroms have always utilized it as a way to transport wealth. And, as the old General said, it could be invaluable in a disaster scenario.

I was fascinated by his talk. It made me realize that except for those of us who are refugees, as Americans we have no concept of what being occupied by a foreign army or, following a catastrophe, what a total breakdown of law and order would be like, and how quickly paper wealth would evaporate. Only those who came to the United States as refugees from Hitler or communism can have any sense of this. The rest of us are oblivious to wealth insurance.

THINK OF RETURNS NET AFTER FEES AND TAXES

Another evening I had dinner with Sam, an old friend, who some 15 years ago sold his company and walked away with a big smile and some serious money. Since then, he has worked intensely at both his golf game and at enhancing this fortune. He has been very successful in both. Along the way, he has come to some interesting conclusions about how tax-paying Americans should manage their money.

To summarize Sam's philosophy, all returns should be looked at after carries and, above all, after taxes. Returns are reported pretax and thus they are an illusion, because achieving high after-tax compounding is what the exercise is all about. Liquidity and transparency of the investment vehicle are crucial. An investor has to have the right to change his mind and get his money back. My friend likes to keep it simple, and, as a result, he doesn't do much in real estate or oil and gas deals: "Too complicated, too illiquid, and the carries are too big. Besides, it's almost impossible to calculate the returns, because they pay the money out over ten years."

Sam doesn't use private wealth management firms to run his money. Their best talent, he says, either invests funds or institutional accounts, and the individual gets short shrift even if he has big bucks. Besides, in the present environment, the best and the brightest inevitably will migrate to hedge funds. He maintains that no major firm, either in Europe or the United States, has its act together on private wealth management. As a result, he has concentrated on hedge funds. He doesn't use funds of funds because he feels he knows as much about hedge funds as they do, and besides their fees take a huge bite out of returns. On the other hand, he concedes they do make sense for less knowledgeable people.

Hedge funds are glamorous, Sam says, and when you are in one that is flying, spectacular top-line (gross) returns can make for great cocktail party conversation. But a tax-paying U.S. citizen must look at the returns after the general partners extract their 20% fee and after taxes on the gains. He invests in hedge funds that have active strategies, that go for it. He is willing to live with the volatility. Market-neutral stock pickers have no appeal for him.

What has worked for Sam is finding a handful of great, enduring funds, knowing the managers well, concentrating on them, and staying with them. Over the past decade, the three great hedge funds in which he has amassed his money have delivered a pretax IRR after carry of 25.4% per annum versus 11.1% a year for the S&P 500. The three great ones had a volatility of 21% over that period versus 15.8% for the S&P, which means 10% declines in a month will occur from time to time. After taxes, the IRR to him, as a tax-paying investor in the United States and California, shrinks to 16.3% as 71% of their gains were short term because they trade a lot. Of course, the S&P 500 return also is before taxes. He finds that as a higher percentage of their funds become tax-exempt institutions, the general partners tend to become even less conscious of taxes.

My friend looks for large funds with stable management that will outperform in up markets and protect your capital in bad ones, which is all you can ask for. You shouldn't expect them to make money in down markets, and you have to recognize that they are going to deliver you a big tax bill. Obviously, for tax-exempt institutions it's an entirely different matter, and Sam thinks hedge funds are the perfect vehicle for medium-sized foundations with unwieldy and ignorant investment committees. Because they don't pay taxes, the compound can be fabulous.

Hedge-fund selection and timing require research and hard work. Entry points are crucial. "Nobody talks about the high failure rate in start-up hedge funds. Just because the managers say they are going to run a low-risk fund and will always have a lot of shorts doesn't mean they can't lose a lot of money. Sometimes the longs go down and the shorts go up." Sam also is very leery of U.S. stock pickers who, "puffed up with success," think they can do macro—international markets and foreign exchange plays. "Currencies and Japan have killed some of my best friends," he says sadly. He also points out that many hedge funds that opened in the late 1990s were really leveraged, long-only funds, and a lot of them got beaten up badly or wiped out in the bear market.

My friend will seed with a million dollars a start-up fund that has credible operators "just for the look." He wants to get to know them better, read their reports, go to their partners' meetings, and understand their style. He will call on them in their offices. If, over a couple of years, he likes what he sees and they do well, he will raise his stake. However, he points out that his results away from his big three funds have been mediocre.

Sam's basic strategy is to have 75% of his hedge-fund money in four or five core, established funds that he feels he knows inside and out. He then has the rest in his "farm team" of around 10 rising stars. Size is the enemy of performance, he admits, but the funds in his core group are big. World-class reputations attract money, and a fund has to have a certain critical mass to buy the best young talent and trading coverage. With all of them, at the first signs of hubris or fading intensity, he starts cutting back his stake. A bad year or a big monthly drawdown, and volatility, doesn't trouble him, as long as he is convinced the managers are staying focused. He wants his hedge-fund managers to be obsessive, self-absorbed, somewhat obnoxious people. It doesn't bother him in the least that the best ones are often very hard on their employees and not popular with Wall Street salespeople and traders because they don't suffer fools. He likes grumps.

The rising stars are attractive because their assets are not so big, and thus they can take meaningful positions in small and medium-size companies. They also can move positions more easily than the giant funds, which is a huge advantage if something goes wrong. All things considered, he thinks hedge funds are the best investment vehicle for wealthy individuals, but they require constant attention and some know-how.

In general, Sam believes in being an owner rather than a lender, and, as noted, he is very tax conscious. As a result, he doesn't have any use for taxable bonds or Treasury inflated protected securities (TIPS), because the taxes eat you alive. "TIPS don't work for individuals," he says, "because you are paying taxes on the inflation component so the *real* return is almost nothing." Real estate investing is tricky, and the funds he has looked at are compensated through transaction and management fees rather than sharing in the profits generated for their investors. In other words, the promoters' interests are not aligned with those of the investors. Oil and gas investing is the same story. The deals always sound enticing, but almost invariably end up with the operators and the general partners getting rich while the investors don't.

Sam has two-thirds of his money in hedge funds. He does think every wealthy person ought to have a lifestyle reserve in high-grade tax exempts. How big should that reserve be? It depends on the age and wealth of the individual. "Ideally," he says, "it ought to be enough to support you in a basic, affluent lifestyle if the stock markets crashed and stayed busted." His concept of a basic lifestyle might be a little exalted, but the concept still makes sense. "Such a dire outcome is unlikely," he adds, "but why take any chances? Besides, tax exempts are relatively cheap now."

VENTURE CAPITAL IS GLAMOROUS BUT RISKY . . . BUT YOU CAN GET A WONDERFUL RIDE

As for VC and private equity, he admits he missed the supposed bonanza of the 1990s. However, he argues VC is vastly overrated as a way to get richer while you sleep. The prevailing myth is that VC is the miracle asset class, and investment advisers cite the fabulous long-term annual returns of long-time professional VC investors such as Yale, J.H. Whitney, and Venrock (all three have done close to 30% per annum for 30 years).

There is no arguing that, when it works and you are with the best, it's wonderful. However, he tells me that, when they are in their cups, the rich, old guys he gossips with admit they got killed in VC. Viewed dispassionately, VC is a risky, brutal business littered with busts, burdened with a high deal-failure rate, and with low barriers to entry for new firms. Furthermore, it is very difficult to exit, because you can't take your money out. However, if you invest at the right time with the right people, you can have a wonderful ride.

The Venture Economics index cited in Chapter 10 reports a mean return of 15.8% annually for the average VC fund from 1969 through 2002, which is about right for a highly illiquid investment. Plain, ordinary big-capitalization U.S. equities (which have instant liquidity) returned 10.6% per annum for the same period. The starting date in computing VC returns is essential. A study by *The Economist* for the period from 1988 to 2000 reported a 12% annual return.

Manager selection is absolutely crucial for venture capital, just as it is with private equity, and very difficult. A recent study from Horsley-Bridges Partners, a San Francisco-based fund of VC funds, reports that between 1990 and June 2003, $195 billion was invested in VC funds. Among all funds, those in the top 25% of performance had $20 billion committed to them and returned to investors $80 billion, presumably with more to come in the future. The rest of the investors in the VC industry, who plunked down $175 billion, have had *no* net return whatsoever, and in terms of cash on cash have *lost* 10%. Obviously, as these VC funds mature and the huge investments made in 1999 and 2000 ripen, the picture may improve, but then again, it may not. Who knows whether current portfolio values reflect business reality in the aftermath of the tech and Internet busts? In fact, there is probably a bias to overvalue portfolios.

The amazing thing is that the Silicon Valley-VC bubble has never really deflated. The overhang of money in the VC business today is estimated at $80 billion to $100 billion, and in the fourth quarter of 2004, $10 billion of new money came in. This overhang exists because, in the glory days, to get entry, prospective investors had to commit their contribution for the life of the fund—with no cancellation provision. Furthermore, they had to agree to pay the fixed fee (usually 2% per annum) on both their invested and their uninvested capital. The VCs obviously have no incentive to give any money back, since they are earning a fee for sitting on it. In the fourth quarter of 2004, the VC industry invested about $7 billion in new ventures—less than the new money that came in. Silicon Valley's delicate entrepreneurial ecosystem is clogged.

I think right now is the wrong time for putting fresh money into VC. As Howard Marks of Oaktree famously wrote: "There's no investment idea that is so good that it can't be spoiled by too high an entry price." VC is a cottage industry that is either in feast or famine. The cycle is almost biblical (seven fat years followed by seven lean), the 1990s were the feast of all time, and the asset class is still working off the hangover. Once, a few years ago, David Swensen showed me the Yale Endowment's private equity returns. Take a look at Table 16.1. Over 25 years, Yale realized compound annual returns of 35% in VC and 31% in private equity *after fees*. I know of no one else who has done as well with a large, diversified program. Note that Yale had a 168% gain on a $2 billion private equity portfolio in 2000. How can you resist returns of this magnitude?

Yale brilliantly avoided the carnage of the tech bust. Swensen is reticent as to how he did it, but I suspect that when the markets got crazy in 1999 and 2000, Yale bought puts and sold short index futures to hedge its exposure to VC and LBO portfolios. Also during the halcyon days when a VC fund took a portfolio company public and distributed shares to its limited partners, Yale promptly sold the shares.

The other issue to consider as an investor is whether you have the intestinal fortitude to withstand the kind of volatility inherent in private equity. For example, look at Yale's LBO returns: up 231% in 1980, and then down 74% in the next three years. Try explaining that to your investment committee in early 1984. In vintage years, the best-performing VC funds have spectacular returns, and stellar performance attracts massive new money and a horde of imitators, many of whom are inexperienced, ignorant, and incompetent. Then the returns disappear, and the horde of latecomers does abysmally, but nobody talks about that.

The *Economist* study also confirms the hazards of selecting a VC fund. In most years, the difference between the top-performing funds and the median is huge. Even in vintage years, many VC portfolios actually lose money. The 23-percentage-point spread between the highest- and lowest-quartile of VC returns over the years is by far the widest of any asset class. Leveraged buyout firms are next, with a 14-percentage-point spread between the twenty-fifth percentile and the seventy-fifth,

TABLE 16.1

Returns of Private Equity Investments of the Yale Endowment

Fiscal Year June 30	Venture	LBO	International	Total
1978	27.2	35.3	na	33.9
1979	−2.2	−3.0	na	−2.8
1980	208.1	231.9	na	225.5
1981	33.3	−16.6	na	−0.5
1982	25.6	−47.5	na	−2.2
1983	123.4	−10.1	na	91.4
1984	3.7	41.6	na	9.2
1985	−10.1	5.6	na	−5.0
1986	2.6	34.0	na	15.8
1987	25.4	23.9	na	24.3
1988	−0.7	7.3	na	3.3
1989	−0.3	38.7	13.4	23.4
1990	15.6	7.8	−4.4	11.8
1991	11.6	14.7	−10.0	6.1
1992	28.3	7.2	4.1	14.6
1993	13.6	57.3	−0.2	32.3
1994	20.2	18.7	24.0	24.6
1995	37.8	26.3	13.1	27.0
1996	124.8	30.9	33.7	60.2
1997	37.6	22.3	90.2	36.2
1998	38.5	46.4	1.9	29.0
1999	133.9	24.8	15.4	37.8
2000	701.0	35.1	38.3	168.5
2001	9.0	−14.7	−3.9	−5.4
2002	−39.9	−11.2	−0.7	−23.3
2003	na			
Last Five Years	107.4	8.4	2.9	39.4
Last Ten Years	53.5	18.9	18.0	36.0
Since Inception	35.3	21.6	15.7	31.4

Source: Yale Endowment

while in the more efficient equity and fixed income classes, spreads are only two to four percentage points.

SELECT HEDGE FUNDS WITH SKEPTICAL CARE

It's crucial to get in the right hedge fund, too. Over the five years ending March 31, 2003, the spread between the twenty-fifth and the seventy-fifth percentile in all hedge funds tracked by the TASS database is 9.5 percentage points (plus 12.7% per annum versus 3.2%, with the S&P 500 down 3.8% per annum over the same period). As you would expect, the volatility of the hedge-fund universe funds is much lower than that of the private equity classes: 15% for hedge funds versus 21% for the S&P 500. As for hedge funds of funds, the spread is smaller: 5.3 percentage points (plus 9.2% per annum versus 3.9%, with a volatility of 12%). Of course, hedge funds are much more liquid than private equity and usually more transparent.

As I reflect on my buddy's strategy and think about the impact of the inheritance tax, it works very well for institutions or portfolios with $100 million or more of investment assets. However, let's say you are retired, have $25 million of financial assets, and a working familiarity with investing. You figure that you need an income after taxes of between $400,000 and $500,000 a year to live in the style you're accustomed to, and you have $150,000 of other income from your pension, social security, and so forth. So you put $5 million into a portfolio of high-grade, medium-term tax exempts, which gives you roughly $225,000. I would buy $2 million ($85,000 of pretax income) of 10-year Treasury bonds as a strategic reserve. Then, with the remaining $18 million, I would buy $5 to $7 million of Vanguard index equity funds. The remaining $10 to $13 million should go to either 5 to 10 hedge funds (if you can identify and follow that number) or a couple of funds of funds. The idea is bonds for income, equities for growth, and hedge funds for all seasons. Obviously, this is a simplistic model, and a lot depends on your level of income, expertise, and the competence of your financial adviser.

Sam also has a good perspective of what is going on in the hedge-fund industry. He says the really big-time legitimate hedge-fund operators with good long-term records are being flooded with money. Because they already have more than they can run fast with, they are laying off much of the new money. They basically put into business young guys who smell like winners. The big-time operator tells his clients that he has this new Emerging Managers Fund with five of the smartest young guys he has seen in years. He reminds them that young guys with no fear and imagination can shoot the lights out, but young guys without fear can also do crazy things. So he, the big-time operator who has seen everything, is going to watch them as closely as a hawk watches mice. The investors eat it up. It's the best of both worlds for them.

For example, Sam says, there is this guy named Jimmy located in Newark, who is a wild trader and has a great record. In his glory days, Jimmy charged 50% of the profits and no fixed fee. Jimmy is not dumb. He knows he can't day-trade billions the same sly, slimy way he ran a couple of hundred million. So he has decided he wants to build a hedge-fund empire, and he has changed his fee to 30% of the profits and 2% of assets. As long as he keeps his golden touch, the money will keep pouring in despite the outrageous fee. To handle the inflow, he is putting kids into business right and left. The story is that last week he took a hot kid from another older hedge-fund guy and gave the kid $300 million. The terms work out to be 15% and 1% to the kid and the same for Jimmy. That kind of money can turn even a good kid's head. On the other hand, over the next year it could give the kid an early ulcer or migraines, because Jimmy is notorious for being a fast hook. You had better perform if you are running Jimmy's money, and if he does hook you, don't expect a golden parachute. Anticipate nothing but public bad-mouthing. As far as Jimmy is concerned, he has never made a bad decision on stocks or people. Any bad performance is because guys let him down.

The funds of funds version of craziness also is looming. Charlie Munger recently remarked, with his ancient tongue firmly in his cheek, that he liked the idea of a fund of funds of funds. Says he, "If a second layer of fees is good, then a third layer must be better." Alas, it is already happening. A London-based $3.8 billion fund of funds, in order to take diversification to the next level and cut risk, is creating a fund of funds of funds, which will invest in 11 underlying funds of funds.

A more recent development is that as banks have entered the funds of funds space, leverage is being offered. A wealthy guy with $2 million to invest wants to buy into a bank's fund.

"I'll tell you what," says his friendly private wealth adviser, "you can see from the record that our fund has low volatility and grinds out its 8% a year. Why not borrow another $4 million from us and, even after paying interest, you are going to be making close to 20% a year. No sweat, no strain."

Now, after almost 18 months of a meandering market in which everyone is struggling, the funds of funds are earning virtually nothing and there is a sea of red ink out there from the double fees and the interest expense. The result is lingering client unhappiness and fund of funds redemptions, which in turn mean redemptions of the underlying hedge funds.

On a bad day the leverage can give me the creeps. Suppose, for whatever reason, that a big fund of funds starts losing money. Knockouts are activated. The fund of funds has to tell its hedge funds to liquidate part of each of their long positions and buy back some of their shorts. The short covering to meet redemptions causes irrational moves. Everyone is raining on his own portfolio, thus triggering further losses and more redemptions. As the ripples and the rumors spread, panic sets in. It's portfolio insurance and LTCM all over again, and although portfolio insurance didn't cause the 1987 Crash, there is no question that it immeasurably intensified it. Leverage is toxic stuff, and as the old saying goes: Liquidity is a coward; it disappears at the first sign of trouble.

DON'T GO HEDGEHOGGING BY YOURSELF: FUNDS OF FUNDS MAKE SENSE

Most funds of funds don't offer leverage, and they provide an essential service for the wealthy individual. My buddy Sam invests in hedge funds directly as the core of his portfolio, and if you are very rich and very plugged in as he is, going direct makes a lot of sense. The problem is the time you have to commit to investing, not as your profession, but at least as your serious avocation. To have hedge funds as your core holding, I think you should have a portfolio of at least 5 funds and preferably 10—5 main managers and 5 on the farm team. At this level, you must spend serious time studying them, calling on the managers occasionally, and probably going to meetings like Morgan Stanley's Breakers conference. Listening to 10 presentations a day is not fun, and doing hedge funds yourself is hard work. You must research your investments. No hearsay. You must understand their investment process. If they can't or won't explain it, walk away. If they talk about the secret investment algorithm they have discovered, say goodbye. Unless you are willing to do this diligently, you should use a fund of funds to invest in hedge funds—and there are a number of good ones. The people that run the good ones are highly professional and they do extensive due diligence and analytics. Sure they add another layer of costs, but the diversity and expertise they provide are worth it for all but the hardworking sophisticates.

History shows a well-managed fund of funds over a period of years at least keeps up with the S&P 500 in good markets, preserves your capital in down markets, and does this with lower volatility. This is no inconsiderable achievement. For the boom-bust five years that ended March 2003 the S&P lost 3.8% per annum and the median fund of funds gained 6.3%. The seventy-fifth percentile fund of funds returned 9.2% and the ninety-fifth showed 15.7%. Funds of funds make all the sense in the world for all but the Sams.

INVESTING IN FINE ART: LOVE IT FOR ITSELF, NOT AS AN INVESTMENT

I had dinner a few weeks ago at the home of a friend who for the past 20 years (since he made some serious money at Morgan Stanley) has collected Western art with passion and discrimination. Now he has the joy of living with his wonderful Remingtons, Bierstadts, and Wyeths and basking in the respect and adoration of his guests. And making money! "I figure the value of my art is doubling every five years," he says, with just a modicum of arrogant smugness. "It's much more satisfying than owning stocks. It would be ostentatious to hang stock certificates on the wall, and besides, they are ugly. Stylish women don't fawn on you because you own Intel."

My friend is probably right that his pictures are compounding at

14% or so, but his taste has been exceptional. This figure does not take into account the high cost of owning art, which includes insurance, security, and expenses for environmental control, and could easily amount to two percent of the value annually. I checked, however, and really good American Western art has kept going up right through the bear market in equities. Art of exceptional quality probably does have fairly immediate liquidity, but this is not true of run-of-the-mill pictures. I should know. For what seems like eons I have been trying to sell a mediocre picture by a mediocre eighteenth-century artist you have never heard of which I bought in a mediocre moment 15 years ago. Nevertheless, my friend is right that great art is the sublime investment medium because it provides high investment returns and esthetic pleasure at the same time. Only owning a farm in some idyllic rolling countryside and watching your cattle get fat or your trees grow is remotely comparable, and even then you wouldn't want to live with the farm every day.

Based on research by art historians like Richard Rush, it seems the long-term return from high-quality art has been around 9% to 10% a year, before carrying costs. There is also evidence that there may be a 50- to 60-year Kondratieff wavelike cycle in art. Past peaks came in 1770–1780, around 1830, in the 1880s, in 1929, and then again in the late 1980s and early 1990s, fueled by manic Japanese buying. As you would expect, bubbles create wealth, and wealth bids up art, and vice versa. From 1990 to 1994, art prices in the major markets as measured by the Art 100 index fell 52%, and an index of nineteenth- and twentieth-century sculpture plunged 60%. But bear in mind that both indexes had astonishing gains from 1983 to 1990. Even with the declines, the compound return for the 10 years ending in 1994 was 11.5%. The standard deviation for that period was 35.7%, compared with 17% for the S&P 500, 30.6% for emerging market equities, and 18.4% for U.S. emerging growth stocks. Since its inception in 1976 to the end of 2004, the Art 100 index has compounded at 10.5%, with a standard deviation of 27.9%.

None of these statistics are precise, because the auction houses and dealers are dedicated to perpetuating the illusion that good art never goes down in price. The weaker dollar also has had the effect of raising prices in the United States and diminishing them in London and Paris.

Liquidity at a reasonable price is not what you might think. The percentage of works that failed to sell at auction has been about 25% in each of the past three years.

Of course, just as with equities, the returns from owning art depend mostly on how individual pictures stand the test of time and fashion. Pictures that prove to be Great Art with a capital G usually turn out to be great investments. Leger's *The Woman in Red* was bought in Paris for 200 francs in 1921 and was held by the same family until it was sold at Christie's last year for $22 million, a return of 19% per annum over almost a century. Van Gogh's *Irises* was painted in 1899 and purchased by Joan Whitney Payson in 1947 for $80,000. Her son sold the painting for $53.9 million a few weeks after the Crash in 1987, for a return of 17.7% per annum for 40 years and a few months. Not bad for a canvas that the Payson family presumably loved looking at all those years. Ironically, the buyer of *Irises* turned out to be Australian beer tycoon Alan Bond, utilizing a line of credit extended to him by Sotheby's auction house. The record price he paid launched a roaring bull market in art from which Sotheby's was the principal beneficiary. Shortly thereafter, Bond's empire stumbled, and he defaulted on the loan. Sotheby's repossessed the picture and later sold it by private treaty (price undisclosed) to the Getty Museum.

Whether a particular piece of art is a good investment is far more a matter of fashion than is the valuation of equities where, in the long run, the growth of book value, earnings, and dividends count most. The bear markets in art have been silent but brutal. Rush's art index rose from 100 in 1925 to 165 in 1929 and then fell to 50 by 1934. Within the long-wave secular cycle, there are also sector cycles driven by fad and fashion where the price changes are even wilder. In the 1780s, Guido Reni was the hot painter, and Catherine the Great bought one of his pictures for the then-princely sum of 3,500 British pounds. But Reni went out of style, and one of his paintings didn't sell for 3,500 devalued pounds again until 1958. Nineteenth-century English collectors were captivated by the strenuous life school, which featured blustery outdoor scenes and stout, hardworking people. Another fad was for misery paintings. Neither is popular today. Could this happen to the cowboy and Native American pictures of my friend? I don't think so, but it's not impossible.

An extreme example of art fashions is that of the eighteenth-century

British portrait painters like Romney, Gainsborough, and Reynolds, who, during their lifetimes, painted ancestor portraits on commission for prices equivalent to $175,000 a picture (at today's prices). A generation later, no one would pay much for pictures of other people's overweight ancestors, and prices fell to 10% of what they had been. During the 1920s, the ancestor genre boomed but then crashed again in the Great Depression. In the summer of 2002, there was a major sale of this genre in London. Gainsborough's *Blue Boy*, which the Duke of Westminster had sold in 1921 to a Midwestern American businessman for £148,000 ($10 million in today's money), went for $1.5 million, and Reynolds's portraits, which, before 1929, had gone for $8 million in today's money, were sold for $300,000 to $400,000.

One of the great art dealers of all time was James Duveen. Although his origins are shrouded in mystery, the charming and impeccably dressed Duveen was immensely successful in his prime. His business plan was simple but daring. He had a low regard for the artistic sensibilities of rich Americans. After World War I he acquired, at distressed prices, a large inventory of ancestor portraits and, over the next 15 years, sold them to *nouveaux riche* American millionaires, his connoisseur clients as he called them, who wanted ancestors to hang in their new baronial mansions in the United States. In his heyday, Duveen liked to boast that no picture sold by him would ever sell for less, and for a few years he stabilized and manipulated the ancestor market—similar to the way the auction houses supported the art market in the early 1990s.

Prices for ancestor portraits held up well for a few years after the 1929 Crash. Then at an auction at Christie's in 1934, a Romney which had been purchased for $700,000 in 1928 (multiply by 11 for today's price) and which was being sold by the owner's executors, attracted no real bids and *was* knocked down for $65,000. This triggered a general collapse in the ancestor market, and by the 1940s most eighteenth-century portraits were selling for a mere 5% of their 1920s highs. The stock market crash wiped out many of Duveen's best clients, including Jules Bache, who ended up owing the dealer $4.4 million. One summer afternoon in 1937, as Duveen was leaving Claridge's Hotel in London, he was accosted by three elderly American dowagers armed with umbrellas, who had discovered that their deceased husbands' art collections were virtually worthless. In the exchange that followed, Duveen was knocked to the sidewalk and kicked. *Duveen* by S.N. Behrman is a wonderfully entertaining and instructive book about the amoral but stylish shenanigans of Duveen and his cohort Bernard Berenson.

Another art fiasco occurred in Japan in the late twentieth century with worldwide aftershocks. The Japanese stock market in the 1980s was a swelling bubble, and by 1990 the wealth it had created had a huge effect on art prices around the world. The Japanese collectors always worked through their dealers, and they had very specific tastes. They liked impressionist, post-impressionist, and modern art created between 1900 and 1950. Some estimates guess they bought about 40% of the impressionist pictures sold at auction between 1987 and 1990, which, incidentally, turned out to be the high for prices.

By the late 1980s, the bull market in art was in full swing, stimulated by the auction houses and dealers, who, with culture and caviar, fattened the innocents for the slaughter. In 1987, Ikkan Sanada, a famous Japanese dealer, brought 18 young but very rich Japanese entrepreneurs and their wives and girlfriends to the United States for an educational buying tour. He worked these beginner collectors, as he called them, up to a frenzy, and they bought half the impressionists at Sotheby's big fall auction and 5 of the 10 most expensive pictures. In the four years up to the peak in art prices in 1990, Japan imported $13.8 billion of art from the West.

By the late 1980s, Japanese banks were promoting loans to buy art. The bankers argued that art was excellent collateral. Japanese corporations and businessmen spent huge sums on trophy pictures. Yasuda Marine & Fire bought van Gogh's *Sunflowers* for $39 million. Ryoei Saito, the chairman of Daishowa Paper, on May 15, 1990, spent $160.6 million on two pictures, a Renoir and a Van Gogh. He paid $78.1 million for the Renoir, and bought the van Gogh, *The Portrait of Doctor Gachet*, for $82.5 million. No pictures before or since have sold at such prices.

At the time, Saito announced, with great fanfare, that at his death both paintings would be cremated with him, but a decade later he needed the money and sold the van Gogh back to Christie's for a price that was said to be one-eighth of what he had paid for it. The Renoir is missing in action but it is believed to have been repossessed by a Japanese bank. Another high-water mark was reached when a Japanese real estate speculator, Tomonori Tsurumaki, acquired a Picasso for $51.3 million on November 30, 1989. The best estimate of Tokyo dealers is that Japanese banks still hold repossessed art purchased for about $5 billion that today could be sold for perhaps $1.4 billion.

I can report firsthand that amateur collecting can be a loser's game if you misjudge future fashions in taste. In the late 1940s and early 1950s, my parents became enamored of glorious, hand-painted, porcelain, life-sized models of birds in their natural habitat that were created by Dorothy Doughty. These bone china statues are delicate and exquisite, and as they were very limited issues, my father became convinced they would become true collectors' items in the years to come. In 1957 Queen Elizabeth II presented a pair of parula warblers to President Eisenhower, and prices of the Doughty birds soared. I believe my parents paid around $8,000 to $10,000 a pair for a number of these limited editions at a time when wonderful art was selling for $50,000 to $100,000 a picture. Fifty years later, the birds are still very beautiful on my mantelpiece and still worth about $8,000 a pair—if you can find a buyer. If a set of the birds had compounded at just 8% a year, 50 years later they would have been worth $469,000 apiece; at 12%, $2,890,022; at 15%, $10,836,574; at 17.7%, or the same pace as Mrs. Payson's picture, $34,580,000. My father was a very good macro stock market investor, but obviously a lousy judge of macro trends in art.

In any case, the bear market in art seems to be over, and prices in general are rising again, but the craziness has not come back—yet. With yields on financial assets so low, the income loss from owning art is much less of a deterrent than it was 10 years ago. On the other hand, CEO hubris and greed scandals have effectively eliminated the corporation as a collector in the United States and Europe. The bubble has been popped, and prices are rising again in a more orderly manner.

When the Nazi blitzkrieg swept across Europe in the early 1940s, Jewish families had to flee to escape the Holocaust. Although many were ostensibly wealthy, their holdings of land, houses, and businesses that they had nurtured for generations were suddenly virtually worthless, because the locals knew they desperately needed to sell. The currencies of defeated, occupied countries were of no value anyway, and there were exchange controls. Jewelry (remember my Chinese General) and art were the only transportable wealth that could be relatively easily converted into cash in the West. At every opportunity, they smuggled jewelry and art to the United States, and, when they finally got to New York, it was their grubstake.

Hedgehogs are big buyers of art today. Some of the acquisitions are trophy collecting; a not so subtle form of bragging. My view is that you should buy a picture because you love looking at it, not as a divisifier or as an investment.

CHAPTER
SEVENTEEN

Three Investment Religions
Growth, Value, and Agnostic

J ust as there are different schools of art, there are three great serious
investment religions: growth, value, and agnostic. Most investors I
know are one or the other. I tend to be a value investor, but I have
an agnostic streak.

IDENTIFYING GROWTH STOCKS
IS EXTREMELY DIFFICULT

Growth stock believers argue that you want to own stock in companies
whose earnings and dividends are consistently increasing. What you pay
for the shares of these companies is important, but not as crucial as correctly identifying true growth companies. By definition, these companies tend to have excellent managements, proprietary positions in
businesses that are not particularly cyclically sensitive, and to be highly
profitable. Ideally, growth stock investors want to hold shares in great
businesses, and they sell only when the business itself falters, not because
the price of the shares has risen. Academics have proved that if you had
perfect foresight and bought shares of the companies with the fastest

earnings growth, regardless of valuations, over the long run you would outperform the S&P 500 by 11 percentage points a year, which is an immense amount.

The problem is that no one has perfect foresight. In fact we are all generally overconfident and overoptimistic about our skill in picking growth companies. Identifying growth *ex ante* is extremely difficult, and as noted previously, growth companies have, for one reason or another, a high propensity to fall from grace, in other words, to stop being growth companies. By the time you the investor can clearly identify a stock as a growth stock, it usually will already be valued accordingly. Therefore, you end up buying the expensive stocks of good companies.

Growth stock investors also are inclined to fall in love with their growth companies that have treated them well. Remember that you are buying stocks, not companies, and don't fall in love. Sell growth stocks when they become outrageously expensive. Fall in love with people, children, and dogs, but not stocks.

A man named T. Rowe Price in the 1930s was the first outspoken advocate of modern rigorous growth stock investing, although some nineteenth-century London merchant banks, Scottish trusts, and Swiss private banks practiced a growth style. With the depression still rattling around in the world's closet, Price at first was mostly focused on dividend growth. Then, after World War II, he broadened his definition of growth, and he and his firm rigorously practiced and popularized the growth concept. In his later years, Mr. Price was a formidable character, and whenever I was in his presence he was very disdainful of those who were not growth-stock investors. "Why would anyone want to own a mediocre company just because it's cheap, when you can own and live with great companies?" He defined a growth stock as follows: "A share in a business enterprise which has demonstrated long-term growth of earnings, reaching a new high level per share at the peak of each subsequent major business cycle and which, after careful research, gives indications of continuing growth from one business cycle to the next, at a rate faster than the rise in the standard of living."

Bob Barker of Capital Guardian, another very successful growth-stock investor, puts it a little differently. "In my firm, we concentrate on finding those few companies that have clear prospects of very rapid earnings-per-share growth over a protracted period ahead. These are the companies in which our portfolio is entirely invested. We pay no attention to all the other companies there are. Think of the time we save by this concentration." Winthrop Knowlton, a wise investor, likened growth stocks to beautiful, giant money trees. He didn't exactly put it this way but I would paraphrase him as saying: Great corporations, like great trees, put their deep roots down years ago, started growing and branching out, and continue to do so. Trees don't grow to the sky, but money trees get pretty close to investment heaven.

VALUE INVESTORS LOVE UGLY COMPANIES

By contrast, value investors want to own stocks that are cheap not only in relation to other equities but also in absolute terms. They believe all investors are fallible and often misjudge the fundamentals of a company. By buying cheap, a value investor creates a margin of safety for his investment. True value investors are not dismayed by unattractive companies; in fact, hard-core value investors sometimes seem to say the uglier the better. They want the three U's—Underowned, Unloved, and Undervalued. Of course they would rather buy a well-managed, good business at a depressed price, but such situations are few and far between. Instead they buy stocks that can be purchased well below their intrinsic replacement-cost value as a business, where current profits are beneath the sustainable earning power of the company, and that also are cheap by the traditional measures of value.

Value investors definitely don't fall in love with their stocks. When the prices of the shares of the ugly companies they own go up, become expensive, and sell well above their intrinsic value, value investors sell them and go searching for cheapness elsewhere. Growth stock investors have portfolios filled with companies with great, growth franchises that they can be proud of. Value investors have portfolios stuffed with the cheap shares of companies that are doing badly and have hair and dirt all over them. Value stocks, by definition, are cheap in relation to their assets and earning power because investors are pessimistic about them. There is usually bad news associated with them, and since investors tend to be extrapolators, they assume the bad news will continue.

Benjamin Graham is the holy father of value investors. Warren Buffett reveres him, although Buffett has expanded Graham's definition of intrinsic value to include the intangible worth of a great franchise or brand. The sheer size of the Berkshire portfolio has forced him to become a buy-and-hold value investor, although that may be an investment oxymoron. Buffett says he likes to buy good companies at great prices. He likes businesses with products he can understand that generate free cash flow. Because technology stocks meet neither criterion, he has never owned them. Ben Graham preached that you always want to buy a common stock (or a corporate bond for that matter) with a *margin of safety*. That margin relates to the liquidating value of the assets of the company (the price an informed businessperson would pay) being well above the price you are paying for the stock. On the flyleaf of Graham's classic book, *Security Analysis,* is the following from Horace's *Ars Poetica*: "Many shall be restored that now are fallen and many shall fall that now are in honor."

AGNOSTICS BELIEVE THIS, TOO, SHALL PASS

Agnostics don't believe in either religion. They say that everything in the investment business is temporary. "This too shall pass" is their mantra. Religious fanatics, they argue, often end up getting burned at the proverbial stake. When growth stocks are relatively cheap and the economic environment favors them, agnostics will own growth. When value is cheap and growth is expensive, they will look for value. Sometimes they will own a little of both. They maintain that there are fashion swings between growth and value that the intelligent investor can capitalize on. The hard-core growth and value investors reply that switching back and forth is a loser's game. I am an agnostic, but because buying cheap beats buying expensive most of the time, I have a strong value bias.

GROWTH OR VALUE: WHICH PERFORMS BETTER?

The performance history of growth versus value is clear. Over a period of years, value beats the daylights out of growth, and small-cap value is by far the best of all. Authorities like Ibbotson and Fama-French have constructed indexes of growth and value and have calculated their performance. Since 1927, according to Ibbotson, large value stocks have compounded at 11.5% a year and small value has compounded at 14.8%. By contrast, big growth has gained 9.2% per annum and small growth 9.6%. Because of the magic of compounding over 75 years, these are staggering differences. One dollar invested in each index in 1927 would be worth today $35,957 if you had put it into small value, $4,802 into large value, $1,089 in small growth, and $820 in large growth! The difference between small-cap value and everything else is astounding. Small value did almost eight times better than large value and more than 40 times large growth. Ben Graham must be smiling. Only in the 1930s and the 1990s has large growth beaten large value for a full decade. Small growth has trailed small value in every decade except the 1930s. However, in any given year the disparity can be incredible. For example in 1998 large growth stocks returned 33.1%, while large value did a mere 12.1%.

If you have to pick only one vehicle, small-cap value is where individual retirement accounts (IRAs) and long-term index money should be in the United States. It's obvious. Equities are a high-return asset class, and small cap is the best of breed. Unfortunately, right at this moment, small cap, both growth and value, are historically expensive relative to big cap. Over the last six years, small caps have done much better than large caps and small-cap value has soundly trounced small-cap growth. I would be patient and wait to buy either small-cap index. Instead, right now in mid-2005, large caps are *relatively* attractive compared to small caps, and large-cap growth is *relatively* undervalued compared to large-cap value. The Leuthold large-cap growth index of 90 companies is selling at 20.5 times earnings and the Leuthold value index is at 11.9 times, which is a growth to value price earnings ratio of 1.68 versus the historical median of 2.5.

For IRAs the Vanguard index funds make sense to me. Sure, you can capture alpha, extra return, if you identify a winner mutual fund, but you are bucking a number of headwinds in terms of higher costs, performance cycles, manager turnover, and so on. When the time comes and small value is cheap again, Vanguard has a Small-Cap Value Index Fund. The stock selection is based on the MSCI Index, which, in making its selection, uses eight value and growth factors including price/book value, dividend yield, earnings yield, sales growth, and long-term-earnings growth. MSCI defines U.S. small cap as those equities ranked from 751 to 2,500 in market capitalization. Based on each stock's score, the computer then places it in the MSCI value or growth index. Not an ideal way to do it, in my view, but nevertheless it captures the essence of the exercise. Equally important, management expenses for the fund are minuscule. There is no sales load whatsoever, and total annual expenses are 27 or 18 basis points, depending on the class of shares owned. Comparable actively managed funds would have expenses of 80 to 150 basis points not including sales charges.

Growth managers argue that the Vanguard and Ibbotson indexes are ridiculously simplistic, and they say their special skill is in identifying companies that are capable of sustained growth and avoiding the losers. They maintain that their portfolios are populated with vision stocks. Arbitrary quantitative groupings, they say, prove nothing. These growth managers sometimes maintain, a little arrogantly, that they have the true *seeing eye* for beauty, and disdain the value geeks who grub in the muck, searching for cheap ugliness. The real test, they argue, is the results of the portfolios of professional growth stock investors versus those of value investors. They also maintain that, for tax-paying investors, the turnover and tax bill in value portfolios is much higher because, in accordance with their religion, value investors have to sell their winners when they go up. By contrast, growth investors can live happily in their eternally growing money trees for decades.

Here is an example of how it can work if your stock selection is fortunate. In the early 1970s, my father was worried about his health and inflation and suspected my mother would outlive him by a considerable number of years. He never was much of a believer in bonds. "Bonds are trading sardines, but good stocks are eating sardines," was an expression he favored. So he constructed for my mother a portfolio of growth stocks (and cyclical growth stocks) such as Phillip Morris, Caterpillar, Exxon, Coca-Cola, AIG, IBM, Citicorp, Hewlett-Packard, Berkshire Hathaway, GE, Merck, Pfizer, and so on—nothing very imaginative, but solid, long-term companies you would want to sleep with. When she died two years ago at age 95, her cost on many of those positions was actually less than the current dividend.

My mother's portfolio compounded over 32 years at 17% a year, and her dividend income grew at about the same rate. I figure the purchasing power of her income stream had compounded at roughly 12% per annum. The only taxes she paid were on those dividends. Talk about tax-free compounding! Of course, as she grew very old, it made little sense for her to sell any of those shares. No matter how egregiously overpriced they became, she held on to them because she would have had to pay a whopping capital gains tax and then her heirs would have to pay a 55% inheritance tax on the proceeds. Of course, the trick is to find and hold growth stocks that can stand that test of time, and obviously it's difficult. My brother Jeremy and I watched her list intently, and, from time to time, we did weed out and replace a few companies that we thought were beginning to falter.

My brother and I were lucky, and we had the wind at our backs. I think it's too dangerous for the amateur to pick individual stocks. As I mentioned earlier, history shows that the lifespan of growth stocks is short, and the fall from grace when it comes can wipe out years of gains. As for mutual funds, their managers come and go, and the fees are high. If you can find someone like Bill Miller at Legg Mason, it's a gift from heaven. As I noted before, an attractive alternative is owning an index fund, and they come in all shapes and sizes with minuscule fees. At least you are going to capture the index return. The two biggest index fund firms by far are Vanguard and Fidelity.

Growth investing, because of its bias toward a buy-and-hold strategy, is inherently more tax efficient. However, for tax-exempt investors, the hard evidence is that the actual portfolios of value managers beat those of growth managers. The New York research firm, Bernstein, publishes an index of growth versus value that is based on the actual portfolio style analysis of six consulting firms as shown in Table 17.1. This index captures the stock selection factor. The incredible swings between the two religions from 1998 to 2001 confirm my determination to be an agnostic. It is also interesting to note that, during one of the great speculative growth stock bubbles of all time, only in 1998 and 1999 did growth absolutely bury value.

TABLE 17.1

Total Return Growth versus Value Managers

| | Large Capitalization | | |
	Value Managers	Growth Managers	Spread (Growth-Value)
1969	−12.1%	−7.2%	4.9%
1970	4.0	−7.4	−11.4
1971	13.9	23.3	9.4
1972	11.0	20.1	9.1
1973	−9.3	−19.2	−9.9
1974	−16.1	−29.8	−13.7
1975	43.8	36.0	−7.8
1976	38.2	21.3	−16.9
1977	1.5	−0.9	−2.4
1978	9.3	10.7	1.4
1979	22.8	24.2	1.4
1980	26.4	38.2	11.8
1981	5.3	−1.3	−6.6
1982	25.0	26.4	1.4
1983	24.6	19.4	−5.1
1984	7.5	1.9	−5.6
1985	31.6	27.4	−4.2
1986	18.9	18.3	−0.6
1987	3.2	6.5	3.3
1988	19.6	12.9	−6.7
1989	25.6	33.1	7.5
1990	−4.3	−0.4	4.0
1991	30.0	39.4	9.5
1992	11.0	7.0	−4.0
1993	14.3	9.0	−5.3
1994	0.6	−0.8	−1.4
1995	34.4	33.5	−0.9
1996	22.4	22.3	−0.1
1997	28.9	30.5	1.5
1998	12.9	32.2	19.3
1999	7.4	33.4	26.0
2000	9.7	−9.3	−19.0
2001	−3.8	−20.2	−16.4
2002	−18.0	−27.3	−9.3
2003	28.6	29.6	1.0
2004	12.5	9.4	−3.1
Q1:05	−0.9	−3.6	−2.7
Annualized Performance			
1969–1979	8.2%	4.5%	−3.7%
1969–2004	12.3%	10.5%	−1.8%
1980–2004	14.2%	13.3%	−0.9%

Source: Sanford C. Bernstein, Inc., Strategic and Quantitative Research Group

CHAPTER
EIGHTEEN

The Trouble with Being Big

I had lunch with Herb today. Herb works at a big investment management firm that is now owned by a financial conglomerate. He was at Morgan Stanley Investment Management for many years, and we always got along well. Herb is not the brightest bulb in the chandelier, nor is he an obsessive investor. He is a good family man and doesn't take much paper home on weekends. He is a nice combination of hustle and charm. His performance on the $4 billion of U.S. equities (part institutional, part mutual funds) that he runs has always been give or take 50 basis points either side of the benchmark. Last year he got paid $1.2 million, part of which was in stock that vests in two years.

BLOATING AND BUREAUCRACY

Herb wanted to talk. He's desperately worried about the future of firms like his, both financially and competitively. He feels that the profitability of the big firms is being consumed by bloated business infrastructures that were built up during the boom years, which are still growing because of inertia and relentless regulatory pressure. The managements of these firms are no longer the investors that built them. They are businessmen/bureaucrats. Because of past sins, real or alleged, they are terrified of regulatory risk, and as a result are adding whole new departments to vote proxies, double-check compliance, and supervise trading.

Meanwhile, investment management fees are under pressure and declining. Inevitably the profit margins of the big firms are eroding. Lower profitability was already eating into compensation levels for portfolio managers as the bear market shrank assets under management, but now the money to compensate all the new administrative hires will have to come out of the portfolio manager's pool. Portfolio-manager compensation may soon have to be disclosed to clients, and unquestionably this will result in messy and embarrassing scrutiny.

Herb is afraid that big asset management firms are in an irreversible decline. The consultants are advising large institutions that investing with big firms is a loser's game. If your portfolio manager does well, he will leave to join a hedge fund. If he does poorly, you don't want him anyway. Portfolio-manager turnover is an anathema to the consultant fraternity. It makes them look bad. Now they are telling their clients that the best, safest place to invest is with smaller, investor-owned investment management boutiques or with hedge funds.

Herb understands all this, and he is worried his compensation will fall. On the other hand, he doesn't want to take the risk of leaving for a boutique or a hedge fund where you eat what you kill. You might say you don't feel sorry for Herb since he is still outrageously overpaid compared to other sectors of the real economy, and you would be right. Compensation levels in the investment-management business are bound to decline. We were all blessed by the great bull market! Anyway, Herb sounded off at me, as though it was my fault, with a diatribe that went something like this:

"Our profitability has been drained by layers and layers of senior management, compliance, proxy, product development, and human resource people. We even hired our own public relations team and a firm historian. The human resource department is continually organizing bonding dinners, new evaluation forms, and birthday parties for secretaries. A university has been created, and a culture committee has been formed. They asked me to be on the culture committee. Management actually talks about manufacturing margins as though we were an industrial company. We have multiples of marketing specialists, most of whom can only sell what is hot anyway. Investment management is a performance business. If you don't have the numbers, all the salesmen in the world can't sell your products. The firm is now run by the business-men rather than by the investors."

Perhaps the fatal trouble with large investment-management firms is that, although they advertise performance, the businessmen that run them don't seem to know or want to know how to create an environment that can produce alpha or generate consistent absolute returns for clients. Instead, they are giant factories, in business to increase fee-paying assets under management. Most of the relatively few firms in business that can generate alpha are smaller, boutique firms, hedge funds, or investment partnerships. They are true alpha shops. Large investment management firms simply have too many structural impediments to overcome to be consistent alpha creators.

It doesn't have to be this way. Large investment firms can succeed, but they need to have managements that have been investors and, there-fore, understand investing. Management must, above all, cherish their true investors and be committed to protecting them from bureaucratic distractions. They have to understand that performance comes first, and then asset growth will follow. It can even be done in the mutual-fund business. Look at Capital Research!

As long as the number of dedicated alpha shops is small in relation to the overall investment-management industry, these firms should be able to earn sufficient alpha at the expense of the asset-collection factories to pay transaction costs and management fees and still leave substantial excess returns for their clients. These fees should be sufficient to allow the good alpha firms to make a lot of money, motivating them to limit capital under management, attract superior talent, and build highly profitable, stable businesses populated with motivated, contented, rich investors.

GREAT MAVERICKS WILL ALWAYS GO THEIR OWN WAY

There are many temptations for talented investors. For example, in the mid-1980s I hired a really smart, personable Englishman (whom I'll call Michael) to develop a London-based international equity product for Morgan Stanley. He hired good young people and built a substan-tial, highly profitable, growing business. However, he didn't want to be absorbed into the body of the beast that is a big, global investment bank such as Morgan Stanley, and he made that point abundantly clear. Although he recognized that Morgan Stanley's name and connections were a valuable asset, he believed that for his entity to thrive, separation was required. He wanted to be left alone by the firm's somewhat bureaucratic management in the London office, and he wanted space in a different location from the rest of the firm. He also didn't want to be distracted by having to attend weekly operating committee meetings with the heads of the other departments in the London office. He had no aspirations to be anything but the best possible investor.

In 1991 the five of us on the executive committee of Morgan Stanley became concerned about the increasing squabbling, infighting, and accounting wars between divisions as the global securities and investment management firm grew larger. To promote cooperative behavior, we began a One-Firm Firm initiative. We decided that at the end of each year, after bonuses had been determined, the executive committee would make special one-time $500,000 awards to managing directors who had made particular contributions to enhancing a One-Firm Firm culture, and that we would fine by an equal amount any who had been negative. Nominations for awards and punishment would be submitted by the various operating units. The program was actually very successful in promoting cross-divisional cooperation. People responded to the carrot and the stick, and in-fighting didn't stop, but it diminished very considerably.

The first year of the program, Michael was fingered by London Investment Banking as being very negative and uncooperative. He had rejected overtures to mix and mingle with the investment bankers, salespeople, or research analysts, even if it was sanitized. He had made it clear he would like to be physically separated from the rest of the firm. I argued vociferously at the executive committee meeting on awards and fines that Michael's point of view was rational, and that he was building a big business for us that was becoming worth a lot of money. I said it would be a big mistake to hit him. He was a proud individualist and he might quit. We had to have a culture that could accommodate very talented, undiplomatic eccentrics. I prevailed, but the other four guys were not happy with Michael's attitude.

That January, I told Michael he had to change his ways, or at least appear to be less antisocial, or he was going to get dinged the next time. I made a considerable effort to integrate him, even taking him to the

Chairman's Cup, a senior-management golf outing. However, it was to no avail. At year end he was again nominated for the fine but by a different division this time. The respected head of the London office, Sir Somebody, said he was a "detrimental influence." I pointed out that his investment performance was exceptional, his business was growing rapidly, and that his people liked and respected him. Fine, said the four other guys, pay him well but he needs to know that his antisocial behavior is going to cost him money. My pleas for mercy and flexibility fell on deaf ears. Although his total compensation was substantial, when I told Michael about the fine, he resigned on the spot.

Shortly thereafter, Michael started his own firm. He has continued to create exceptional alpha with his value style, and his firm now runs something like $12 billion! The fee is 1%, and the money is run in four separate, pooled accounts. The back-office is outsourced. As I understand it, he has 15 or so investment professionals and a few client service people, which is all you need. You do the math! The firm must be incredibly profitable. Recently I had dinner with Michael in London, and he seemed very content.

In the end we survived Michael's departure because we had depth. At the time, Michael had a superb, young lieutenant who stepped up when Michael left, grew the business, and Morgan Stanley's international value record today is first decile on a huge asset base. It is the crown jewel of the asset-management division. Thinking back on it, in many ways the loss of Michael was inevitable because of the kind of person he was and because Morgan Stanley was becoming a big firm.

Everything the big investment-management firms are wrestling with raises the danger of a vicious circle. Investing and career choices are all about getting into the flow of virtuous rather than vicious circles. Bureaucratic diversions and the inevitable erosion of compensation from the profit-margin squeeze are driving the best investment managers to boutique investment management companies and hedge funds where there are fewer distractions and more potential. If they lose their talented investors, inevitably the big investment-management companies will leak assets. As time goes on, the giants will become dinosaurs, stocked with mediocrities and closet index-fund managers, and, before long, the fee pressure will spread to their institutional businesses as well.

Working at a big investment-management company is an uphill battle. Lawyers and businesspeople, not investors, run those firms, and, without meaning to, they are killing the geese that laid the golden eggs. Capital Guardian and maybe Fidelity, which are run by investors, are the exceptions. Both of these firms have another advantage. They are not publicly owned. Publicly owned firms with business managements have to run their businesses for short-term profits. This means selling to clients what is hot and deemphasizing what is cold. This is the wrong way in the long run to manage the business. I fear that investment management companies that are part of investment banks labor under an even heavier burden because of the perceived conflicts, most of which are a bad rap. With the exception of the Michael matter, I never experienced any pressure or interference in the 30 years I was chairman of Morgan Stanley Investment Management. It's not impossible for big firms to be successful and profitable. It just takes enlightened management and it's hard.

PATIENCE IS A VIRTUE—BUT IT'S SO TOUGH TO PRACTICE

Another example of the right way is that of Jeremy Grantham of a Boston investment partnership, Grantham, Mayo, Van Otterloo & Company. Jeremy Grantham, a contrarian, value-oriented, somewhat irascible fellow, has always been regarded as a serious thinker. He is a hungry observer of the investment life around him, a seeker of truth, a man of the mind. He doesn't care what the world thinks. He is an *irregular* person. He has a hard glitter to him, if you know what I mean.

In 1995, Morgan Stanley; Grantham, Mayo; and three other firms were each given $1 billion by the Verizon pension fund. We were all paid a small fixed fee but could earn a substantial incentive fee if we beat Verizon's benchmark global allocation. The program was the brilliant brainchild of John Carroll and Britt Harris. As I recall, Jeremy Grantham became bearish about equity markets in general and tech in particular around 1997. As a result his performance versus the benchmark and the rest of us was lousy. In fact by the spring of 2000, Grantham, Mayo was in last place, 500 basis points a year behind us, and I think at the time we were the leader.

We actually did okay versus the benchmark in the three-year bear market that followed because we also were bearish, but Grantham, who had stuck to his extreme position and was very overweight bonds and underweight stocks, positively soared. He passed all of us like we were standing still. He made up for four years of lousy performance in two years! It was unbelievable! It is to the great credit of Britt Harris, then the chief pension-fund officer of Verizon, that he stuck with Grantham through thick and thin. Britt knew Grantham's thought process, had confidence in Jeremy's integrity, and he never wavered. Very impressive! Most pension-fund officers would have fired the consistently worst performer, but not Britt.

But that isn't the whole story. In the late 1990s, the firm, Grantham, Mayo, had a very rough time. The firm's assets fell almost 40% as disgusted clients closed their accounts, and his more bullish partners left to form their own firms. Grantham, Mayo went into the red, and Jeremy was mocked as a stopped-clock contrarian. He was undaunted. He kept paying his good investors and spent money on client services and seeding new investment lines like timber and hedge funds. The firm's headcount actually increased almost 50% even as it was losing money. That's very hard to do.

Then when the bubble burst, Grantham, Mayo reaped the rewards. Not only was their performance superb during the bear market, when the rally began in 2003 they did well, particularly in emerging markets. Their emerging markets fund soared 70% in 2003 versus 51.5% for the MSCI emerging markets index, and the money poured in. By the end of 2003, assets under management had tripled from the low to $60 billion, and emerging markets alone had $10 billion with a rich fee. So what did Jeremy do? Because he felt that it was just a rally in what was still a secular bear market and that emerging market equities in particular had run too far too fast, he closed the strategy to new investors at the end of September 2003.

In the summer of 2005, Grantham described his role as "trying to thrive in a secular bear market." He believes deeply in "reversion to the mean" as a fundamental tenet of investment life. Markets are shockingly inefficient, he said, and as an investor you should wait for the fat pitch. Big portfolio bets should be tempered until valuations move to extremes. Patience is an investment virtue, but he concedes that it can be difficult to practice because mean reversion can take a long time. These are all adages that most of us give lip service to but have great difficulty following. Jeremy talks about them and rigorously practices them.

Presently he is still cautious on most equity classes. Expectations are still too high, and there are a number of things that could go bump in the night. Equities, particularly in America, remain expensive because valuations and returns have to revert back to equilibrium fair values. Assuming that they will over the next seven years, returns on all asset classes will be meager. He calculates the compound annual real return from large cap U.S. equities will be minus 1%. Treasury bonds are only slightly better, but international equities and emerging market debt will return 2.5% to 2.7% annually. The best asset classes will be emerging market equities and timber, which will earn 6%. Remember these are real returns and are therefore before manager alpha and inflation. Despite his negative outlook, since equity markets turned in the spring of 2003, his asset allocation accounts have performed very well.

What does Jeremy think are the big bets now for a long-term investor? First, move money out of American equities and into international. Emphasize high-quality, lower-volatility stocks and reduce small-cap, high-volatility, more-speculative equities. His specific advice is to move into conservative hedge funds, timberland, commodities, and conservative fixed income.

Jeremy is 66 years old and going strong. He continues to be committed to preserving his firm's independence and to investors, not businessmen, running the firm. He told *Institutional Investor*, "What we did when we were losing money, the stance we took, would have been impossible if we were beholden to an owner demanding quick results. The stance we are taking now of closing winning strategies would also have been difficult. I am convinced that independence is in the best interests of the firm and our clients." Boy, that is integrity!

I suspect that to be truly great, an investment-management firm has to be modeled on Plato's Academy. Plato wanted to create a fertile atmosphere at his Academy where brilliant young men could be trained to be statesmen, and in this way the future political leadership of Greece would be enhanced. His theory was that the cross-fertilization of profound minds working in different disciplines (historians, artists, mathematicians, philosophers) mingling with each other would enrich the thought processes and insights of all. The intellectual sum of the whole would be far greater than the sum of the parts.

ALPHA INVESTING IS A ZERO-SUM GAME

I remember a talk I had in early 2004 with Joan, another old friend from a major investment-management company, who runs big Europe, Asia, Far East (EAFE) portfolios for large pension funds. Her accounts are $500 million to $1 billion in size, and the fee is 30 to 40 basis points. Joan invests macro, in other words, top down. She is a solid, experienced investor, her international portfolios have done well, and her clients know and respect her. Furthermore, they are nice, intelligent people. However, both they and their consultants are enmeshed in a system that is mostly oriented to *current* performance *relative* to the benchmark.

In the big-pension fund world of long-only managers, *absolute* return is not relevant. Plan sponsors view their roles as making the allocation decision among stocks, bonds, real estate, private equity, and so on. Within the equity asset class, for example, they decide how much should be in the U.S., international, emerging markets, and all the capitalization subsectors. Each class has its own benchmark. The plan sponsors then hire investment management firms to create alpha in their category, and if they don't, the sponsors fire them. The institutional investment world runs on alpha, the beloved alpha. This is understandable, but it can be counterproductive. The pressure for short-term performance versus a benchmark can easily disorient the investment brain of a portfolio manager. What should matter is capital enhancement in bull markets and capital preservation in bears; in other words *absolute*, not relative, returns.

In this sense, professional alpha investing is not a winner's game but a zero-sum game, because for every winner there has to be a loser. In fact professional investing is even worse than zero-sum games like the NFL, where every Sunday the number of winners matches the number of losers, because transaction and management costs make investment management marginally a negative-sum game. Because compensation levels for portfolio managers are exalted, the game attracts the best, the brightest, and the most obsessive. Of course there are some incompetents out there, but not many as they tend to get weeded out, so earning alpha is a hard, grinding task.

I know that over the past three- and five-year periods, Joan's portfolios have earned around 300 basis points a year of excess return over the EAFE benchmark, which puts her close to the top quartile of all EAFE managers. However, when this conversation occurred in the spring of 2004, she was bemoaning her most recent performance and worrying about explaining it to her clients in upcoming meetings.

"What were you up for the year that ended March 31?" I asked.

"Fifty-one percent," she told me.

"Sounds pretty good to me!" I said. "The S&P 500 was up 32%."

"It's not good enough in my world," she snapped. "My benchmark, the EAFE index, was up 56%, so I underperformed by 500 basis points. It's how you did versus the benchmark that counts. I am being put on the watch list by two of my big accounts that I have had for years."

"They are harassing you because you were behind the benchmark for the latest 12 months when your three- and five-year record versus both your benchmark and other managers is good?"

"Apparently. No one has fired me yet, but I'm on probation and I'm sweating it. The firm is sweating it, too. I'm worried they are going to ding me on comp this year."

It's ridiculous! A performance monitoring system run amok! March 31, 2003, was about two weeks after the equity markets of the world bottomed and embarked on a huge rally. In addition, for most of the next 12 months, the dollar was falling like a stone, and the international currencies were soaring, so the rising yen and euro were huge additives to the local currency return of the EAFE markets. The EAFE index for the period was up 36% in local currencies but earned an astounding additional 20 percentage points from the currency factor. An EAFE portfolio had to be 100% invested in equities to capture that 20% ride, since EAFE portfolios are not allowed to hold cash in foreign currencies.

The real sticking point, however, is that after the horrendous three-year bear market, in early April 2003 it would have been almost imprudent not to have held some cash. Everyone was tearing their hair and gnashing their teeth in despair because the world was about to come to an end and deflation loomed. However, once the equity markets turned, having cash proved to be a tremendous drag because of the huge rise in stocks and the massive appreciation of foreign currencies. In other words it's really tough to beat the index in a rip-roaring bull market.

As I think about it, it seems to me that the right way to look at *relative* performance is *relative* to the dimensions of the gain. In other words, if the index was up 10% and the portfolio was 5%, there is negative alpha of 500 basis points. That *is* a big deal! The relative underperformance to the benchmark is 50% (−5% of alpha is 50% of 10%). But if the index is up 56% and the portfolio is up 51%, that's a relative underperformance of only a little more than 9% (−5% of alpha is 9% of 56%) and a minor event. Besides, it's the three- and five-year performance numbers that really count.

Joan worries about being on her clients' watch list and frets about her performance. She is seriously stressed from the clients' pressure on her to create alpha, and I am concerned that she will press too hard for alpha. It's ironic, but the more you want performance and push for it, the more difficult it is to get. It's like playing a sport. The more confident you are, the better you play. A *relaxed*, obsessive investor is best.

I thought about it some more. Demanding performance versus a benchmark and focusing on short-term results are the two great banes of investing. Warren Buffett is the Investment Folk Hero of modern times, up there in the Hall of Fame with Lord Keynes and Ben Graham. He also is everybody's All-American guy because in this day of greedy, get-rich-quick yuppies and conspicuous consumption, he still lives in the same old house in the same old town out on the same old prairie. Nobody cares if he travels in his own jet. As he so succinctly put it, "I used to think corporate jets were the indefensible; now I think they are the indispensable."

Buffett once said that the great thing about being an investor is that you're like a batter in a baseball game in which there are no called strikes. They can throw you General Electric at 45, he said, and you don't have to swing. They can throw you Microsoft at 28 and you don't have to swing. They have to keep pitching and you don't have to swing. So if you're patient, the odds are with you. You can wait until you get a big fat one right where you want it. You might not swing for six months; you might not swing for two years, but the odds of hitting it out of the park are a lot better when the pitch is fat. You must be patient!

That's fine for Buffett to say with his *private investor* hat on, but those of us who have *public investors* and consultants looking over our shoulders don't have the luxury of letting pitch after pitch go by. We have to swing. The umpires who are the consultants and the clients often aren't patient, and they call strikes on us and watch our batting average almost from day to day. Running a hedge fund, the pressure is for *absolute* performance with no monthly *drawdowns*. Drawdowns are declines in net asset value. Under pressure from some of our investors, we now provide net asset values twice a month, but at least we aren't fretting about beating a benchmark, although we certainly keep a wary eye on the S&P 500. Poor Joan, however, has both tensions. Her clients demand she produce performance above her EAFE benchmark, and they also want short-term performance. Neither demand is conducive to good long-term investment thinking nor does it prove much of anything.

So whose fault is this distortion? I think it's a vicious circle in which the clients, consultants, and we money managers are all to blame. Clients want performance; they need it whether they are an individual, a company, or a foundation, because the portfolio or the pension plan is a profit center for which they are held accountable. As a result, they put pressure for performance on the administrator of the portfolio, yet if they are CEOs, they lament out of the other side of their mouths that they can't run their companies properly because the money managers who own their stock are so oriented to quarterly results. Investment managers complain about the short-term horizon of clients, yet they buy and sell stocks with hair triggers. The consultants pour gasoline onto the fire and rub their hands. Manager firings mean more searches for them. Everyone blames everybody else, but the process is circular.

What's the answer for the lonely soul looking for a long-term relationship with a solid investment manager? First, go easy on the pressure. Second, get someone who is battle tested and as close to having a private investor mentality as possible. Third, find a firm that is comfortable with itself and its financial status. Fourth, go with a firm that is owned and run by investors. Examples would be an investment counselor who is established but who is not trying to dress up the daffodil for sale, or a hedge fund where the partners have plenty of their own skin in the game. And there are some very good people working in private wealth management at big firms.

CHAPTER

NINETEEN

Bubbles and the True Believer

Since time immemorial, the financial markets of the world have been prone to bubbles in everything from tulips and art to shares and houses. Therefore, obviously it is very important for investors to understand them. All bubbles start as powerful fundamental developments and legitimate investment opportunities. They become bubbles or manias or whatever you want to call them when investors in their euphoric optimism project future results, not based on rational fundamentals, but on a continuation of past results. The Internet, instant information, thousands of new Certified Financial Analysts, and the SEC's program to create a more level playing field will not result in more *efficient* markets or fewer bubbles. Markets are inherently *inefficient* and always will be because of human nature, because of greed and fear, because of the herd instinct. As Seth Klarman puts it: "People don't consciously choose to invest with emotion—they simply can't help it."

Each bubble is different. Two recent excellent books on bubbles of all varieties are *Devil Take the Hindmost: A History of Financial Speculation* by Edward Chancellor and *Markets, Mobs, & Mayhem: A Modern Look at the Madness of Crowds* by Robert Menschel. The most poetic and dramatic evocation of the chaos and sense of hopeless of a financial panic is in the opening lines of W.B. Yeats' epic poem *The Second*

Coming. Yeats describes the falcon turning aimlessly in a widening gyre, unable to hear the falconer. "Things fall apart," he writes, "the center cannot hold." Anarchy reigns and a "blood dimmed tide" engulfs the world. But the great lines that capture the despair of the bottom of a bear market, a panic are: "the ceremony of innocence is drowned; the best lack all conviction while the worst are full of passionate intensity."

TWO TYPES OF BUBBLES: BAD AND VERY BAD

There are two general varieties of bubbles. The first, as bubbles go, is less malignant; the other, pure cancer and very dangerous. The happier varieties are bubbles in the securities of productive assets like technology, railroads, and capital equipment underwritten by the financial markets, in other words, stocks and bonds. The bad kinds are in nonproductive assets like tulips, Tokyo golf courses (in 1990 membership in one Tokyo club sold for $5 million in yen-equivalent current dollars), real estate, or collectibles when the bubble's assets are used as collateral for loans from banks. Obviously the most dangerous of all is a bubble that sucks in a large percentage of the population of a country, such as a bubble in residential real estate. However, a housing bubble is slower moving because the price appreciation is not so readily apparent and because it spreads by word of mouth. As of mid-2005 I do not believe the United States yet is in a full-blown, nationwide housing bubble. Are house prices over the moon in certain fancy areas of the country? Absolutely! But the same does not apply to the broad mass of housing. Could house prices in America be flat for five years? Sure. Could mortgage equity extraction cease with a knock-on effect on consumer spending? Of course. But is it the 1930s again? I don't think so.

When a bubble in nonproductive assets financed by banks bursts, the consequences invariably are deflation and depression. The tech bubble of the 1990s was in a highly productive asset, and it was financed by stocks and bonds, not the banking system, so its aftershocks may be relatively minor. Of course a lot of ridiculous ventures were financed and a huge amount of stupid, speculative money was devoured, but that's the way of the world. By contrast, the bubble in Japan in the 1980s was in nonproductive assets (zaitech, land, golf courses, art), and it was mostly financed by the banking system. The consequences have been much more severe.

It's excruciatingly difficult to figure out when bubbles are going to burst. They have a nasty tendency to last much longer than even the most experienced, patient student of financial markets and crowd psychology can believe. Bubbles always flow from powerful substance so it's the rational being taken to the irrational to the mystic. Valuation and overbought technical metrics invariably signal the bust far too early. Bullish sentiment goes from being crazy to euphoric to mad. I have mentioned *BusinessWeek* covers as a powerful contrary indicator. In the first six months of 2000, as the bubble was peaking, *BusinessWeek* ran no less than five gushing cover stories on tech and the new economy.

Observing market action doesn't help, either. There were several times in the late 1990s when it appeared the mania had finally peaked and the meltdown was under way. I remember April 1999. It seemed as though things couldn't get crazier. The Internet index (IIX) had soared 340% in eight months. Even the bears were becoming mute. Suddenly out of a clear blue sky, the stocks collapsed. By early August the IIX was down 30%. Many of the high flyers like eBay, Amazon, Yahoo!, and AOL fell 50%. The crucial trend lines and support levels had been broken. It appeared it was the beginning of the end!

But it wasn't. In the next seven months, the IIX tripled again. eBay went from 70 to 250. Huge market capitalizations like Cisco and Intel doubled. We bears began to despair of it ever ending. Then, fitfully, the bubble began to lose gas. In the early spring of 2000 the Internet stocks collapsed. The IIX fell from 690 to 400 in two months. This sharp drop was shrugged off as an aberration in an already inflated specialty market. That summer, the big tech names began to drift sideways, but inexplicably the IIX rallied back to 560. Once again, all seemed right with the tech and Internet worlds. "The pause that refreshes," said one market letter writer.

In July 2000 *The High Tech Strategist* published a table that shows the average price/earnings ratio for the 40 largest Nasdaq stocks was 230 times earnings. Then, in late summer, there began to be rumblings that the overall economy was beginning to falter. In September, the tech stock carnage really began and it was frightening to behold. In five weeks Intel fell 45% with a loss of $240 billion of market value. There would be periodic rallies over the next two years, but the bubble had been burst and the great secular bear market in technology and Internet equities was under way.

When a bubble finally bursts, the so-called *fallacy of composition* comes into play and inflames mob psychology. This theorem says that, in a crisis, the action that is rational for each individual is irrational for the group as a whole and creates a disastrous outcome. The classic example is that when there is the cry of "Fire!" in a crowded theater, it is rational for each individual to save himself to rush toward the exit. However, when everyone does it simultaneously, there is a panic, and a crush results. In a financial panic, each individual is acting rationally when he sells his stocks, or would be were it not for the fact that others are doing the same thing. Each participant, by rationally trying to save himself, contributes to the ruin of all.

THE PROVERBIAL LONG WAVE IN THE ECONOMY

Somewhere embedded deep in the investor psyche in the early twenty-first century there is a sense of foreboding and disaster. Everyone knows the old saw that every boom is followed by a bust, and all know well the history that after a bubble bursts there are long, agonizing periods with dismal returns for years with occasional sharp fool's rallies. The bears are fascinated with the doomsday of an impending great depression and the apocalypse of a market crash. They sense there is something ominous, derivatives, debt, housing, terrorism, lurking out there—a great cancer growing secretly and inexorably in the bowels of the world.

The long cycle has been a recurring phenomenon in human economic history. Not until the late 1920s, however, when Nikolai Kondratieff's essays began to be published in *The Long Waves in Economic Life* (*Voprosy Konyunktury*, Vol. I No 1, 1925), was the phenomenon formally identified. Kondratieff described a recurring 50- to 60-year economic cycle, driven by the ebb and flow of innovation and capital investment that had social implications. Writing in 1922, Kondratieff identified a long wave that began around 1790 and lasted until 1843, a second that ran from 1843 to 1896, and a third that should extend to around 1950. His charts and papers, which relate to the United Kingdom, the United States, and France, analyze commodity prices, interest rates, and wages.

Nikolai Kondratieff had an interesting resume. In 1920 he had designed the first five-year plan for Russian agriculture, and his planning was highly regarded by the commissars. Jealous rivals pointed out that their revered agricultural economist's long-wave theory argued that the downturns in capitalist economies were not attributable to inherent defects within the system and furthermore were self-correcting. The commissars were surprised but not amused. In 1924 Kondratieff was put on trial for economic heresy, found guilty, and sentenced to Siberia where he spent the rest of his life making big stones into little ones. It is believed he died in the early 1930s. As noted above, in 1926 his theories were noted but officially disparaged by other Soviet economists.

Kondratieff's papers were generally ignored until the 1970s when Professor Jay Forrester of the Sloane School at M.I.T. became fascinated with them and refined their application to the modern world. Actually Kondratieff identified rather than analyzed. Forrester believed the waves could be explained by capital investment. Each cycle ends with excessive capital equipment accumulation and increasing use of leverage for speculation, and a long period in which the excesses are purged by a secondary depression, a collapse of the capital goods sector, and a long period of stagnation. Stagnation tends to be characterized by protectionism (the 1816 tariffs, Smoot–Hawley) and a massive debt overhang. Accumulating physical depreciation then sets the stage for the next growth phase. In effect, as Forrester wrote, a major depression rebalances the economy, liquidates debt, and clears away the accumulated excesses.

A Kondratieff pattern is discernible in the economic history of the United States. Forrester argued that the late 1940s was the end of one and the beginning of a new long wave. The Vietnam War and inflation ended the first phase, and a primary depression followed in 1974 followed by a plateau, then one more growth burst, a secondary depression, and a long period, 15 years or more, of stagnation. Kondratieff's theory probably would not expect this long wave to end until around 2010, but the tricky issue is whether the 1990 recession was the secondary depression he would expect or whether we had it in 2000–2001. In other words, are we close to the end of the stagnation period or 14 years into it? In either case, the Kondratieff wave cycles don't fit as well this time.

Today most economists deride the long-wave theory as being in the same league with astrology or palm reading. They argue that advances in economic theory, the much greater role of government in the economy, and expanded international cooperation in the past half century have permanently mitigated the steepness of the economic cycle. Technological change occurs faster than it used to. Instead they concentrate on the conventional three- to four-year inventory cycle. A few focus on the 7- to 11-year fixed investment, or Juglar, cycle. At one time, a 20-year building, or Kuznets, cycle was popular. By way of comparison, one Kondratieff equals roughly three Kuznets, six Juglars, or 12 inventory cycles. I dislike agreeing with economists, but I tend to feel that Kondratieff is intriguing but black magic.

The problem with doomsayers, perpetual bears, and gloomy Guses is that they are broken records. Of course occasionally their forecasts do come true. But even stopped clocks are right twice a day. Or as Nietzsche so elegantly put it: "Stare too long into the abyss and you become the abyss."

THE TRUE BELIEVER: DISCIPLE OF GOLD

Peter Palmedo has stared into the abyss, and in a way he has fulfilled Nietzsche's prophecy. Peter is a great old friend from mountain-climbing days. He lives in Sun Valley and runs an investment-management company/hedge fund that specializes in gold.

A horse I have never quite been enamored with in the ride to riches is gold. I have shunned gold for all the conventional reasons: Gold has a negative yield because you have to pay for storing it, there is no intrinsic valuation equation, and its only worth is as expensive apocalypse insurance. I accept that gold has its allure. It was thought by the early Egyptians to be the skin of the gods, and it has *preserved* its purchasing power over the millennia. The Old Testament recounts how, in 600 B.C., one ounce of gold bought 350 loaves of bread. As of today, one ounce will still buy 350 loaves of bread in the United States. However, this often-cited example also shows that gold has been a sterile investment; it has not *enhanced* the purchasing power of its owners over the millennia. Enhancement, not just preservation, is why we play the investment game. Over the past century, equities have appreciated 10 times faster than gold.

Peter and I have talked about all this for years as we climbed mountains. I once wrote a piece about Peter when I was at Morgan Stanley. I do think there is a plausible case that a professionally managed, hedged portfolio consisting of the metal itself and gold shares could realize returns of 10% real and maybe 12% to 13% nominal per annum but with a lot of volatility. Here is the story.

I know a number of investors who are deeply, almost fanatically committed to an investment philosophy. They are the true believers. The purest, most steadfast disciple of an asset class I know of is Peter, who is a gold disciple. By definition, a true believer has to endure long, lonely stretches out there in the cold and bleak winds of the investment wilderness as an exile from the herd, when his or her style doesn't work and the world thinks he is both terminally wrong and crazy. Certainly in the late 1990s value investors had a very tough couple of years because if you didn't believe in tech in the late 1990s, you were nuts and obsolete. But other than Peter, no one I know has suffered a decade of anguish and still persisted.

Peter is a really interesting guy. Now 50 years old, he has boyish good looks, is very fit, is soft spoken, but has always had a rebellious streak. If his prep school basketball coach told him to practice foul shots, Peter would work on three pointers. Told by authority, "It's either my way or the highway," Peter instinctively heads for the highway. After majoring in economics and option theory, he joined Morgan Stanley's equity derivatives group in 1980 and did a lot of everything. In the summer of 1987, using a series of quantitative models he had developed, he became convinced that dynamic disequilibrium, a three-standard-deviation event, was imminent. He persuaded the firm and certain accounts to buy deep out-of-the-money S&P 500 puts, which he demonstrated were very underpriced (in addition he bought a load of them for himself). Then came the Crash!

With a nest egg, Peter began to think the high stress and travel Morgan Stanley required were not his thing, considering that he had a wife and three young children. A skier, climber, and biker, he moved his family to Sun Valley, Idaho, and began to search for an asset class to *immerse* himself in. *Immerse* is the operative word. Peter's style has always been to focus intensely on one thing, study it, build models on it, and develop an analytical edge. He came up with gold because it was complex, misunderstood, underresearched, and susceptible to his option-pricing theories. In 1990 he founded Sun Valley Gold.

Over the next decade, Peter became arguably the most knowledgeable gold analyst in the world. He totally immersed himself in the study of gold, always applying his option-pricing theories. Over time he built a four-man research team of geologists and mining engineers who probed mine sites and generated detailed inputs for cash-flow and resource-value models. In addition, he uses dynamic valuation modeling and warrant-theory cash flow to determine accurate and consistent corporate valuations. For the metal itself, he built models that attempt to predict the effect of small changes in the variables of the supply and demand curves. Gold is an intriguing commodity to model because there is a huge above-ground stock and limited production increases. Quants tell me that Peter's models and equations are highly sophisticated and that Sun Valley Gold has the best mining research. As he studied the literature, Peter focused on a long scholarly piece written in 1988 by Lawrence Summers (later secretary of the treasury and now president of Harvard) and Robert Barsky entitled "Gibson's Paradox and the Gold Standard." Summers and Barsky argued that the relative price of gold is driven by (and is the reciprocal of) the real rate of return from capital markets and that this relationship has strengthened since the price of gold was floated.

> *Gold is a highly durable asset, and thus, as stressed by Levhari and Pindyck (1981), it is the demand for the existing stock, as opposed to the new flow, that must be modeled. The willingness to hold the stock of gold depends on the rate of return available on alternative assets. We assume the alternative assets are physical capital and bonds.*
>
> "The Pricing of Durable Exhaustible Resources,"
> The Quarterly Journal of Economics

Peter gave me a copy of the Summers–Barsky thesis, and it's too dense a thicket for me. He has written a succinct paper that is comprehensible. In it he points out that this relationship to the capital market's real return and particularly to the stock market has proved stunningly consistent since that paper was written. Since 1988 the price of gold has had a negative 0.85 coefficient of correlation with the S&P 500 and an R^2 of 72%. As things got crazier since 1994, the negative correlation rose to 0.94, with an R^2 of 88%. In other words, the stock market explains 88% of the weekly price fluctuations of gold over the past eight years. The long-term correlation with Treasury bonds is not as high but still very significant.

As Peter explains it, the so-called problem with gold, which causes its erratic price behavior, is that "the elasticity of a positively sloped investment demand function overwhelms the inelasticity of supply." I didn't understand it either until he explained. You see, only 18% of the gold mined throughout history is held in investment form, or slightly more than $200 billion. The investable capital markets of the world are estimated to be about $60 trillion. In a low return cycle for stocks and bonds, monetary and investment demand for gold turns positive, and there is a dramatic shortage of available metal. This large differential can only be solved by much higher prices. The point is that it is not inflation or deflation that is the principal driver of gold, but the return from other long-term financial assets, particularly equities. Peter's model of this relationship is shown in Figure 19.1. As you can see, in times of bleak returns, gold beats everything else.

Peter maintains that the long-term equilibrium or inflation adjusted price of gold in today's dollars is about 520/ounce, as compared to the current price of about 425. Summers and Barsky also say that there is a secular trend toward a higher real and nominal price. Population and income growth exceed the constrained growth of the physical stock of metal, which has been a mere 1.75% over the centuries. In addition, in the modern world, monetary growth far exceeds economic growth.

FIGURE 19.1
Expected Real Return Matrix

Capital Markets					Gold
10%	–		–		–8%
8%	–		–		–3%
6%	–		–		2%
4%	–	↔	–		7%
2%	–		–		12%
0%	–		–		17%
–2%	–		–		22%

Source: Sun Valley Gold LLC

However, gold was not a happy place to be in the roaring 1990s. Gold was still correcting the excesses of its huge bubble of the late 1970s, so the market price was in the process of not only reverting to the mean, but dramatically undershooting. The best company-specific research and the most sophisticated models were for naught in a secular bear market. Peter was viewed as "that guy who used to be smart that went crazy and became a gold bug." However, he didn't care because he was convinced that double-digit real returns on financial assets were unsustainable. He is a true believer, and while his family grew up in Sun Valley, he climbed every mountain in sight and waited for his time to come.

Peter thinks of his benchmark as being gold bullion and gold shares, each at 50%, in a range from 70% to 30%. Allocation can add a couple of hundred basis points a year to gold's return. Gold shares tend to have twice the volatility of the base metal because of their inherent operating leverage. Sun Valley Gold's record is that active management of a gold-shares portfolio can add 500 points of alpha to the return of the gold-shares index. This strikes me as optimistic, but the gold-shares market is very inefficient, and analytical resources can make a huge difference.

How much you should have in gold on an investment, as opposed to a trading basis, depends on how long-term bullish or bearish you are. If you believe Peter's story and think the real return from world capital markets (in other words, equities and fixed income) over the next half decade is going to be 4% per annum, the real return Peter would be shooting for from a managed gold portfolio is going to be 12% to 15% real (+7% metal, +1% allocation, +14% gold shares, plus 6 to 8 percentage points of alpha). That would be spectacular! I don't disagree with his 4% real return forecast, but I do wonder if Peter can generate that much alpha, particularly as his fund is now considerably bigger.

Owning some gold is a wonderful diversifier. Gold goes up when stocks and bonds go down. Therefore, if I were running a giant pension fund with $30 billion assets and $5 billion in absolute return strategies, my allocation to *managed* gold would be 5% to 7% of the absolute return portion. A risk-averse individual might want to do 10%. But I don't see owning gold, the metal, outright except as a trading sardine.

TWENTY

Divine Intervention, or Inside Information?

A Tale that Will Make Your Blood Run Cold

The poet Robert Service long ago wrote "there are strange things done 'neath the midnight sun by the men that search for gold." He added: "The arctic trails have their secret tales that would make your blood run cold" ("The Cremation of San McGee"). If you hang around the investment business long enough, eventually you experience some mysterious, almost supernatural events because the stock market is a capricious beast, almost a force of nature like the sea or the arctic. It can be bountiful and loving in its embrace but also hard and cruel and sadistic. Making your living from the stock market is a strange, hazardous, yet beguiling occupation. It's a little like being a ship's captain back in the time of wind and sail. As the master of a whaler out of Nantucket in those days of yore, in good

An earlier and different version of Chapter 20, "Inside Information," was printed in the *Institutional Investor Magazine* of July 1971.

times when the whales were everywhere and the wind was warm and fair, you blissfully rode the ocean's friendly currents. Then suddenly, without warning, the sea would turn and you would find yourself driven helplessly toward some distant rocky shore by one of its fierce, irrational storms. Men and women who live at the mercy of the whims of the sea and weather are a superstitious lot.

I don't expect anyone to believe Judson Thomas' story. It's too incredible. It's the old magic slipper, fountain of youth yarn that everybody dreams about but nobody thinks could really happen, not in cold, hard daylight in malignant New York City on that wretched Wall Street where there is no love or mercy, just numbers and dollar signs. Sometimes truth is stranger than fiction.

When all this happened, Jud was maybe 50 years old. I had known him for 20 years. Maybe 10 or 12 years before I had introduced him to Jim Gantsoudes, who was then running institutional sales at Morgan Stanley. Jim hired him, I'm afraid, partly on my recommendation. Jud never really got into it at Morgan Stanley, either in terms of the business or building relationships. He could handle the menial stuff like arranging lunches and taking an analyst around, but he lacked sales charisma. He would assiduously take notes in the morning research meeting but then be unable to make the story or the IPO sing. Jud was an affable empty suit, not a guy who could make a difference. After a couple of years, he was let go. I've always felt a little guilty about that episode, both in terms of misleading Gantsoudes but even more because I think it permanently undermined Jud's confidence.

Anyway, after leaving Morgan Stanley, Jud was on the beach for a while, but he finally settled at Hudson & Company, a second-rate research and trading boutique that had a technician and a couple of decent analysts. He got paid strictly on production, and I know he had to scramble and scratch for every trade. My impression was that even in the bubble years he never took home more than $125,000, and he told me he sometimes found himself awake at night worrying about his production and lack thereof.

I wouldn't say I was really a friend of Jud—I never saw him socially or anything like that—but we had that peculiar intimacy of two guys in the same business who had spent chunks of dead time together over the course of many years, in our case waiting on the Port Chester station platform. He was what is known in the dismissive vernacular as a nice guy, but from all those snatches of conversation I never got an original idea or perceptive insight. He knew infinitely more about the Giants and the Yankees than the stock market. I can see him the way he used to be before it happened, struggling every morning up that long flight of pockmarked cement steps to the platform, a big, beefy middle-aged man, faintly disheveled, his shoes spotted. The face was good—strong, sturdy features arranged honestly—but the eyes had been shot away a long time ago and now there was nobody home a lot of the time.

Those mornings Jud moved gently, as if he had a headache, maybe a mild hangover, which was not an overwhelming surprise to anyone who had any idea of his daily martini consumption. "Got that burned-out feeling," he would say. "Damn business." Being an institutional sales-man is an occupation that makes some unusual demands on one's psyche and soul, and Jud drank at least one martini at lunch, two on the train going home while he played cards in the bar car, and at least two more at home with the "old lady" (as he called her) to "dull the pain."

He never defined to me what particular pain he was trying to as-suage, but I'm pretty sure it stemmed from his uphill struggle to survive and a nagging lack of what the industrial psychologists call job satisfac-tion. Jud had been in institutional sales for a long time. For Hudson, he covered 30 of the big New York and Boston institutional accounts, and he dispensed the buzzwords like *robust* and *granular* while throwing in *fulsome* indiscriminately so it was obvious he really didn't know what the word meant. He had seen portfolio managers come and go, but as he got older they seemed to get younger, and he confided to me that it became increasingly more difficult for him to relate to the new ones.

These days institutional sales is a young man's game. A smile and a shoe shine count for nothing. A really good institutional salesperson is a portfolio manager's friend and confidant, and an idea generator. It is not easy for a 50-year-old man to get close to the latest 30-something rising star at Fidelity or at Moore Capital. The traders at the big institutions are inclined to go out drinking or to a ball game with guys their own age or with some fellow who had played running back for the Packers. As for the serious hedge-fund guys, they had no time for him at all. Jud knew all the big names in the game like Kingdon, Cooperman, and Druckenmiller, but they disdained him as a hack.

In fact, most of the time he was lucky if he even got past their dulcet-voiced secretaries or some junior trader. The fund managers

themselves were inaccessible and arrogant when they were doing well
and whiners and grouches when they were running bad. But Jud always
maintained that Dick Rhinelander of Pinnacle Partners was the worst.
Back in the late 1990s Pinnacle had a good run, and then in 2001 and
2002, Pinnacle was net short and posted two 20% years back-to-back,
growing to $4 billion. However, some guys whispered Rhinelander
wasn't that smart—it was just that in those bear-market years, anyone
who had the guts to sell short tech faster and more indiscriminately
could look good. Then the weather changed, and more recently Pinnacle had struggled. A few guys said Rhinelander was a one-trick pony.

Anyway, most of the time when Jud would phone Pinnacle, his call
would be shunted into voice mail. Once in a while, if the secretary remembered the Christmas chocolates and if the great man was in a condescending mood and had nothing better to do, Jud would get a chance
to blurt out Hudson's latest spiel to him. Rhinelander, the portfolio
manager from Harvard, wouldn't say anything. He'd say absolutely
nothing except "thanks" when Jud was finished. "Thanks" and a click.
Most portfolio managers would at least kibitz or say, "yeah, yeah," even
if they couldn't have cared less. Not Rhinelander. He gave no playback
at all; it was like talking to yourself in an empty room. It left you feeling
stupid and emasculated, but Jud had to do it because Pinnacle gave him
a little business.

Of course the quick, young fund analysts he sometimes got shunted
off to were just as bad. They acted like they already knew everything he
told them, and they asked him obtuse business-school questions about
enterprise value and free cash flow he couldn't answer as they shredded
his story. Actually I'm pretty sure that after the last martini on Friday
night, sitting with that white haze enveloping him, his eyes not focusing
on the blaring television, Jud would admit to himself and the old lady (if
she ever asked him) that the money managers and their analysts didn't
care what stocks he liked and only bothered to listen at all because of
that compulsive money-manager fear of missing something.

They thought he was just a big dumb salesman, a loser, not even a
has-been, just a never-was, and he didn't blame them. He almost always
was wrong on the market, and his stock ideas had an uncanny way of
dying horrible deaths. His buy recommendations never failed to disappoint—wildcat strikes, antitrust suits, bad earnings, or maybe the CEO
dropped dead from a heart attack. If his idea was a short, there would be

a tender from out of the blue or wise guys would engineer a squeeze. Something bad if he pushed a long or something good if it was a short always happened.

THE MYSTERY OF JUD'S *WALL STREET JOURNAL*

So each morning when Jud bought his *Wall Street Journal* in the crush of commuters in the crowded Port Chester station house from the garrulous, old blind man who had been there for years selling newspapers and coffee, it was without enthusiasm or anticipation. Some guys seemed literally to devour the *Journal*; to them it was crisp and full of hope and new moneymaking messages, but to Judson reading it was a task, a dull ritual of superficial scanning, all the time knowing he should read more carefully but not really caring. Once in a flash of originality that surprised me he said, "Trying to determine what is going on in the world by reading newspapers is like trying to tell the time by watching the second hand of a watch."

Up to now I've just been building the background, and at this point the story of Jud and the *Wall Street Journal* really begins, and I'll tell it as he told me that day propped up with an oxygen tent behind him in the hospital. Anyway, this particular morning in February, Jud got on the usual train that looked as bedraggled as he felt and glanced at the *Journal* in his normal, desultory, distracted fashion. He carefully read only the front page, looked up a few stocks he owned, and scanned the most active list. Then he tried halfheartedly to read several Hudson research reports but instead dozed the rest of the way to New York. He usually left his *Journal* on the train, but this particular morning in his stupor, he found as he got off the train that he still had it and stuffed it into a newspaper bin on the platform in Grand Central.

In the elevator on the way up to the Hudson offices he listened idly as two well-dressed young brokers chattered about the previous day's market.

"Fidelity must have been the seller of that ten-million-share block of GE."

"Yeah, no one else who has that much stock would dump it so hard. Most active stock and down three."

Jud recalled seeing that block print. Something jogged his memory now. Strange, he distinctly remembered reading in the *Journal* this morning that Intel had been the most active stock and was up 4 to 80. The company's third-quarter earnings had been surprisingly good. GE had been about sixth on the most active list and he remembered it as being up 1.45. Odd! He'd check on it when he got to the office.

That morning he was busy with the usual trivia of phone calls relaying the morning meeting and asking clients to a research lunch. About noon he was standing in the trading room when an order came in from one of his accounts, Omega, to buy 100,000 Intel. The stock was trading around 76, and his trader had already bought 50,000 shares when the earnings for Intel's third quarter printed. Since they had been in the *Journal* that morning he didn't bother to flash Jack, Omega's trader.

Abruptly Intel began to run. The stock printed 20,000 at 76.70, 10,000 at 77, and then 200,000 at 79. Jack was on the phone now.

"Did you buy that last 50,000?"

"No, I didn't, Jack. The stock has jumped to 79 here in the last few minutes and you said to buy it around 76."

"Goddamn it, Jud, that was before they reported earnings up 25% and had very positive guidance. Did you see the release? Why didn't you call me?"

"I saw the earnings on the tape, Jack. I didn't flash you because they were in the *Journal* this morning."

"You're crazy. They were not. They just came out. Why do you think the stock has been running wild in the last 10 minutes?"

"I'm sure I saw them in my *Journal* this morning."

"Get on the ball, dude! You don't know what you're talking about. The stock's flying and the big guy is all over me. Wonderful execution! You tell me how good you are at working an order, and then, when I finally give you one, you blow it. Cancel the last 50,000."

Shaken, sweating a little, feeling the eyes of the order desk traders on him, Jud picked up the *Journal* on the next desk. He turned to the earnings reports. No Intel figures. Then he flipped to the most active list again. No Intel. Like the guy in the elevator had said, GE was the most active. He checked another *Journal* and then asked his friend Fred Zuch if he had noticed the Intel earnings release that morning in the paper.

"No, Jud," said Zuch. "They only came out this afternoon and they were much better than expected. You saw what they did to the stock!"

"Yeah, I saw," mumbled Jud.

By this time the market was closed, and now the most active list was about to print. Feeling discombobulated, Jud stared at his Bloomberg screen. There it was. Intel was the most active up 4 to 80. Jud rubbed his eyes in a daze. He still had that dull headache. Damn! He was going to have to cut back on his martinis and start reading the newspaper more carefully. It really did make a difference. Omega's trader had been very sore about missing that execution because Cooperman probably had screamed at him. These days, 100,000-share orders were hard to come by. But that evening on the train, his resolve was forgotten as he got into a card game and had a couple of drinks.

A COLD SHIVER RUNS UP JUD'S CREAKING SPINE

The next morning he almost missed the train and barely had time to buy his paper at the station newsstand. The express was two cars short and standing, swaying unsteadily, he glanced through the *Journal*. Suddenly, as he looked at the most active list, he felt a cold shiver run up his spine. Intel was not listed as yesterday's most active stock. Amgen was and it was up 6 to 45. The second most active was Texas Instruments, down 4.20 to 31.45.

That morning in the hospital Jud told me his hand was shaking as he turned to the market commentary column. "Amgen tacked on 6 as it announced FDA approval of a new drug for irritable bowel disease while Texas Instruments fell over 4 after a disappointing presentation at a Goldman Sachs conference.

The train was in Grand Central Station now, and Jud was swept out into the dimly lit platform, the *Journal* clutched damply against his body. As he walked down the platform and the crush of commuters dissolved, he abruptly, impulsively opened the paper and turned once more to the stock tables. Intel: Open 82.25; High 83; Low 78; Close 78, minus 2 on the day. Now moving instinctively, almost desperately, he crammed the paper into the same trash container as yesterday.

When he got to the office he was still sweating, a cold, clammy perspiration that was like the sweat of a fever, and his mouth was dry. On the street he had desperately wanted to buy another *Journal*, but somehow he was afraid; something restrained him. The act of acquiring the paper might be enchanted, part of the spell, and he was terribly afraid to tamper with it.

"Say, Fred," he said to Zuch, "can I take a look at your *Journal*? I left mine on the train."

And, of course, it was as he half-hoped, half-feared. The *Journal* showed Intel as the most active and there was no mention of the Amgen announcement or Texas Instruments' drop. Jud handed the paper back. He felt punchy, dazed, but off somewhere in a back room of his mind it was as if a cell phone was beginning to ring insistently.

It was now 9:00 A.M. and he had to begin making his morning research calls. Usually he hated this job as a menial clerk's task. Mostly he left messages on portfolio managers' voice mails, and he knew most were peremptorily erased after a few sentences; only occasionally did he get through to the portfolio manager himself. This morning by chance the almighty Rhinelander picked up.

"What have you got?" he snapped.

"Amgen has an announcement coming today about a new drug for irritable bowel syndrome. It's not a blockbuster but it should put four or five points on the stock. I hear Texas Instruments is struggling and they're going to have disappointing things to say at the Goldman conference. You'd better sell your stock this morning."

"How do you know that?"

"Well, I . . . I heard it from this consultant. . . . I was just kind of thinking. . . ."

"Don't waste my time with that know-nothing crap," Rhinelander said curtly and hung up.

Jud could feel congealing on his face that tense, frozen expression he always got when someone treated him like he was a babbling fool. Suddenly the confidence of real knowledge surged through him, warm and utterly powerful. "Know-nothing, huh? Rhinelander will soon see who is the babbling know-nothing."

The market was open now, and he had CNBC on his screen. Intel was opening at 82. On impulse he called Omega's trader.

"Say, Jack, I'm sorry as hell about missing that 50,000 Intel yesterday."

"You ought to be. Lee was pissed, and I got chewed out good. The stock is trading at 82, up 2 more."

"Yeah," said Jud, "there it goes at 82.55 and now a big block at 83."

"And I've got 50,000 to buy with a limit of 80."

"Listen," said Jud, "give me that 50,000 and I guarantee you I'll get it for you below 80 today."

"What are you talking about, Jud? Guarantee what? Are you crazy?"

"I'll get 50,000 shares below 80 or the firm will make good."

"Old-timer, you're cracking up. You must be drinking already. That stock just broke out on the charts. It'll never see 80 again."

"I'll stop you at 78.50."

"Okay, okay. You've got the order with an 80 limit so it's not worth anything. Those other guys at Hudson hear you talking like this, Jud, and you'll be on the beach and there won't be any sun."

Intel traded actively between 81 and 83 until around 3 p.m., when a large seller came in. Jud bid 78.26 for 25,000, and his bid was hit at 3:30. The market overall got sloppy in the last half hour, and Jud bought the last 25,000 at 77.76 minutes before the close.

"Say, Jud, that was some execution," Cooperman's trader said when Jud called after the close. "Well, never follow excessive strength on a most active after a fast spike," said Jud, astounded at how easily the words came out. "I've always had a good feel for the market in hot stocks."

"Yeah, well, I guess you do after all. I'll mention it to Lee. He remembers things like this."

"YOU'VE GOT THE HOT HAND, KID"

The next morning once again his *Wall Street Journal* was for the following day. Superstitiously, afraid to jinx the genie or whatever it was, he read only the most active list and the market column. The only big action was Motorola, up 5 to 85. Then, moved by some primeval instinct, he buried the *Journal* deep in the same newspaper bin.

When he made his research call to Pinnacle that morning, the secretary said Mr. Rhinelander wanted to speak with him. "Arrogant bastard," thought Jud, "wants to *speak* not *talk* with me. Typical. If my special paper keeps coming, I'll be the one who's deciding whose speaking to whom."

"Say, Jud," Rhinelander came on with that Harvard accent, "you sure were right on that Amgen announcement and the Texas Instruments meeting. That was good stuff."

"Well, anyone closely following Amgen's research filings should have known they were close, and the industry data on TI's product lines has been softening the last month or so," Jud heard himself saying with a glibness he didn't recognize.

"Well, I guess so," Rhinelander replied. "My guys didn't pick it up, though. What else has Amgen got coming?"

"Nothing right away, but I'll talk with my consultant again early next week and let you know if anything big is up."

"Yeah, sure," said Rhinelander. "Do that. What else do you like now?"

"Well, I think Motorola is going to be very upbeat on its 3G cell phone line today. My guess is that it's going to announce a new product with a lower price and a built-in camera. But I see it as just a trade. I've got no feel longer term."

"Yeah. If they do have a camera in the phone, the stock will go up. The Street will be positively surprised. The stock has been dead for a while. Why don't you buy me a hundred thousand."

Jud had read that Motorola was up over five points after the announcement, but carelessly he hadn't noticed the time of the announcement. As a result, that morning he was afraid of missing the execution, so he put the entire 100,000 in at the opening and got hit immediately at 79.80. By 11:00 in a sloppy market, Motorola was down 2.20 from the previous close to 77.80.

"Great execution," Rhinelander snarled. "Haven't you ever had a 100,000-share order before?"

As a matter of fact, he hadn't had many recently. But early that afternoon, the Motorola story started printing as the company made its presentation. The stock began to get active, and there was a block print at 80. Next, the guys on CNBC were interviewing analysts and babbling hysterically, and the stock was at 82.50. Then trading was suspended, and just before the close it opened at 85.

Rhinelander called after the close. "Hey, Jud, you're the man. You sure had that Motorola figured. What do I do tomorrow—hold her or should I kick her out?"

"Let me sleep on it. I'll let you know in the morning."

"Okay, doctor, okay. If you say so. You've got the hot hand, kid."

But the next morning when Jud carefully, religiously followed the ritual and waited until he was on the train to open the *Journal*, he found himself staring at yesterday's prices in a perfectly ordinary newspaper. Oddly, this discovery, though a shock and a letdown, was not terribly disconcerting and was almost a relief.

Jud was neither a profoundly imaginative nor an introspective man, especially when sober, and the phenomenon that had been happening to him was so bizarre to begin with that he was not particularly inclined to analyze or to worry about its temporary disappearance. In a strange, fatalistic way he was quite confident his "special" *Journal* (as he now thought of it) would come again, and all that was required of him was to adhere faithfully to the routine. As a matter of fact, far from being unnerved or distracted, that morning Jud read the newspaper with unusual attention, and when Rhinelander called, calmly told him his guess was that Motorola had a little more upside in it. As it turned out, the stock did go up a couple of more points over the next few days.

Well, that was the way it all began. As time went on, Jud got his special *Journal* about once a week but in no regular pattern. He could detect no divine intervention at the newsstand. There was a stack of *Journal*s and it was first come, first served. Once the blind newspaper vendor in the Port Chester station was ill for 10 days and the old man usually took the last two weeks of August off, and during those times there were no specials. When the special came, it was always the next day's paper, and Jud made a point of never reading more than the most active list and the "Abreast of the Market" column. To read further, he sensed, would have been an abuse and possibly could have endangered the very existence of his special. He never confided in anyone about the secret of his newfound success. Why, he couldn't say. It was just a strong, spooky feeling he had.

Anyway, despite his misgivings, through it all Jud was quite clever in achieving maximum exploitation of what was essentially only an occasional one-day edge. He was canny enough to keep his mouth shut or be noncommittal on the off days. Sometimes, the special told of extreme market strength or weakness, and Jud used these insights to build a reputation for having a great short-term market feel. Wall Street and the hedge-fund community have much-publicized shortcomings, but the apparatus for identifying a moneymaker, a winner, is highly efficient. Within six months, Jud was being talked about as a big hitter, and after a year he was known as one of the great traders and had become a recognized name.

The portfolio managers flocked to him and with good reason because a chat with Jud, early in the morning on a day he had picked up his special, could make a purchase or sale look brilliant. Lunches tended to be less rewarding, and, of course, four out of five days there were no startling insights whatsoever. Nevertheless the money managers were so mesmerized, so intrigued with the idea of having lunch with the great Jud and then being able to say they had picked his brain, most of them never noticed they weren't getting much in the way of sustenance. CNBC continually invited him to appear, but he never succumbed, figuring it couldn't do him any good. Perhaps hubris would anger the genie.

Jud did his best to pad the off days with liberal helpings of Irish charm and Wall Street patter. By saying nothing when he had nothing, he made sure nobody got hurt. Once in a while, someone would be so uncouth as to jokingly wonder where he got his inside information, and with everyone buggy about the subject, he made sure to clothe his tips in fundamental gibberish like "My analysis of Chinese business conditions leads me to believe iron ore prices are about to rise incrementally" the morning before Cleveland Cliffs jumped four points. He carefully avoided acts-of-God news events like deaths of company presidents, and he seldom passed on advance word of merger announcements or legal actions.

By the end of the first year, Jud was riding high. He had become a star, and he produced immense amounts of business for Hudson. One big hedge fund offered to make Hudson its prime broker if Jud would cover it, and Sonny Linthicum offered him a consulting fee. The partners of Hudson didn't know what to make of it. The guy had been a dud for years, but now he was red-hot. If he was really that good, should they let him trade firm capital? Instead they offered to make him a managing director, but he declined, saying he wanted a direct payout on his production. The talk was that he took home $4 million in 2003.

As you would expect, Jud's lifestyle changed as well. He began to dress elaborately but mod with tapered Hugo Boss suits and fancy shirts from Pink like the swinging young money managers wore. His hair was longer now, and he drank less. He bought a very expensive set of season tickets to the Giants' games. He never called his wife the old lady anymore, and even vaguely began to talk of collecting art. Of course, he still rode the train out of the Port Chester station, although now he often took a car home.

An ironic quirk of the whole thing, Jud told me that day in the hospital, was that he never made any real money in his own account. There were so many rules about front running and he was so preoccupied with his sales calls that he never got around to trading for himself. And even if he had, he said, he really needed long-term capital gains, and, therefore, his one-day edge was relatively meaningless.

At about this point, I came into the story. I had continued to see Jud most mornings at the Port Chester station and I was aware of the spectacular improvement in his fortunes. Although Jud and I were not confidants, I guess I was as old and as good a business friend as he had; however, I had no more idea than anyone else of the providential and mystic source of his investment advice. My hedge fund even did some business with Jud, but we were not a big enough trader to be on his first-call list, and he never gave me any tips on the occasions we walked off the train together. I am embarrassed to say I had not noticed anything unusual about his morning paper routine.

That June my elderly maiden aunt was convalescing in New York Hospital with a broken hip. Because we had always been close, I visited her once or twice a week. One morning in mid-June there was much talk on the commuter train that the previous day Jud had suffered a heart attack on the train, and that he had been taken off at 125th Street on a stretcher and rushed to New York Hospital. That afternoon, after visiting my aunt, I stopped by Jud's room. He was in an oxygen tent and there was a rather grave-looking private nurse in attendance. I was with him for only a few minutes and murmured the usual banalities before being ushered out.

Two days later his doctor called me at my office. Jud, it seemed, was most insistent on seeing me again immediately. "He's out of the oxygen tent temporarily," the doctor told me, "but normally I wouldn't let him have a visitor except that he's absolutely insistent you come. He says he must talk to you. I want to warn you that his condition is still extremely critical. On the train he had some kind of shock which caused a massive heart attack, which could reoccur at any time. His heart actually stopped beating for perhaps 60 seconds, and there may have been some brain damage from the lack of oxygen."

That afternoon I found Jud propped up in bed looking pale and haggard but alert. He came right to the point.

"The doctor told you my condition? Assuming I'm going to live, and for reasons I'll get to later, I'm sure I *will* live, I'm going to have to take it easier in the business. I simply won't be able to hustle what I think of as my *edge* the way I have." He paused.

"As I'll explain," he continued, "I think I've got what you might call a truly *unique* edge, and I'm going to propose I join your firm. I'll supply the stocks that are going to move that day for your fund to buy, and you handle the executions. In fact, about all I'll do is ride the train to Grand Central in the mornings and talk to you afterward. We can work out the particulars of my participation in your firm later."

About then I thought his brain had been severely damaged, but then he told me the story that I have just recounted. Let me say, hearing him tell it, all the while sitting there looking at him, I believed it implicitly. It was simply too fantastic *not* to be true. And don't forget I had seen at close hand the seemingly miraculous transformation of an affable, slightly alcoholic loser of a salesman into an uncanny short-term trader.

"So you see," Jud was saying, "we can make it big. I get the same stuff, but I give it only to you, and no one will be the wiser. I think we could add at least 10 percentage points a year to your performance. And if your fund grows, as of course it will, it will still work. There has never been any evidence that its potency is affected by the amount of my buying. As for it being inside information, they'd laugh Eliot Spitzer and the Securities and Exchange Commission out of court. But let me tell you what happened last Tuesday, which makes it even bigger and better."

The previous Tuesday, it seemed, he had got a special, but this one was different. This *Journal* was not for the next day, Wednesday; it was for the *following* Wednesday.

"Do you see what this means?" asked Jud, leaning toward me, eyes intent. "Think of the moves in stocks we can catch with a six-day instead of a one-day edge! And imagine the market trading profits we can make. Before long we'll be the biggest hedge fund in the world. Now I know one issue doesn't mean that they're all going to be long-term specials, but if even a few are . . ."

Visions of sugar plums danced in my head, but at this moment the nurse came in. We had been talking for more than two hours, she said, and she insisted I leave. We shook hands, and as I turned to go I said something inane like "Take care of yourself."

Suddenly Jud was somber. "Say," he said, "I didn't go into what else was in that special I got last Tuesday."

"Well, no, you didn't."

"There was a notice on page C-2 right next to the 'Abreast of the Market' column dated June 23, next Wednesday, that Hudson & Company announced with deep regret the death of their beloved friend and senior associate, Judson Thomas."

I stared at him, horrified. He gazed back at me, his eyebrows arched quizzically.

"So you see," he went on, "the luckiest thing that ever happened to me, next to getting the specials, of course, was to get hit with this heart attack last Tuesday. Probably the emotional shock of seeing my name and that notice triggered the heart attack, but just to be sure, I'm having them move me back to intensive care and I'm climbing right back into that oxygen tent Monday and Tuesday and not getting out until the danger period is over. I told the doctor to be around Tuesday also. I'm not taking any chances."

I was tongue-tied. I couldn't help thinking that if there had been no evidence his buying and selling changed the next-day prices in the specials, why did he think he could alter the *Journal's* news this time? But what could I say? I just nodded and left.

I had long-standing plans to go to Florida for that weekend, and when I called the hospital Saturday, the nurse told me he was back in the oxygen tent and unable to speak on the phone. She said it in a funny way. Jud had said not to worry, but . . . I was worried. I called again the next day, but the nurse said he was still in intensive care. I asked her to have the doctor call me, but he never did.

I didn't sleep well Tuesday night worrying about Jud and I got up very early the next morning and went to the station. The newsstand had just opened, and I turned to page C-2 and there the death notice was, right where he said it would be next to the "Abreast of the Market" column. But maybe it had been set in print the night before.

I bought a *New York Times* and the obituary was there, too, with an old picture. So he was definitely dead. Even with the doctor, intensive care, and the oxygen tent he couldn't change the notice in the special that said he had died.

This all happened a few years ago. As time has passed I've begun to wonder if maybe Jud imagined the whole thing. After all, the doctor said there had been some brain damage when his heart stopped during that first attack. Maybe he was hallucinating. But if he dreamed it all up, then he sure had one hell of a hot streak going on his own. The stock market is a mysterious thing, like the sea, and "there are strange things done 'neath the midnight sun by the men who search for gold," so who knows.

I still buy a *Wall Street Journal* every day at that same newsstand, but there have been no "specials" for me.

C H A P T E R
TWENTY-ONE

John Maynard Keynes
Economist, Hedge-Fund Manager, and Fascinating Character

O ne evening last year at a dinner I was seated next to Bill
Miller of Legg Mason, a man whose U.S. equity fund has beat
the S&P 500 for something like 11 years in a row! We got to
talking about books, and he mentioned that one of the best,
most fascinating books he had ever read was Robert Skidelsky's
three-volume biography *John Maynard Keynes*. Intrigued, I bought it,
and although it took me almost three months to work my way
through its 1,600 dense pages, I was absolutely enthralled. So fascinated, in fact, that I did additional reading about Keynes. This chapter,
therefore, is based on a number of sources besides Skidelsky's epic.

THE MOST INFLUENTIAL ECONOMIST
OF THE TWENTIETH CENTURY

The first two volumes, *Hopes Betrayed 1883–1920* and *The Economist as
Savior 1920–1937*, are by far the finest, truest biography I have ever
read, and I have read a lot of them. The third volume, *Fighting for Free-*

dom 1937–1946, drags. The first two volumes describe the journey and fantastic character of John Maynard Keynes, a brilliant, troubled, passionate, crapulous man, but they are much more than that. They are about the social climate at the end of the Victorian era, when Britannia still ruled the world, and the mistakes at the end of World War I that produced depression, deflation, and another conflagration.

Keynes was by far the most influential economist of the twentieth century. Keynesian economics rescued the post–World War II world from depression and deflation and may have had as much impact in saving us from socialism and communism as Winston Churchill, Franklin Roosevelt, and Ronald Reagan combined. Every serious investor needs to understand the Keynesian model, for it is an integral part of the way the world works.

But these volumes are far more than just history and economics. They are also about passion, emotion, and both gay and heterosexual love. They transformed my view of gay relationships. Until Keynes was almost forty, he lived in two worlds. One was the avant garde, Bohemian, wildly promiscuous, highly intellectual, and very gay world of the Bloomsbury Group. Bloomsbury included the artist Duncan Grant, the philosopher Bertrand Russell, Lytton Strachey (*Eminent Victorians*), the poet Rupert Brooke, and the novelist Virginia Wolff. Historians now maintain that the Bloomsbury Group, in addition to its cultural impact, was a major force in ending the Victorian era and changing forever the way the British upper class behaved.

The other world Keynes moved in was the aristocratic milieu of Cambridge, the British Treasury, and international finance. Keynes was not just a man of the English establishment; from birth he was part of the elite of each establishment of which he was a member, which included Eton, King's College, and the prestigious secret society, The Apostles. He was an aristocrat with a dazzling intellect and a razor-sharp mind. He was the intimate of one prime minister and the counselor of many. As the chairman of the National Mutual Life Society he was at the very center of England's financial oligarchy. He was a man of great expectations. When he was five, his great-grandmother wrote to him: "You will be expected to be very clever. . . ."

Then, in his late 30s, he fell deeply in love with a Russian ballerina, went straight, married her, became even richer, and ended up as Lord Keynes of Tilton. The dancer, Lydia Lopokova, had a trim figure, but she was rather plain. She was not cultured or intellectual, and she often mangled the English language. To the dismay and anger of Bloomsbury, Keynes, in the sunshine of her smile, remained enchanted with her for the rest of his life, and gradually became estranged from his old crowd.

Skidelsky's books are also about investing. Keynes was a macro investor, a hedge-fund manager, a generation before Alfred Jones. He made his money between 1920 and 1940, investing in the most difficult and volatile asset markets of all time. The ebb and flow of his performance saga, the evolution of his modus operandi, and his investment insights are fascinating. It is oddly reassuring that this brilliant analyst with his penetrating powers of concentration was almost carried out three times in the course of his highly successful investment career. However, as a reader, don't get turned off by the sometimes heavy intellectual and economics content in certain sections. Judiciously skip. The experience is enriching and worth the time.

Keynes' principal biographer, Robert Skidelsky spent 20 years writing the three volumes that were published by Penguin Books beginning in 1983. It is a masterful biography, and Skidelsky, a superb economist in his own right, is both descriptive and analytical on Keynes' thinking and economic theory. Skidelsky withholds nothing, and I mean nothing. He discusses Keynes's homosexuality, his extreme mood swings, and his investment triumphs and disasters. He includes passages from the love letters members of the Bloomsbury Group exchanged, and describes the difficult passage of Keynes and Lydia to physical and social happiness. It is never prurient, but instead the biography is an incredibly revealing view of the soul of a very complicated, sensitive, and sensual man. It is an economic treatise and a great love story at the same time.

INTELLECTUALLY BRILLIANT EVEN IN HIS YOUTH

As a young boy, Keynes was tall, gawky, and not particularly athletic. He was bullied and mocked because his lips protruded and his nickname was Snout. He became convinced that he was physically unattractive, and he developed a stammer. Skidelsky postulates that these early afflictions lead to a cerebral childhood and his central need to give and receive affection that dominated his life. Always an avid reader, by the time he was 12, his intellectual brilliance set him apart, and the bullying stopped. At Eton, his scholarship impressed both the masters and his fellow students, and toward the end of his time there, he thrilled to the ancient games, particularly the Wall Game. It was probably the last time he broke a sweat.

By the late 1890s, the great British public schools had been somewhat reformed so that they were more structured, supervised, and less barbaric than they had been earlier in the century. Nevertheless, the boys lived in a feudal, *Lord of the Flies* society. For example, eyeglasses were not permitted at Eton, so a short-sighted boy could not play ball games. Eton was a closed, male society, and the boys had no opportunity to have relationships of any kind with girls. Homosexuality was rampant, and Keynes had several long relationships, the most intense with the son of a bishop who was Keynes's chief rival for academic honors. Thus, by the time Keynes went to Cambridge, he already was deeply inclined to intimate social and physical relationships with boys.

Keynes left Eton with a brilliant record that he continued at King's College, Cambridge. King's was not that different from Eton. At King's, Keynes flourished. Again his scholarship and his mind awed everyone. He was tapped for the elite secret society, The Apostles, in his first term, a rare honor. The society introduced him to the great intellectuals of Cambridge, and his life became portioned into two parts. One was passionate philosophy, aesthetics, intellectual intercourse, and homosexual love, and the other was scholarship and the study of political and practical affairs. The former had definite precedence. The traditions and secrecy of The Apostles bred an attitude of elite superiority, and the members developed intimate associations with each other. The criteria for membership were "great cleverness and great unworldliness."

The Apostles had always been riddled with homosexuality. Keynes's best friend and lover in his last years at Cambridge was Lytton Strachey, but their relationship was marred by a ferocious competition for the affections of a young freshman, Arthur Lee Hobhouse, with whom both fell in love. Skidelsky points out that Keynes and Strachey had been brought up to believe that women were inferior in mind and body. "Love of young men was, they believed, ethically better and more enriching than love of women." They called it Higher Sodomy, and they believed future generations would regard them as pioneers, not criminals. It is intriguing to note that at the turn of the century, the time of

Queen Victoria's Golden Jubilee, when the British Empire was beginning to fade, Britain was like so many other ancient dynasties; it was permeated with homosexuality.

The Apostles were a Cambridge institution dating back to 1820. In 1904, a London offshoot, the Bloomsbury Group was formed, fertilized by new blood that had not attended Cambridge and even by some women members. Bloomsbury was even more enlightened than The Apostles, and the members scorned rationality in favor of sensibility and sensuality. Bloomsbury espoused a new attitude toward the visual arts, design, and literature. They dismissed organized religion and refused to take it seriously. They mocked the Victorian way of life, conventional heterosexual relationships, and were stridently antiwar. They were committed cultural and sexual revolutionaries, and maintained that civilization has nothing to do with morals, democracy, patriotism, technology, social justice, or the life of action. Action, they said, is the disease of those incapable of passionate love. Keynes himself disdained politics as no more than "a fairly adequate substitute for bridge."

As time went on, Bloomsbury evolved into a collective lifestyle that included widespread homosexuality, bisexuality, and, as Skidelsky describes it, "a sexual merry-go-round as friends became lovers and then went back to being friends." People came and went, attractive young men were discovered and exploited, nobody seemed to work, but members were expected to be creative. Discussions sprang up and then were forgotten. Plays and charades replete with double entendres, satire, and political implications were held every evening. It was never quite clear who was occupying what bedroom or with whom. The members of Bloomsbury claimed to disdain jealousy as a plebeian emotion, but when Keynes' great love of the time dumped him for another man, his letters reveal deep emotion. Skidelsky writes that Keynes' first great love affair was back at Cambridge with Hobhouse, and that over the next two decades he had several serious love affairs and considerable casual sex. The most powerful of these love affairs was with the beguiling artist Duncan Grant. The affair lasted from 1908 to 1915 and was traumatic, subject to interruptions, but very passionate. Skidelsky believes Keynes was always disposed to worship "the artist with inner integrity but with an outward need for protection." When the affair ended, Keynes was brokenhearted. Although he had many subsequent attachments, he never found a true emotional replacement until he met Lydia.

BECOMING A POLITICAL THINKER

The Apostles and Bloomsbury were the center of Keynes' personal life until he met Lydia. He loved them because they were gifted, creative adolescents playing in the enchanted garden that to him symbolized civilization. As time went on, he assumed the management of their investments. In turn they loved him for his slashing intelligence, his restless mind, and his imagination, and they were amused by his roving eye. However, they continually badgered him for not leading the true artistic, aesthetic life. He was a man of action, a man of affairs, and that was virtually traitorous to the Bloomsbury ideal. They particularly objected to his role at Treasury and in the peace negotiations after World War I. They said he was worldly, manipulative, and domineering. And they criticized him for being rude, acerbic, moody, and gross.

While this was going on in his emotional world, in the other world, the world of Whitehall and Cambridge, Keynes, the intellect, the political thinker, the economist, was assuming ascendancy. Everyone, admirers and critics alike, were awed by his ruthless powers of concentration and brilliance. In 1908 he took the civil service examination and finished second in the country. "I want to meet number one," said Virginia Wolff when he told her. The Treasury offered him a position, and in 1910 he took a leave of absence from teaching at Cambridge to work for the Treasury. He relished the discovery of statistical relationships. "Nothing but copulation is so enthralling," he wrote Duncan Grant in 1912.

At the end of World War I he was sent to the Versailles Peace Conference as deputy for the chancellor of the Exchequer. He had a grandstand seat and argued vociferously from the second row that punishing Germany would only cause an economic catastrophe and its radicalization. However, he was merely a deputy, and he watched powerless as Georges Clemenceau outmaneuvered Woodrow Wilson, and a humane, sane peace was replaced by a vindictive one.

Disgusted with the outcome of the conference and disillusioned with politicians, in 1919 he resigned. Then, later that same year, he published *The Economic Consequences of Peace*, which, written in anger and with foreboding, became an international bestseller and brought him worldwide fame. Schumpeter described Keynes and the book as "bursting into international fame when men of equal insight but less courage and men of equal courage but less insight kept silent." The amounts demanded by the Allies, he wrote, were so immense that Germany would be permanently impoverished. He was right, and the result was Hitler.

KEYNES AND HIS HEDGE FUND

Meanwhile as his intellectual presence grew, he was gradually maturing and becoming more conventional. The rough edges were being smoothed. His table manners improved, he dressed better, although he never really tempered his arrogance to lesser minds. His cultural interests also broadened. In 1918 with the sound of German guns echoing, at a panic auction in Paris he bought at rock-bottom prices for the British Museum five pictures by Corot, Manet, Gauguin, Delacroix, and Ingres. He also acquired an excellent Cezanne, a Delacroix, and an Ingres for himself. This was the beginning of a very lucrative collecting career.

Around 1915 Keynes had begun speculating in stocks and currencies. In the speculative boom following World War I, he made big money by selling sterling short against the dollar but long the pound versus the mark, the franc, and the lire. Encouraged by these results, in late 1919 he created what was essentially a hedge fund with his friend and broker, Foxy (not a propitious name for a broker) Falk. Falk was an experienced speculator and, in contrast to Keynes, broad-shouldered, handsome, charming, and a fine golfer. They raised a substantial amount of money, and the sleeping partners included Keynes's father, brother-in-law, Duncan Grant, and other Apostles and members of Bloomsbury. The fund began operation on January 1, 1920, and by the end of February was up more than 20%. In March and April, performance stalled as gains on other positions were offset by a loss from being short the pound versus the dollar when the Bank of England raised rates unexpectedly.

That spring Keynes must have been infected with a touch of hubris because he took a group of his investors including his lover, Duncan Grant, on a six-week tour of Italy. The climax of the excursion was a grand dinner party given by a wealthy American art collector to introduce Keynes, the famous English economist, to Florentine society. Keynes and Grant thought it would be an amusing practical joke if Grant pretended to be Keynes and babble economic nonsense while Keynes became Grant and appraised their host's art collection. When the prank was subsequently discovered, their host and his guests were decidedly not amused.

While Keynes was cavorting in Italy, the world began to fall apart. The postwar boom suddenly hit the wall. Unemployment in England over the next six months was to rise from 4.5% to over 20% of the work force; wholesale prices began a 45% decline with wages and retail prices soon to follow. A week after returning to London, Keynes's fund was in serious trouble. The European currencies had rallied against sterling for no plausible reason, and although the rally was brief, it lasted long enough to wipe out the highly leveraged fund. Keynes's personal losses were more than three times the profits from his earlier sterling position and he owed a substantial sum to his broker. He now had a negative net worth. Amazingly the Bloomsbury investors did not reproach Keynes. They never lost faith in his financial genius, and the next year he formed a new fund, which eventually recouped their losses and restored Keynes's wealth.

In the 1920s, Keynes taught at Cambridge, was an adviser to the Treasury, lectured, and wrote books and articles. In 1921 he published *The Tract on Monetary Reform*, which argued for a managed currency and a stable standard of value. The Central Bank must lower interest rates when prices tended to rise and raise them when prices tended to fall. Inflation, he said, inflicts the most injury by altering the distribution of wealth. Deflation's damage comes from retarding the production of wealth. "Thus inflation is unjust and deflation inexpedient. Of the two perhaps, deflation is, if we rule out exaggerated inflations such as Germany, the worse because it is worse in an impoverished world to provoke unemployment than to disappoint the *rentier*." Later when unemployment soared in the depression, he changed his mind. It was in this book that he described the gold standard as "a barbarous relic" and made his famous comment that "this *long run* is a misleading guide to current affairs. *In the long run* we are all dead."

THE NEED FOR A CONVENTIONAL LIFE: TO BE TAKEN SERIOUSLY AS AN ECONOMIST

The 1920s also saw a dramatic transformation in his personal life. Lydia Lopokova, when Keynes first became fascinated with her in 1918, was a well-traveled Russian dancer-actress (almost a chorus girl) eight years younger than Keynes who was, by all accounts, rather plain with a "compact, well-formed little body" and a protruding nose. She also had a husband, a lover, and a checkered past. From the beginning, Keynes was enchanted by her "peasant-like charm," but the romance flickered over the next four years. At one point, Lydia disappeared back into Russia where she shed herself of husband, lover, and other attachments. By mid-1922 she and Keynes were deeply in love, although oddly Keynes had not given up his latest gay lover, Sebastian. But in the months that followed, his physical relationship with Lydia developed, and in 1924 they finally were married. The biography includes the most intimate correspondence between them, which is very explicit and moving. "You do develop my cranium, nicely, Maynarochka," she wrote him, "and I am so glad that I live with you and I am intimate with your little holes your soul your breath and kisses." Lydia tenderly introduced Keynes to heterosexual sex, and once there, he never returned to his previous ways. Neither seemed in the least troubled by the other's promiscuous past.

Skidelsky believes that Keynes' marriage to Lydia was the transforming event in his life, and I agree. Bloomsbury was too exotic (and erotic) a launching pad for the Keynesian revolution in economic statesmanship. Could a grown man, no matter how brilliant, who sometimes walked across the Cambridge campus *pumping* (urinating) and who was famously gay, lecherous, and notoriously promiscuous have led a revolution in the world's economic management? After all, Oscar Wilde was thrown into jail for such activities, and Keynes's landlady in London had hinted at blackmail. In addition Keynes could be very rude, haughty, and sarcastic. A colleague complained he used his brilliance "too unsparingly . . . he never dimmed his headlights." Lesser mortals' feelings often were wounded. Arguing with another economist, Keynes reduced him to tears with "the whole battery of . . . wit, petulance, rudeness, and quick unscrupulousness in argument." Before his marriage, his Bloomsbury nickname was Pozzo because it was said his mind was like a gutter.

To be truly taken seriously as the economic savior of civilization, Keynes needed to present a more conventional face to the world. He also required a secure emotional and physical base, which was what Lydia gave him. All his life he had searched for affection and intimacy, but he had never been confident of his previous relationships. With Lydia, he was secure emotionally and physically. Marriage softened Keynes and made him more human, more conventional, less bizarre and relentlessly

brilliant. Whether it was the environment or Lydia herself, marriage un-
locked his creativity, and his most productive years followed.

KEYNES' INVESTMENTS DURING
THE GREAT DEPRESSION

Keynes, like practically everyone else, did not anticipate the Wall Street
Crash in 1929, and he underestimated its effect on the U.S. and world
economy. His experience with the efficacy of cheap money in the depression of 1920–1922 caused him to believe it could work again. In
late 1929 he predicted that cutting interest rates would revive business
all over the world and that commodity prices shortly would recover. As
it turned out, the severe collapse in the general price level in 1930 completely overwhelmed any effect of cheap money, as *real* interest rates
rose even as nominal rates fell. These events shook Keynes' belief in the
ability of monetary policy to cure a severe slump that included deflation. Lowering interest rates was not enough. Fiscal policy had to be activated. The consumer had to be given a transfusion. The Bank of Japan
and the Ministry of Finance had to learn this lesson again in the 1990s.

Keynes' wealth, accumulated over the 1920s, was hit hard by the
Crash, but not because he owned U.S. stocks. By the late 1920s he had
been speculating for a number of years quite successfully in commodities and had become a reasonably rich man. In early 1929, he was long
rubber, corn, cotton, and tin when suddenly prices collapsed. His commodity losses forced him initially to sell stocks into a falling market to
meet margin calls. Then commodities fell further, and he suffered grievous wounds. By the end of 1929 he had nothing left but some tag ends
and a massive position in the Austin Motor Company, which had collapsed to 5s from 21s earlier in the year. His net worth had plunged 75%
from its high and fell even more in 1930.

Keynes fared much better with the hedge fund he then was running.
Once again he was in partnership with Falk, but they had divided their
investors' capital in two, finding that doing so focused and sharpened
their judgments. In 1929 Keynes's segment declined 15% but Falk's fell
63%. Unfortunately Falk had turned bearish in 1928 but, against
Keynes's advice, had gone back into U.S. equities in the summer of 1929.
He ended up having to put up his country house for sale, which Lydia

said served him right. A year later Keynes was so strapped for cash that he even tried to sell his best pictures but withdrew them because the bids were so pitiful. All these travails demonstrate that in a massive secular bear market in both real and financial assets, there is no escape. Personal relationships also suffer in hard times. Falk and Keynes' long friendship and collaboration soured, and when Falk, pressed for capital, had to sell his country house, Lydia laughed. As the Great Depression unfolded, other friendships deteriorated. The same pattern exists today in the hedge-fund world. Wrong moves, disagreements, and losses shatter relationships that, when things were prosperous, appeared to be forever.

In September 1931, close to the bottom of the great secular bear market, Keynes wrote a memo discussing the future investment policy of the National Mutual Insurance Company, of which he was the chairman. Some members of the board were advocating dumping stocks, but he argued that "a drastic clearance would be a mistake." His memorandum deals articulately with some of the classic dilemmas of institutional portfolio management. Its principal points were:

- The tendency of a deflation will be sooner or later towards very cheap money.
- Some of the things which I vaguely apprehend are, like the end of the world, uninsurable risks and it is useless to worry about them.
- If we get out, our mentality being what it is, we shall never get in again until much too late and will assuredly be left behind when the recovery does come. If the recovery never comes, nothing matters.
- From the point of view of our credit etc., a recovery which we failed to share would be the worst thing conceivable.
- I hesitate before the consequences of the doctrine that institutions should aggravate the bear tendency by hurrying each to be in front of the other in clearing out, when a general clearing out by the nature of things is impossible . . . and would bring the whole system down. I believe that there are times when one has to remain in the procession and not try to cut in.

Keynes's setbacks in the Crash changed his personal investment approach. In the 1920s he saw himself as a scientific gambler playing the economic cycle by speculating in currencies and commodities. He knew leverage was dangerous but believed he was nimble enough to escape any disaster. Once, in a falling market, he even had to take delivery of a month's supply of wheat from Argentina. His plan was to store it in the King's College chapel, but in the end he devised a scheme to object to its quality, knowing that the cleaning would take a month. Fortunately, by then the price had recovered, and he escaped. However, after 1930 he dismissed this kind of activity as "a mug's game" because rational analysis could be defeated by the "radical uncertainty" of random events. After the Crash he concentrated on equities, where value could be identified, and he operated as much more of a long-term, value investor. However, he always used leverage to magnify his returns.

As equity markets rose and fell in the 1930s, Keynes resolved to follow an investment philosophy of buying, not selling, when investors panicked and prices fell. Go against the psychology of the crowd and buy the shares of sound, undervalued companies with good businesses that were out of favor. He also decided to concentrate his equity positions in a few, carefully investigated stocks—his pets as he called them—holding them steadfastly through thick and thin, and trading less. In 1932 he bought U.S. shares, in particular the preferred shares of the great public utility companies, which his analysis showed to be depressed far below their intrinsic values. When South Africa left the gold standard, he acquired shares in a South African gold mine run by an old friend. In the 1930s, when prices were deeply depressed, he also was a very successful buy-and-hold investor in art, manuscripts, and rare books.

However, despite his good intentions, Keynes never really changed his ways. He was always a speculative and aggressive investor in the financial markets. He didn't seem to realize that his use of leverage and the attacks of nerves he was prone to when prices were falling were inconsistent with his new buy-and-hold investment strategy. He also was not good at identifying irrational exuberance and market tops. He was to take another big hit in the 1937–1938 bear market.

THE GREAT GAME AND THE GAMBLING INSTINCT

Did Keynes invest so aggressively because he needed the income? The record is that he could have lived comfortably, but not as luxuriously as he preferred, on his noninvestment earnings. He also liked the challenge of the great game. In his most important work, *The General Theory of Employment, Interest, and Money*, he wrote this revealing sentence. "The *game* of professional investment is intolerably boring and over-exacting to anyone who is entirely exempt from the gambling instinct; whilst he who has it must pay to this propensity the appropriate toll." Keynes loved the investing game because it pitted his mind and intuitions against the markets. He was right that the game is intolerably boring and exacting if you don't love it. I have known plenty of investment professionals who didn't truly love the game and without exception they were all journeymen at best. As for leverage and nerves, Keynes knew of what he spoke since three times—in 1920–1921, 1928–1929, and 1937–1938—he had paid a high price for his use of leverage.

As the now happily married Keynes moved into the 1930s, his lifestyle and persona became even more conventional. However, at the same time his work was increasingly creative and influential. In 1936 *The General Theory of Employment, Interest, and Money* was published. The book was to have an immense impact. Economists were charged with being activists, not just theoretical intellectuals. The world of the 1930s was a dreadful mess, ravaged periodically by depressions, deflations, and rampant inflations. Extreme economic distress was the root cause of the violent social disorders that were shaking the very structure of Europe and even the United States. Keynes had warned of this in *The Economic Consequences of Peace*, and now the world was reaping the whirlwind. The issue Keynes was addressing in his new book was whether the inherited economics nostrums of the past were adequate to these new and different maladies.

His answer was a resounding no! In addition Keynes made a powerful and optimistic point. The world's economy and social system had not been ruined by wickedness but by bad economic management and the stupidity of adhering to the obsolete doctrines of what he called "classical theory." "Practical men," he wrote, "who believe themselves to be quite exempt from any intellectual influences, are usually the slaves of some defunct economist. Madmen in authority, who hear voices in the air, are distilling their frenzy from some academic scribbler of a few years back."

The book was extremely controversial and generated great emotion. Young economists at Harvard, Yale, and Cambridge embraced it, while the older traditionalists, seeing their religion under attack, were deeply disturbed by its radical nostrums, and rejected it as heresy. Arthur Pigou said: "We have watched an artist firing arrows at the moon. Whatever be thought of his marksmanship, we can admire his virtuosity." Paul Samuelson 10 years later wrote: "It is a badly written book, poorly organized. . . . It is arrogant, bad-tempered, polemical, and not overly-generous in its acknowledgements. . . . It abounds in mares' nests and confusions. . . . Flashes of insight and intuition intersperse tedious algebra. When it is finally mastered, we find its analysis to be obvious and at the same time new. In short, it is a work of genius."

The book made a compelling case for reflation by deficit finance. Keynes argued full employment in mature capitalist economies could be maintained only with the help of government spending. In downturns, governments should consciously practice deficit spending to fulfill the role of private demand. The government's budget should not just be for the purpose of sound financial planning for expenditures and revenues, but as a major instrument in the stabilization of the national economy. Deficits and surpluses should be used to regulate the growth of the economy. He said deficits were not necessarily bad, which to many seemed heresy. He urged make-work projects to raise income and stimulate demand. This idea, variously called the *buried rubbish solution* by his admirers or the *rubbish paragraph* by his critics, generated intense controversy.

> *If the Treasury were to fill old bottles with bank-notes, bury them at suitable depths in disused coal-mines which are then filled up to the surface with town rubbish, and leave to private enterprise on the well-tried principles of laissez-faire to dig the notes up again . . . there need be no more unemployment and, with the help of the repercussions, the real income of the community, and its capital wealth also, would probably become a good deal greater than it actually is.*

Keynes' thought process and analysis, of course, was influenced by the Great Depression. He attributed much of the depression and deflation the world was suffering to unspent savings, *the paradox of thrift.* "The more virtuous we are, the more determinedly thrifty, the more obstinately orthodox in our national and personal finance, the more incomes will have to fall when interest rates rise relative to the marginal efficiency of capital." In a healthy economy, there must be continual investment. Ancient Egypt, he wrote, was doubly fortunate in that it had pyramid building and the search for precious metals "the fruits of which, since they could not serve the needs of man by being consumed, did not stale with abundance." The same applied to the Middle Ages with cathedral building and singing Masses for the dead. But, he said, two pyramids, two dirges are twice as good as one, "but not so two railways from London to York." The key phrase was *stale with abundance*.

The General Theory founded modern macroeconomics, and virtually all of the subsequent work in that field emerges from it. The Roosevelt Brain Trust instinctively understood its concept of deficit spending stimulating demand and employment. New Deal disciples maintain that Keynesian economics was the backbone of the New Deal, and that it was what brought the U.S. economy back from the Depression to full employment. The United States in turn resuscitated the world. The skeptics argue that it was another event called World War II, not Keynesian economics, that revived the world.

Keynes believed that in rich societies capital investment would be inadequate to sustain growth because of the high propensity of people to save. He also was pessimistic about the falling birth rate of the 1930s. This led him to worry about "secular stagnation," the inability of mature economies to sustain recoveries. Both these problems still plague Europe today.

Is it possible that the sharp decline in the birth rate in Japan, which is the cause of so much secular pessimism about Japan's future growth, could be a function of 15 years of hard times? Keynes did not minimize the vicious cycle of the Great Depression, commenting in 1933 at the time of Roosevelt's inauguration. "Even I would hardly think that I could know what to do if I were President, though I expect I should when it came to it." In fact, Keynes in 1933 wrote an open letter to the president, which was published in the *New York Times*, which advocated increasing the national purchasing power resulting from government expenditures financed by loans—that is, the buried rubbish solution.

The *General Theory* also included Keynes most brilliant stock market insight, in which he compared the stock market to a hypothetical newspaper-sponsored beauty contest in which a substantial money prize was to be awarded to the participant who guessed which of the photographed faces would be judged to be the most beautiful.

> *It is not a case of choosing those which, to the best of one's judgment, are really the prettiest, nor even those which opinion genuinely thinks the prettiest. We have reached the third degree, where we devote our intelligences to anticipating what average opinions expect the average opinion to be. And there are some, I believe, who practice the fourth, fifth and higher degrees.*

Keynes made both his intellectual and financial fortunes in the 1930s. As an academic, a lecturer, and a writer, his income was modest, probably at the peak $200,000 a year in today's terms. By standing fast and buying his pets when prices collapsed, he had affected a miraculous recovery in his wealth. By the end of 1929, he had lost most of his capital, but by 1936 his wealth came to more than £500,000 or roughly $45 million in today's terms. His net worth had appreciated 23 times from 1930 to the end of 1936 over a period in which the U.S. stock market tripled, and the U.K. market did very little. The portfolios he oversaw for various Cambridge college endowments and insurance companies also vastly outperformed the indexes and similar institutions. The more control he had, the better the portfolio did. In one case, he complained that it took him so long to convince the insurance company's investment committee of the merits of equities, that by the time they acceded, it was invariably too late.

SUFFERING (PERSONALLY AND FINANCIALLY) DURING THE LATE 1930s AND WWII

Keynes suffered a heart attack in mid-1937, and his recovery was not hastened by another severe bear market in late 1937 to 1938. The U.K. and U.S. economies abruptly collapsed into recession again, and the war clouds were gathering in Europe. Stocks broke sharply in November 1937 in the major markets. Keynes was heavily committed and highly leveraged in both New York and London. His health deteriorated as his portfolio declined. He wanted to stick with his philosophy of faithfulness to his pets, but the leverage ate at him. "I've not gotten to the point of being a bear," he wrote to a friend that September, "but I am *much* more disinclined to be a bull on borrowed money. And to bring down some loans is a necessarily tedious and difficult process." Those of us who run hedge funds can empathize with his agony!

On October 21, 1937, Keynes wrote that ". . . my hunch is that prices must now be near bottom." Nine days later, Wall Street took another plunge, and by March, with prices drifting lower, he conceded it was only prudent to reduce his debt even if it meant selling blue chip stocks. By the end of 1938 his capital had shrunk to £140,000, down 62% from the end of 1936, and, since markets had already rallied, his losses must have been even deeper at the bottom. It was the third time he had been almost wiped out, and he frequently complained to Lydia about fits of depression and attacks of nerves. In the years that followed and particularly during World War II, his investing was less aggressive, but his portfolio became even more equity oriented. He could never resist an intriguing story about a stock. At his death in 1946 he had an investment portfolio of about £400,000 or $32 million in current purchasing power. He also had an art and rare book collection worth around £80,000. In other words, it appears he never returned to the high-water mark of his net worth achieved at the end of 1936.

In 1938, with the bear market still in full force and even though still convalescing, Keynes found himself in the uncomfortable position of having to justify his bias for equities to the investment committees of the institutions he advised and who had also suffered heavy losses. "I feel no shame at being found still owning shares when the bottom of the market comes. I would go much further than that. I should think it is from time to time the duty of a serious investor to accept the depreciation of his holding with equanimity and without reproach himself." Even at the darkest moments in 1940 and 1941, Keynes was convinced that England and the United States would win and that the postwar world, if properly organized, would be prosperous. If this didn't happen, it wouldn't make any difference whether an insurance company owned stock or not. When the chairman of National Mutual and its board found this reasoning odd, Keynes resigned in disgust.

Keynes suffered from heart disease off and on during the war, but he had an office and staff at Treasury and then after the war served as Britain's negotiator with the United States. It was a difficult time. He was enfeebled, and Lydia rationed his time. He disliked Henry Morgenthau, and he thought the United States was too harsh in its demands on Britain. Keynes forcefully argued that England had stood alone and saved the world, and had bankrupted itself in the process. The U.K. economy was in a state of collapse and on the verge of class warfare. In the end he prevailed.

In July 1944, Harry Dexter White, who represented the U.S. Treasury, Keynes, and a host of functionaries met at Bretton Woods, New Hampshire, to create a new economic order for the postwar world. Keynes argued that before 1914, the Bank of England for 50 years had skillfully run the international monetary system. World commerce had prospered. After World War I, Britain was so weak that it had been unable to fulfill this role, leaving a vacuum that destabilized trade and exchange rates. A new system had to be created, he said, to extricate the postwar world from stagnation and deflation. Keynes and White conceived of a new world order based on fixed exchange rates, the dollar, and a gold peg. They created the World Bank and the International Monetary Fund. Over the next quarter of a century when combined with the Marshall Plan, their model performed spectacularly. World trade, which had actually declined in the 1930s, grew at more than 7% per annum. World industrial production in the same period compounded at 5.6% a year. Keynes and White had to an important degree brought a final end to the Great Depression.

Ironically, the two men detested each other. Keynes, by now Lord Keynes of Tilton and an English aristocrat, thought White was obnoxious and rude. "He has not the faintest conception of civilized behavior," he wrote. White referred to Keynes behind his back as "your royal highness." Keynes once, in a response to a question, said White was a "queer man." White's rejoinder was to the effect that he objected to being called queer by a queer. Both men had their own guilty secrets (White was a Soviet agent), but they actually worked well together.

Keynes's legacy lives on. The second generation of Keynesian economists who came into positions of influence in both government and international institutions, with the election of President John Kennedy, ran the world economies for many years. Keynes's prescriptions for diseased economies became the medicine of choice, and their dominance was capped by Milton Friedman's famous assertion in 1965 that "we are all Keynesians now."

John Maynard Keynes died of cancer in 1946. He was only 63 years old. Lydia, his lover, confidante, and sometimes nurse for the last 25 years of his life, lived another 30 years. Without the intellectual stimulation of Keynes, her vitality faded. As time went on, she reverted to her simple, Russian peasant ways, became reclusive, and lived completely in the past.

As I have tried to describe in this book, there are many brilliant and bizarre characters in today's hedge-fund world, but Keynes surpasses them all. Hedgehogs would have liked and appreciated him. What would he have thought of us?

It's an incredible story!

CONCLUSION

Although those quantitatively inclined would disagree, to me, investing is much more an art than a science. Intelligence, experience, diligence, a knowledge of history, an open mind, and an obsessive nature are all important ingredients for the successful hedgehog—as are intuition, imagination, flexibility, and maybe just a touch of the seeing eye. How you mix and match, or what is the optimal combination of these characteristics, is beyond me. There is no single style.

It's not a resume thing, and investment success, in my opinion, has nothing to do with age. As that old cynic George Bernard Shaw put it: "Men are wise not in proportion to their experience, but to their capacity for experience." I have tried to explain in these pages that there is no checklist, no one single model for a long-only investor or a hedgehog, but I do think that to flourish, the professional has to relish and be invigorated by intellectual competition and be able to handle stress and adversity. It's not a game for the fainthearted or for the intellectually lazy. Being obsessed and driven by greed is not sufficient; you want your money manager to truly love and be fascinated with the complexity of the game. Obviously, however, as I have described, the game does burn out some of its most committed devotees, and the amateur as an employer must be alert for signs of combat fatigue.

It's hard to be a hedgehog and it's far from easy to be a user of hedgehogs. All I can say is good luck.